Studying Shakespeare
on Film

Related titles from Palgrave Macmillan

Mark Thornton Burnett and Ramona Wray (eds), *Shakespeare, Film, Fin de Siècle (2000)*

Deborah Cartmell, *Interpreting Shakespeare on Screen (2000)*

Robert Shaughnessy (ed.), *Shakespeare on Film (1998)*

Studying Shakespeare on Film

MAURICE HINDLE

First published in 2007 by
PALGRAVE MACMILLAN
Houndmills, Basingstoke, Hampshire RG21 6XS and
175 Fifth Avenue, New York, N.Y. 10010
Companies and representatives throughout the world

PALGRAVE MACMILLAN is the global academic imprint of the Palgrave Macmillan division of St. Martin's Press, LLC and of Palgrave Macmillan Ltd. Macmillan® is a registered trademark in the United States, United Kingdom and other countries. Palgrave is a registered trademark in the European Union and other countries.

ISBN-13: 978–1–4039–0673–1 hardback
ISBN-10: 1–4039–0673–4 hardback
ISBN-13: 978–1–4039–0672–4 paperback
ISBN-10: 1–4039–0672–6 paperback

This book is printed on paper suitable for recycling and made from fully managed and sustained forest sources.

A catalogue record for this book is available from the British Library.

Library of Congress Cataloging-in-Publication Data

Hindle, Maurice.
    Studying Shakespeare on film / Maurice Hindle.
        p. cm.
    Includes bibliographical references and index.
    ISBN-13: 978-1-4039-0673-1 (cloth)
    ISBN-10: 1-4039-0673-4 (cloth)
    ISBN-13: 978-1-4039-0672-4 (pbk.)
    ISBN-10: 1-4039-0672-6 (pbk.)
        1. Shakespeare, William, 1564–1616 – Film and video adaptations.
    2. English drama – Film and video adaptations. 3. Film adaptations – History and criticism. I. Title.

PR3093.H56 2007
791.43'6—dc22   2006050779

10 9 8 7 6 5 4 3 2 1
16 15 14 13 12 11 10 09 08 07

Printed and bound in China

To the memory of my parents
William and Florence.
And for my son Matthew

... nowadays we see before we hear

Sir Richard Eyre
Shakespeare stage and screen director

Contents

Contents

List of Illustrations

Acknowledgements

I must first of all declare an enormous debt of gratitude to those writers from whom I have learned and borrowed much in my Shakespeare on film studies, but especially the work of Roger Manvell, Jack J. Jorgens, Kenneth S. Rothwell, Anthony Davies and Samuel Crowl. At a more personal level, I am grateful to have received encouragement and advice from various quarters over three years of part-time research and writing, most especially from Owen Gunnell, whose immense knowledge of Shakespeare in performance in Britain since the sixties has been a real boon to me in discussion. In the latter stages I was most appreciative of the advice and support from a number of people, especially the very detailed feedback and suggestions given by my Open University colleague Anita Pacheco, and also for the comments of David Johnson, then chair of the Open University *AA306 Shakespeare: Text and Performance* course team. The encouragement, suggestions and moral support given by Luke McKernan, Robert Shaughnessy, Tony Howard and Peter Holland were also most welcome at this time. Help from Luke's colleague Sergio Angelini at the British Universities Film and Video Council was much appreciated. Two one-month periods of leave from my Open University duties in the Faculty of Arts were of crucial importance to me in this project, and I am grateful to Richard Allen for being instrumental in facilitating the arrangements. I would also like to thank all those Open University colleagues in London who have periodically helped simply by showing constructive interest in my work, particularly Bob Owens, Naoko Yamagata, Alice Whieldon, Michel Petheram and Jeanette Robinson. I also wish to thank Judith Buchanan, Peter Barham and especially Matthew Hindle for taking an interest. I am very appreciative of the help given to me by the staff of the British Film Institute library, by Daniel Wiles of The South Bank Show, by Louise Gray at the BBC, by Andrew Roach at 2 Entertain, by Gitesh Pandya, editor at BoxOfficeGuru.com, by Tamar Thomas at Renaissance Films plc and especially for the invaluable assistance of Jerry Whelan at DD Home Entertainment. Finally, at Palgrave I want to thank my editor Kate Wallis for her support and patience, and also for the help given by Sonya Barker and Felicity Noble.

The author and publishers wish to thank the following for the use of copyright material:

Ethan Hawke and Miramax Films, for the film still of Ethan Hawke, from Michael Almereyda's *Hamlet* (2000), on p. 203; Kenneth Branagh and Warner Bros. Entertainment Inc. for the film still of Kenneth Branagh, from *Hamlet* (1996), on p. 195; London Features International Ltd. and the British Film Institute, for the film still of Laurence Olivier and Jean Simmons, from *Hamlet* (1948), on p. 188.

Every effort has been made to trace the copyright holders but if any have been inadvertently overlooked, the author and publishers will be pleased to make the necessary arrangements at the first opportunity.

Abbreviations/Acronyms

BAFTA	British Academy of Film and Television Arts Awards
BBC	British Broadcasting Company
BFI	British Film Institute
CBC	Canadian Broadcasting Company
F	Folio, first collected edition of Shakespeare's plays (1623)
LWT	London Weekend Television
PBS	Public Broadcasting Service
Q1, Q2	Quarto, individual edition of Shakespeare play, many of which were published in the author's lifetime
RADA	Royal Academy of Dramatic Art
RNT	Royal National Theatre
RSC	Royal Shakespeare Company
RTC	Renaissance Theatre Company

Introduction

Shakespeare has always had an audience. Up to the beginning of the twentieth century, that audience, whether elite or popular, experienced Shakespeare exclusively in a theatrical space, and was relatively small. The invention of moving pictures changed all that. Not so noticeably in the silent era or in the 1930s, it has to be admitted, since it is only with the success of Laurence Olivier's wartime production of *Henry V* (1944) that one can talk of a film adaptation having for the first time found favour with a mass moviegoing audience. Olivier's achievement and popular success also went beyond issues of patriotism and propaganda, with at least two of the finest adapters of the Shakespeare play to the big screen being inspired by Olivier's filmic example to produce Shakespeare movies of their own: Franco Zeffirelli and Ian McKellen. Enthused by Olivier's *Henry V*, Zeffirelli went on to take Shakespeare to the mainstream movie audiences of the 1960s with his Burton/Taylor vehicle *The Taming of the Shrew* (1966) before bringing a large youth audience to the hugely popular *Romeo and Juliet* (1968), a success partly repeated with his Mel Gibson/Glenn Close *Hamlet* (1990). For McKellen it was a viewing of Olivier's *Richard III* (1955) at the Bolton Odeon which inspired: 'A spell was cast as I watched the shadows of great actors and had confirmed my juvenile sense that Shakespeare was for everybody' (1995, 37). The experience of feeling that Shakespeare 'is for everybody' also drove Kenneth Branagh to produce a *Henry V* to rival in popularity Olivier's 1944 production, a move that reinvigorated the Shakespeare film adaptation genre in 1989. Although in terms of output it is the prolific and committed Branagh who still dominates the continuing post-1989 era of Shakespeare movies, I would like to focus here a little on Ian McKellen and Richard Loncraine's fine adaptation of *Richard III* (1995).

I do this not because their *Richard III* broke any box office records – far from it – but because its realisation reveals an imaginative understanding at work of what matters in the tricky business of translating Shakespeare to the big screen for a modern audience. I deliberately use the word 'translating' because, as Jack Jorgens has observed, 'in a sense *all* Shakespeare films are translations', creative attempts 'to recast and reimage a work conceived in a different language and for a different culture' (1991, 14). Well aware that 'Translation is an inexact art, carrying responsibilities to respect the author's ends, even as you wilfully tamper with the means,' McKellen's strategy of extracting a screenplay from Shakespeare's *Richard III* play text was governed by the decision 'to shorten it but without losing any of the detailed development of plot or character'. As a great Shakespearean actor also familiar with the language of cinema, McKellen offers a useful insight into how Shakespeare's own changing language use, developing as it does in sophistication over time, can have implications for the way big screen adaptations are to be approached:

> Some reduction of the play's verbal impact was inevitable but much less damaging than in, say, *Macbeth*, where every poetical line is interdependent on the rest. The verse and language of *Richard III*, a much earlier play, are less dense than in the great tragedies. Although the young Shakespeare was writing almost entirely in verse, he frequently captured a conversational tone ... It is a tone that is ideal for cinema (1995, 17).

Based on a theatrical production which had already 'updated' the play by relocating it to a 1930s Britain where a dictatorship like Richard's might plausibly have assumed power, *Richard III* was shaped and directed by Richard Loncraine to create a convincingly authentic 'period look'. Far from being an end in itself however, the film is 'just borrowing the period' (as McKellen pointedly says): 'We weren't pretending that Shakespeare had anticipated modern tyranny, but just saying that he would have understood it' (1998, 47). This approach to reimaging and translating has the film using its casting, costumes, locations and incidents such that throughout (in Peter Holland's words) 'authenticity is subordinate to argument'. One good example (which must suffice) of how the movie avoids what Holland calls the 'cheap paraphernalia of filmic naturalism' (Holland, 1996, 19) is by having the characters who smoke (everyone smoked in 1930s Britain) do so in ways that indicate and enhance character: Richard's own chain-smoking suggests the anxieties of the restless, haggard killer, ever on the watch; Buckingham's fat cigars stress the greasy grandee on the make; the Duchess of York and Queen Elizabeth convey upper-class female elegance by using cigarette holders; military subordinates like Ratcliffe and Tyrell smoke furtively while waiting upon or serving Richard, their master. Many more features of this film dramatisation of *Richard III* are considered in Part III and in the essay on it in Part IV.

The principal aim of this book is to help students of Shakespeare on film develop a critical approach to their studies by offering exploration, discussion and analysis of how film adaptations of the plays communicate as *film* texts, rather than as plays on the page or for the stage. These explorations are begun in Part I with a discussion of the different ways in which stage and film convey the performance of Shakespeare's plays to their audiences. The purpose of giving a history of Shakespeare on film in Part II is partly to demonstrate how the products of this genre have been conditioned by interlinked but shifting developments over time in film technology, directing, acting and shooting styles, and so on, and also by the changes in social, cultural and political domains of experience. The history also allows me to give a more extended account of some of the more significant films I could not find space to write essays on in Part IV. Part III explores the various modes, styles and genres which have been used to communicate Shakespeare on film to its audiences. Part IV offers a series of 'exemplary' essays on various film adaptations of Shakespeare comedies, histories and tragedies that build on the discussions of the first three parts. To conclude, Part V examines the way Shakespeare plays have been adapted for TV audiences, discussing various examples. Since all five parts are concerned to draw attention to the distinctive ways in which film's visual language and grammar are deployed to communicate meanings and effects to a Shakespeare on film audience, I have throughout emboldened many of the technical terms used in making or discussing filmed drama, and these are explained in the Glossary at the end of the book.

I should perhaps say something about my assumptions in writing and presenting what follows. I have not deemed it part of my task to introduce readers to Shakespeare's plays, but assume there will already be some familiarity with them. Quotations from or allusions to Shakespeare's play texts refer to *The Norton Shakespeare* (1997), based on the Oxford edition. With the special exceptions of silent films and Kurosawa's *Kumonosu-Jô* (his version of *Macbeth*), I have throughout confined my discussions to filmed adaptations of Shakespeare's plays that use the dialogue of the Shakespearean text. There are many other adaptations I should like to have discussed, such as Derek Jarman's *The Tempest* and Celestino Coronado's *Hamlet* (both 1979) or Jean-Luc Godard's *King Lear* (1987) – to mention only three. But space forbids me from including discussion on these as well as other productions, such as Peter Greenaway's *Prospero's Books* (1991) or Al Pacino's *Looking for Richard* (1996). Beyond these, there are also the many films for which Shakespeare's plays have provided plots, characters and ideas, such as Ernst Lubitsch's *To Be or Not to Be* (1942), Fred Wilcox's *Forbidden Planet* (1956, drawing on *The Tempest*) or Jocelyn Moorehouse's *A Thousand Acres* (1997 – borrowing from *King Lear*). These 'Shakespearean cinematic offshoots' have been intelligently and entertainingly discussed by Tony Howard (Jackson ed., 2000). I also need to point out that all of the Part IV essays are about films which at the time of writing are available on DVD or video; it would seem futile to write at length about film texts which cannot easily be obtained or seen.

Finally, it may be appropriate to say a word about what might be called the critical self-positioning of the various discussions that follow. Like other areas of critical study in literature and drama over the last 25 years, Shakespeare film studies as a discipline has become a contested domain, a site for debate, some of it quite wide-ranging and polemical. I am acutely aware that any performative representation or discussion of Shakespeare's drama may trigger questions concerning race, class and gender. But the book that follows is practical rather than polemical, the scope for debating the ideological contexts of Shakespeare on film being limited. The reader seeking a broader grasp of the range and reach of the discipline as a whole is therefore encouraged to look at some of the publications listed in the 'Suggested further reading'. I could not recommend a better place to start for accessible and lively essays on race and gender (and much else besides) than in the two *Shakespeare the Movie* collections edited by Lynda E. Boose and Richard Burt.

Maurice Hindle
London, 2006
www.mauricehindle.com

Part I

Shakespeare and the Language of Film

1

Filming and Staging Shakespeare: Some Contrasts

It seems obvious to state that the conditions of performance and reception of a Shakespeare play produced for film on the one hand, and stage on the other, are going to be different. However, exploring some of these differences will provide us with a useful way into studying Shakespeare on film. To start with a very broad contrast between the two forms of production, it has been said that 'in the theatre we accept theatricality; in the cinema we demand actuality' (Manvell, 1979, 266). This requirement for an impression of actuality, or reality, is directly linked to the fact that film is a *recorded* medium of performance, a completed 'product' that is played back to cinema/video/DVD audiences watching in a space and time entirely remote from the original performance. Very obviously, a film audience can play no part in affecting the performance they are watching; in the theatre by contrast, where the performance is continuous and live, there is always some kind of interaction between the stage and those watching. If a **narrative film** (as most Shakespeare film adaptations are) is to communicate accessibly and coherently with a film audience, it therefore needs to be made as realistically involving as possible, for an audience that will always be 'virtual'. As we all know, a continuous film performance is made from many smaller bits of filmed performance, edited together. The very different *conventions* of performance and reception operating in theatre and film also mean that movie actors need to use rather different performance techniques if they are to communicate with us well. The sound amplification technology, enabling a cinema audience to hear what is being said from anywhere

3

in the screening auditorium, means that the actors are not required to 'project' their voices the way stage actors do: they need instead to speak more at the level used in the social interactions of everyday life. Without a live audience to cater for, film actors instead perform more exclusively to/with one another such that the 'eye of the camera' is satisfied, the ultimate decision in this regard normally remaining with the film's *director*. The director usually has final say over whether their visualisation of the script the movie is following has been successfully realised into filmed performance. This decision-making process points to another of the vital differences between the playing conditions of film and theatre. In a theatrical production, the cast frequently rehearses a play for weeks before it opens to the public, hopefully to ensure a high level of artistic performance. For a film, without a live audience, a scene can be repeated again and again until played and filmed to the satisfaction of the director (budget permitting), mishaps being eliminated and the best shots or shot sequences (**takes**) chosen for the 'final cut' of the movie. Once shot and edited into the connected sequences of the finished product, a filmed performance is 'fixed' for ever, in and of its time of making. It provides a record of what all who have been involved in the production no doubt hope is the best that can be dramatically achieved, a complete recording 'secured' for all subsequent viewers of the film, who may eventually watch in many thousands of locations all over the globe: wherever cinemas are accessible, or where DVD/video playback facilities are available.

2

The Audience: Individual and Collective Experience

Most new theatres these days are replacing the 'two room' division of spaces produced by the old-style **proscenium arch** with more prominent stages bringing actor and audience closer together in 'one room'. At the time of writing, the main house of England's Royal Shakespeare Theatre at Stratford-upon-Avon is being restructured to this design. In the words of current Royal Shakespeare Company (RSC) Artistic Director Michael Boyd, it will have a 'bold **thrust** stage, inspired by the Renaissance courtyard', the aim being 'to articulate what's distinctive about theatre through the intimacy of the relationship between actor and the audience, and the audience with one another'.

The sense of intimacy experienced by a cinema audience is very different from that achievable in even the most intimate of playhouse spaces. However emotionally involved they may become in the events replayed on screen, since they are physically 'detached' from what has been filmed and edited in another time and place, moviegoers will be in quite another form of relationship to what they are watching to that of the theatregoer. How film spectators receive, decode and engage with movies is therefore of prime importance to those who create the drama projected on screen, since producers, directors and actors all want to attract and to hold the attention of audiences who have paid to watch. This is why audience 'test screenings' are used so much in an era when the high costs of commercial film production mean that directors, producers and distributors need an assurance that film audience members will understand, like, and be held by (especially the opening of) a film if they are to make a profit for their enterprise, or, in the case of **arthouse** movies, at least to recover their financial outlay. Filmgoers are most likely to be appealed to as 'self-contained' perceiving *individuals*, screen images and sounds being geared to producing an emotionally and psychologically engaging *private* experience, this audience requirement therefore being quite different to that made on a live theatre spectator. In the theatre, although each individual's response to stage events will finally be their own, meanings and effects are generated in the context of a public, more *collective* interactive experience. A feature of this collective experience is that it is 'pluralistic' and relatively unpredictable, the theatrical spectator choosing which aspects of the performance to look at and focus on. The cinema or small-screen audience's focus on the other hand will be dictated by what the *camera* 'sees', and *only* by what the camera sees. Consequently, the film viewer's sequential perception of the actions and images of the filmed story is wholly governed by what the film director, principally, chooses to show. Quite literally, it is the producer, the director and the editor who in the end 'call the shots' to be transmitted on celluloid, DVD or video.

To the extent that the audience's viewpoint can therefore be directed by the sequence of images and actions put up on the screen, there is great scope for the audience's viewpoint and feelings to be *shaped* or manipulated in certain ways. (Once alerted to the fact, watchers of Kenneth Branagh's Shakespeare films will notice just how much their music soundtracks are used to stir and shape the emotions of his film audience.) On the other hand, the act of watching a narrative film can be and often is acknowledged to be a complex process. The manipulation of cinematic techniques of **montage** and **mis-en-scène** by film-makers in telling a story always makes demands on the perceptual capacities of the viewer, their ability to 'construct' from the sequence of images shown, an understanding of what is being conveyed. With a stage performance, our impressions are overwhelmingly defined by the strong presence of actors communicating with us through the mutually accepted pretence of *stage conventions*. The impressions we experience from a narrative film however are instead created by what Christian Metz calls our 'constant impulse to invest' those 'ghostly creatures moving on the screen' with 'the "reality" of fiction'. This 'reality of fiction', he says, 'comes only from within us, from the projections and **identification**s that are mixed in with our perception of the film' (Metz, 1974, 10). Constituting the total world of the story some film theorists call a film's **diegesis** (Greek for 'narrative'), this comprises everything we assume to exist in the world the film depicts – characters, settings and so on. Besides the explicitly presented events we all watch, as mesmerised viewers we will also be subjectively adding 'unseen' elements into the 'fictional mix'. Such elements will include presumed and inferred events, objects and places, as well as our feelings, fantasies and valuations about the characters depicted – the 'projections' and 'identifications' Metz speaks of – so that we can each construct and internalise a story making some kind of sense to us.

Whatever the 'impression of reality' we negotiate for ourselves in the transaction between the images on the screen and our own perceptions of them, it should not be forgotten that what is seen will also be dependent on an economic process and reality, lying behind the process of production. The range of cinematic techniques available to be used at any one time by a director will vary, partly depending on the production budget available, and partly depending on the connected question of the kind of cinema audience being targeted. A small but apt example concerning Shakespeare adaptation and budgetary issues concerns film director Roman Polanski. He has stated that he would now use the **digital imaging** techniques available to modern filmmakers to create the outdoor castle sequences, were he to make a film of *Macbeth* nowadays; in 1971 he was forced to use the unpredictable, time-consuming and expensive methods of location shooting to get the results he wanted for his movie.

The way economics relates to the respective targeting of arthouse or popular film audiences can be made briefly and broadly by contrasting the approaches taken to filming Shakespeare by Orson Welles and Baz Luhrmann. In each of his three adaptations (*Macbeth* (1948), *Othello* (1952), *Chimes at Midnight* (1965)), Welles's highly individualistic cinematic style makes no concession to the requirements or perceptual capacities of a worldwide popular movie audience. This meant his having to work within severely constrained production budgets for each film, which in turn also ensured that the audience for his films would only ever be arthouse, that is, in commercial terms extremely small audiences attending a limited range of cinematic venues. In the case of Baz Luhrmann, from the start he aimed to communicate with an MTV-influenced youth audience for his *Romeo + Juliet* (1996). His stylistic approach and casting were designed to have large-scale international appeal, which attracted ample funding from Hollywood both for making and (a long lead-time of) publicising the film. As a result, backed by highly successful test screenings, it was almost guaranteed that the movie on release would **open wide** (i.e. simultaneously across over 1000 cinema screens in the USA), massive audiences and profits being the result.

3

The Space of the Movie Screen

Unlike the Shakespeare *stage* play, the Shakespeare *screenplay* is liberated from the confines of the theatre's acting space by cinema's photographic technology. This offers the potential of virtually unlimited playing spaces, the range of interior or exterior locations only being constrained perhaps by time and cost. Before Laurence Olivier's film of *Henry V* was released in 1944, the battle of Agincourt in Act 4 had only ever been conveyed in stage productions by the reports of characters or spoken interactions between characters involved in the battle. In both Olivier's film and then in Branagh's 1989 *Henry V* movie, the battle was realised in outside locations in more or less convincing ways. We are not therefore wholly reliant on what the characters *tell* us through the dialogue to experience the force and impact of the battle scenes on the French and the English sides: we actually *see* both sides battling it out. The film medium can also move us about instantaneously from one location to another, ensuring that we experience a sense of time passing but without the effects of discontinuity which stage convention practice forces on us in the theatre.

However, because actors on screen are only ever 'discovered' by the watching audience as *already* being within the space of the film frame we focus on (i.e. in the ***mis-en-scène***), the dramatic events on screen are experienced as happening more *naturalistically* than can be the case on stage. It is as if we are being given a 'window' on to a realistic world of events which really seem to be happening. In a theatre setting, by contrast, before they can start performing, the actors must somehow physically enter the playing space, and are frequently perceived by the audience to be doing so. (Nowadays, scenography – the sophisticated manipulation of lighting, sound and scenery whose use in fact reveals the influence of film techniques on stage practice – makes this less of a problem.) Such choreographic considerations are eliminated in filmed narrative drama, where the well-edited movie creates such a seamless continuity of storytelling that the viewer, once engrossed in the succession of screen images, need never have the illusion of screened reality broken, from beginning to end. The spatial possibilities offered by location shooting are frequently exploited by moviemakers to model the visual realities of the 'external' world on to film in a convincing way; the more they do so, the more our capacity for absorbing such images of visual mimesis increases. Our human visualising processes are already conditioned to register the actually moving world around us through continuous coherent images being focused on our retinas like a kind of internal screen, a phenomenon that by definition involves us in perceiving our living environment. The twin cinematic phenomena of **critical flicker vision** and **apparent motion**, which movie cameras and projectors use to delude us into thinking that the succeeding film images we watch in the movie theatre are *moving* when they are not, are similarly effective in making us think that what we see on screen in the well-edited film is also 'real' (Bordwell and Thompson, 2001, 2).

When location filming is used for Shakespeare adaptations, which was occasionally done from earliest days up to the middle of the twentieth century, more frequently in the post-war period, and then almost every time for the larger budget films of the 1990s onward, the effect is almost always beneficial. This is especially so where the numerous dramatic themes and turns created in Shakespeare's scripts can be reinforced and made more emphatic by using carefully chosen settings: Mogador for Welles's *Othello*, Tuscany for Branagh's *Much Ado About Nothing*, Mexico City for Luhrmann's *Romeo + Juliet*.

Just as scene locations may be multiplied for the film medium, so can the number and range of actors used be greater than are employed for stage productions. A staged Shakespeare play invariably requires a cast of trained actors practised in verse speaking to perform much of the play text, if the play's dramatic content is to be got over successfully to a theatre audience. It is difficult to disentangle the relative importance of the words as opposed to the gestures employed by stage actors in the business of communicating the drama and meaning of a Shakespeare play effectively to a live audience. But one thing cannot be doubted: the audience will rely heavily on the *words* they hear as their primary means of understanding and enjoying what is being dramatically communicated. With the audience for Shakespeare film adaptations enlarging to include a non-traditional Shakespeare audience becoming younger and younger from the 1960s onward, the use of the pared-down, image-led screenplay text now expected for filmed Shakespeare has enabled actors less experienced in Shakespearean performance to be cast for many of the screen roles. Good examples are Zeffirelli's and Luhrmann's film versions of *Romeo and Juliet* (released in 1968 and 1996, respectively), where neither of each movie's male leads had ever acted in Shakespeare plays before, on stage or in film. And what is true for lead roles is also true for smaller parts: whereas success for the Shakespearean stage hinges crucially on an actor's skills in manipulating theatrical convention, on film it is possible to hire actors to perform Shakespeare who have had little or no experience in playing classical theatres.

This last circumstance hints at another of the 'advantages' of film's performance conditions: since the main dramatic resource of the narrative movie is the **reaction shot**, where the camera cuts from the actions or speech of one character to show us another character's reactions to these, film often requires an actor to perform only for a short time in front of the camera, in brief **takes**. Consequently, unless a long take is undertaken for the sake of preserving a stage-like continuity of performance or effect (as with some of the long scenes in Welles's *Macbeth* or Branagh's *Hamlet*), the use of short takes means that an actor does not have to learn long speeches or sequences of lines. A director is therefore able to hire actors not necessarily accustomed to performing long continuous scenes, or who have little experience in remembering lots of lines in the way that stage actors frequently must do; that is to say, they can employ movie actors or stars. As short takes become the order of the day, actors in filmed Shakespeare may therefore not always need to be available to perform for any sustained period of time. Stage actors on the other hand must obviously always be *present* in 'real time' to play their ensemble part live in each unique theatrical performance.

4

Imagery: Verbal and Visual

The greatest single difference between the communicative methods of stage and cinema is that the theatre is essentially a *verbal* medium foregrounding the spoken word, while film communicates using predominantly *visual* techniques. Shakespeare has become the acknowledged leading playwright of English drama because the language of his plays, endowed as it so frequently is with imaginative verbal imagery, metaphor, and rhythmic word patterns, contributes powerfully to the creation and dramatic interaction of characters whose identities are often complex and rarely one-dimensional. Many people therefore enjoy reading a Shakespeare play for its literary qualities alone, just as one may gain pleasure from reading a novel or a poem. In fact, essayists of the Romantic period of English literature (*c*.1780–1830) like William Hazlitt and Charles Lamb valued Shakespeare's plays far more highly as texts to be *read*, than as dramas to be performed and watched by a theatre audience.

No one is likely to accord such high literary values to a film script or screenplay. The reason for this lies in the predominantly visual bias of the cinematic medium, where *speech is only one part* of the dramatic totality being communicated to us from the screen. Setting aside for a moment the fact that all modern playhouse audiences for a Shakespeare play will need to accustom themselves to the archaisms of a 400-year-old vocabulary, it is vital to recognise the following: *that the dialogue of any play performed from the stage must **in its own right** command the attention and interest of an audience.* The play dialogue in other words must have the capacity to be 'pitched up' by the actors beyond the requirements of normal speech, such that it has the dramatic power to convey emotional tension, psychological involvement, wit or humour. At every point, the words spoken need to underline and create the kind of character being portrayed, and to convey clearly the issues being explored.

The performance of screen actors must also be expressive. But the *scale* of their verbal projection will be much less, bodily gesture or facial expression often being as important, or even *more* important as a mode of communication, than verbal expression. What is shown and seen can also take precedence over what is heard on the stage too, especially in a period when the potent visual images commonplace in film, TV, advertising and mass culture persuade theatrical directors to use more and more visual effects to create dramatic impact. Yet because film accentuates the intimacy of every detail of acting through the **close-ups** afforded by the camera and the sounds recorded by microphones, dialogue on the screen usually needs little more projection than that required for the close proximities of everyday social situations. Dialogue not only can be spoken at everyday levels, but altogether *less* of it may be necessary than is required for stage performance. In fact, the emotional intensities or reactions of a character filmed in close-up are often revealed without recourse to verbal expression, a visual image of their actions and expressions being sufficient to show us all we need to know.

Such revelation can sometimes be elaborated on by use of the **voice-over** technique, as when the eponymous characters of Olivier's *Hamlet* or Polanski's *Macbeth* speak soliloquies revealing their private thoughts. Film terminology calls this **internal diegetic sound** – sounds having their source in the film's story world (diegesis), inside the character's mind here for Hamlet and Macbeth – though not in the 'real' space of the scene played. Not only is the effort to externalise emotion required less for a screen performance than it is for the stage, but *showing* such effort can be damaging, as actor Micheál Mac Liammóir noted from his experience of playing Iago in Orson Welles's film of *Othello*:

> Find out what I have long suspected: (a) that one's first job is to forget every single lesson one ever learned on the stage: all projection of the personality, build-up of a speech, and sustaining for more than a few seconds of an emotion are not only unnecessary but superfluous, and (b) that the ability to express oneself just *below* the rate of normal behaviour is a primal necessity ... One single sudden move of eyebrows, mouth or nostrils and all is registered as a grotesque exaggeration. (MacLiammóir, 1994, 96)

The implications of this shift in perceptual emphasis for the successful adaptation of Shakespeare plays to the screen are both profound and may be, for some, troubling. For if it is as *viewers* rather than as 'hearers' that cinema audiences are required to 'decode' the screen images and sounds created for them, there is bound to be a *cutting* of the Shakespeare text. Even in the theatre it is very common for the text of Shakespeare plays to be cut, since in today's time-starved post-industrial societies it is only the most dedicated of Shakespeare lovers who will want to attend live performances of three-hours-plus duration. The 'two-hour's traffic of our stage' mentioned in the Prologue of *Romeo and Juliet* relates to a historical epoch when the stage language and vocabulary heard by most (if not all) of the orally orientated Elizabethan audiences would be accessible to many of them. Furthermore, the accessible dramatic language used by Shakespeare and his fellow actors would have been performed from the stage far more rapidly than it is possible for actors of modern productions to perform, simply because modern audiences would fail to follow the lines quickly enough to gain and retain sufficient understanding of what is going on.

5

Putting It All Together

To summarise, modern audiences of film drama are accustomed to watching a succession of 'action-driven' visual images accompanied by a relatively undemanding level of spoken dialogue. Such audiences 'read' a film largely by following the *visual imagery* of actors who supply the dramatic input we are *looking* to experience from the screen; we gain this experience from their *showing* us what they are thinking or feeling, rather than by using the kinds of *verbal imagery* so plentifully supplied in the texts of Shakespeare's plays. In order for a film audience to follow a screen narrative primarily transmitted through succeeding visual images, these images – camera shots in effect – must usually be made to flow coherently and connectedly. The process of creating a seamless flow of images an audience can follow without effort involves skilful **continuity editing**. The principles of such editing have always dominated mainstream cinema around the world, but from the 1960s onward the pace of cutting (editing) from shot to shot became more rapid. Fast paced TV commercials and French New Wave cinema seem to have influenced this change, and certainly since **digital** editing made the fast cutting of shots even easier, this style has come to govern film-making, not only for action films, but also in dramas, comedies – and many Shakespeare adaptations.

Most films on general release will eventually be seen on DVD or video and many film directors have felt that fast cutting can help to hold a small-screen viewer's attention more effectively, so they shoot their films accordingly. For those directors making Shakespeare films, movies which are ultimately likely to attain their largest audience over time on the small screen, an even more important change has taken place. Since **long shots** on TV have little visual impact, directors typically frame their shots of actors more tightly, so that we now find many more **close shots** or ultra-close shots on the big screen than in the older days of cinema. The **medium shots** in more traditional film-making certainly showed the actor's face, posture and gestures, but a newer, *intensified* continuity concentrates its efforts on faces, and in particular, the actor's eyes. With the 1000 or more shots that comprise a Hollywood entertainment film, the choice and editing together of such shots (from the many more produced while filming) is a vital component for achieving a seamless narrative. One modern expert film editor has commented on the criteria for shot-choice by reporting that 'The determining factor for selecting a particular shot is frequency: "Can you register the expression in the actor's eyes?" If you can't, the editor will tend to use the next closer shot, even though the **wider shot** may be more than adequate when seen on the big screen' (Bordwell and Thompson, 2001, 289).

So we see how the needs of the home-based small-screen viewer are being catered for, even at the stage when a film is actually being shot. In the Shakespeare film drama adaptation, since much of the close interest for audiences will be on the screen performances of the actors and the way they as characters interact with one another, directors will therefore create shots that provide a single 'centre of interest', something to grab the visual attention of the small-screen audience. Even in Shakespeare films, where long takes are still sometimes used to give actors an opportunity to produce a 'theatricality' of effect, still the tendency is towards closer and shorter shots.

Furthermore, there is an inclination to avoid complex patterns of staging. The movements of the actors tend to be kept fairly simple, with the camera moving around them in different ways, creating the kind of kinetic energy that provides small-screen viewers with the visual interest and variety they need. Such mobile camera movements can be achieved in a number of ways. These include the camera slowly tracking in toward each character in a **shot/reverse shot** exchange; the camera tracking in a circular pattern *around* a group of characters; or a complex series of moving camera shots, created with the use of a **Steadicam**. The latter two techniques are very evident in Branagh's Shakespeare films, the circular camera tracking movement being used most effectively in *Hamlet* (1996), especially at that point (in 3.1) where Rosencrantz and Guildenstern are reporting their findings on Hamlet's 'crafty madness' to Claudius and Gertrude. The Steadicam is used to great effect in the unbroken two-minute climactic sequence concluding Branagh's *Much Ado About Nothing* (1993).

Part II

The History of Shakespeare on Film 1899–2005

1

Silent Shakespeare

The story of Shakespeare on film starts at the very end of the nineteenth century in the context of a theatrical performance. On 20 September 1899, a production of *King John* opened at Her Majesty's Theatre in London, with the theatre's owner and actor-manager in the title-role, Sir Herbert Beerbohm Tree. On the same night a short film recreating scenes from the play was premiered at the Palace Theatre, London, and at other theatres in Britain, Europe and America. Four scenes from the play had been filmed earlier in September at the British Mutoscope and Biograph Company's open air studio on the embankment of the River Thames, each scene lasting about a minute.

The only fragment that survives of **Sir Herbert Beerbohm Tree's King John (1899)** the first ever Shakespearean film, recreates part of Act 5, scene 7, the final scene of the play. It shows Beerbohm Tree as King John in a long white gown, poisoned and writhing in his death throes on a chair in front of a backcloth palely depicting classical columns and a flowering bush. (In the play, John has insisted he be brought outside into an orchard so that his scorching, poisoned 'soul hath elbow-room' to 'out' (5.7.28–29).) Tree is flanked by his youthful son Prince Henry (Dora Senior) and the Earl of Pembroke (James Fisher) on one side and by Lord Robert Bigot (F. M. Paget) on the other: all sport mediaeval period costumes. A hint that this is a Shakespearean 'first' on film is suggested by the fact that just before these attendants turn to gaze concernedly upon their king in his death agonies, we see them all glancing toward the camera before moving 'into character'; evidently they have waited with some amusement for the 'Action!' signal to come from film company director and photographer William Kennedy-Laurie Dickson.

As a film, *King John* is clearly limited, its primary purpose being to promote Beerbohm Tree's stage play. Surviving publicity material for the Palace Theatre film exhibition calls it 'A SCENE – " 'KING JOHN, NOW PLAYING AT HER MAJESTY'S THEATRE" ', while a 1902 catalogue of the American Mutoscope and Biograph Company advertises it as 'BEERBOHM TREE, THE GREAT ENGLISH ACTOR, With leading members of his company in the death scene of "King John". Taken with all the scenery and effects of the original production' (McKernan and Terris, 1994, 81–2). Exaggeration prevailed in advertising then, as now: it is unlikely that the scenery and effects of the theatre production could have been used for Biograph's historic Thames-side open-air studio shoot. Nevertheless, there is something to be learned from viewing this earliest of Shakespeare films. Beyond the fact that the whole action consists of a single shot from a fixed camera, and that it was made to entice the public into a Shakespearean theatre production, the first thing to strike us is that Beerbohm Tree performs as if to a stage audience. The film is mute, yet he speaks his lines and moves his body about using the exaggerated gestures we associate with late-Victorian theatre. As a record of the acting style he and other actor-managers of the late-nineteenth century (like his rival Sir Henry Irving) had practised, the movie is a valuable celluloid document of theatre history.

Important though it might be as a 'first' in showing Shakespeare on film, Tree's brief attempt has to be seen as a device that simply *photographs* actors in moving pictures for promotional purposes; at the dawning of the film era it is unfair to judge it as a Shakespeare on film adaptation as such. But as there were about 500 silent Shakespeare films of different sorts released before talkies started to be made, and since not one word of the play scripts Shakespeare wrote could ever be heard being spoken in these movies, we may be entitled to ask, why did silent film-makers even make the attempt to turn Shakespeare into films in the first place? Those who enjoy Shakespeare's plays in the theatre are likely to say that their great appeal lies in hearing the author's magical use of language acted out, in words that *need* to be heard in order to be felt, understood, and enjoyed. How can we take pleasure in what Stephen Greenblatt calls Shakespeare's 'infinite delight in language' (1997, 1) when we cannot hear the silent film actors speaking their lines on screen? In fact, posing the question in this way takes no account of how 'pictorial' theatrical Shakespeare had become by the end of the nineteenth century, as indicated by *The Era* reviewer of Beerbohm Tree's theatre production of *King John* in September 1899, who states that the play presented itself as

> without central purpose, but very eventful; and Mr Beerbohm Tree has done the best thing possible in the circumstances by cutting away the super-fluous matter, arranging the piece in three acts, and by a succession of splendid tableaux, giving us a grand idea of the pomp and circumstance of war and politics in the thirteenth century.   (Quoted in Ball, 1968, 22)

The omission of any reference to the play's verbal text, much of which was no doubt considered 'superfluous matter', is utterly significant. The emphasis on creating pictorial stage realism begun by Garrick's mid-eighteenth century withdrawal of the playing space into the **proscenium arch** picture frame had by 1899 been taken by Irving and Beerbohm Tree as far as it could go. The projection of Shakespeare in their theatrical productions virtually replaced the nuances of verbal interpretation by what the audience now wanted – visual spectacle.

The advent of the film at the dawning of the twentieth century brought in a visual communicative technology of artistic and commercial potential, so Shakespeare, already a staple of theatrical spectacle, was bound to be taken up and adapted for the screen in some earnest. American critic Kenneth Rothwell sets the scene of what was now to come, rather well:

> The history of Shakespeare in the movies has [been] the search for the best available means to replace the verbal with the visual imagination, an inevitable development deplored by some but interpreted by others as not so much a limitation on, as an extension of Shakespeare's genius into uncharted seas.   (Rothwell, 5)

All kinds of attempts to bring Shakespeare to the screen would be made during the century by enterprising directors committed to taking Shakespeare on film into 'uncharted seas'. Yet it is important to see that this 'inevitability' of Shakespeare being translated to film was also triggered by specifically commercial motives. The popularity of silent cinema grew very rapidly, and so did the silent film trade's need for source material, for 'stories' they could turn into films. Inevitably, texts by a variety of established literary and dramatic authors would be sought out for adaptation. Shakespeare was known as a great storyteller as well as a brilliant poet and dramatist – a tried and tested 'property', in the language of film commerce – so his plays were bound to be exploited, especially since copyright presented no problem.

Another compelling reason existed for film-makers wanting to bring Shakespeare to the cinema screen. Almost from the outset, the film trade was sensitive to its lowly reputation as a supplier of popular entertainment, a 'lowlife' reputation akin to that enjoyed by the music hall – vaudeville. Of course, such entertainment had no pretensions to providing 'high culture' – far from it. Shakespeare the cultural icon could therefore be drawn on to 'elevate' the status of the film medium as such. This process would not only help to make films seem more 'respectable' by linking them to the world of the theatre (cinemas were already beginning to be designed like theatres), but it also added up to a bid to enlarge the existing (working class) film audience, by drawing in the middle class as well.

Conveying filmed Shakespeare in silence

Of the many films produced, it is well worth briefly exploring some examples. I shall say a little about some of the short silent films transferred to the BFI DVD *Silent Shakespeare* (2004) and two other longer silent movies, James Keane's American *Richard III* (the very first American feature film) and Svend Gade's *Hamlet* (the so-called female Hamlet).

The **British Clarendon Film Company's** *The Tempest* **(1908)** is a charming example of how a Shakespeare play can be 're-imagined to suit the means available' (McKernan, in McKernan and Terris, 3). Running at about 12 minutes, the film shows 11 scenes re-telling the story in the simplest of terms, intertitle cards clarifying the scene from the plot depicted. The first scene shown (the opening titles are missing) is not part of the play's action at all, but usefully fills in **backstory** for narrative purposes by depicting Prospero arriving on the island with his little daughter Miranda. Although the crude **flats** stepped through by Prospero show us the kind of scenery we associate with the stage, the film is conceived mostly as a piece of cinema in its own right, the use of **stop-motion** shooting to create some scenes of magic being one obvious example of this. Its most ostentatious cinematic sequence occurs when the camera places us near to Prospero and Miranda as they gaze out at the sinking ship through a kind of proscenium arch. Scratches on the print are here used to suggest lightning, while layered effects of superimposition to depict near and distant actions simultaneously are created by rewinding the film in the camera and re-shooting over the same strip of film.

The Vitagraph Company of America was the largest of the pre-Hollywood studios (bought up by Warner Brothers in 1924), specialising in so-called quality films, movies based on historical, biblical and literary subjects. A contemporary review of one Vitagraph movie shows how the company's effect on a growing mass consumer market was both designed and perceived to be 'in the nature of an educational service which is deserving of the heartiest support of all who are working for the improvement of humanity' (Pearson and Uricchio, in McKernan and Terris, 202). With extensive production facilities in Brooklyn, New York, Vitagraph made fourteen Shakespearean adaptations over the period 1908–12, the largest number of Shakespeare films ever made by one company. *Macbeth* was the first of seven movies released in 1908, producing admiring comments in the London-based *Kinematagraph and Lantern Weekly*:

> This firm are to be congratulated on the masterly way in which they have staged Shakespeare's tragedy. The famous play contains many situations which lend themselves admirably to effective treatment in picture form, and the company have made the most of them. Thus in the first scene, when the three 'Weird Sisters' prophesy that Macbeth shall be King we are shown him as in a vision, in the King's robes and crown [...] Then in order are pictured the other famous scenes of the play, culminating in Macbeth's death.
> (Quoted in Ball, 42)

But there were anxieties too. The Chicago police lieutenant who functioned as guardian of his city's moral health when censoring the film, though clearly an admirer of Shakespeare, was worried by the graphic representation of Duncan's murder on screen:

> The stabbing scene in the play is not predominant. But in the picture show it is the feature. In the play the stabbing is forgotten in the other exciting and artful and artistic creations that divert the imagination. On the canvas [i.e. film screen] you see the dagger enter and come out and see the blood flow and the wound that's left.   (Ball, 42)

In saying this, the police censor unwittingly reveals two of film's key features compared with the stage: its capacity to show scenes that Shakespeare chooses merely to report, scenes which convey realistic images that can impact viscerally on the viewer's imagination and feelings. The accusation that Roman Polanski had made his version of *Macbeth* too realistically bloody would be levelled at the Polish film-maker sixty years later.

A Midsummer Night's Dream **(1909)** was a hit film of the year for Vitagraph, and as with the Clarendon *Tempest*, part of its charm lay in its use of trick photography. A key feature of the movie is its attempt at filmic realism. Trade papers of the time sang its praises for effective location shooting, the woodland scenes being shot in summertime near Vitagraph's south Brooklyn studios. This outdoor location allows the actors to create interesting performances as they move through or hide behind the trees, light and shade adding realism and mystery to the setting. The film was marketed imaginatively too, for although this *Dream* was filmed in summertime, release was delayed until Christmas day 1909, a seasonally festive moment for a festive comedy.

Other silent adaptations that did more than merely 'entertain' also sought to make artistically informed and inventive use of film's possibilities in order to communicate effectively with the film audience. **James Keane's *The Life and Death of Richard III* (1912)**, starring American veteran stage actor Frederick Warde, was the first American feature film. Much of Warde's over-demonstrative and stagey performance is mercilessly exposed by the camera. But Keane's use of (what later became known as) *mis-en-scène* cinematography, altering the relationships within the film frame to convey visual meaning, cumulatively creates a series of silent images which clearly and dramatically tell the story using film language. A scene standing out for its creativity in combining clever camerawork, lighting and a dramatic *mis-en-scène*, is one of Keane's own invention – 'Death of Lady Anne'. As James Loehlin puts it, the action here 'occurs in three distinct planes, all held simultaneously in focus'. While Anne is seen lying prone in bed, well lit in the foreground, an attendant half in silhouette behind her prepares to give her wine, whereupon Richard appears from a passageway behind him, **back-lit**, putting most of his face in shadow: he comes urging the attendant to add poison to the drink, which is done, and as the wine brings on Anne's collapse, Richard slinks away. As Loehlin says, such filmic techniques look forward to the scary expressionist effects to be created by Murnau's *Nosferatu* (1922) as well as the **deep-focus** camerawork of Orson Welles's films (Loehlin, in Burt and Boose, 2003, 184).

An even more sophisticated approach to rendering Shakespeare on silent film comes with **Svend Gade's *Hamlet: The Drama of Vengeance* (1920)** starring Danish film actress Asta Nielsen, a film which Rothwell claims 'struck a great blow in liberating the Shakespeare movie from theatrical and textual dependency and moving toward the filmic' (Rothwell, 21). The movie marks this filmic advance in a number of significant ways. Running at 134 minutes in its original German release, it was a full-length feature made primarily as a vehicle for Nielsen, Germany's most popular film actress and an international movie icon of the period. The film's script was based on Edward Vining's eccentric 1881 theory that Hamlet is a woman who must for reasons of state conceal her true sex and appear as a man, even though she loves Horatio, who in turn is in love with Ophelia. Despite the bizarre re-fashioning of Shakespeare's text, Nielsen's playing of this Hamlet with a shocking 'secret' produces an intriguing effect, her androgynous appearance and sexual ambivalence creating both compelling interest and suspense. However, of even greater interest than Nielsen's cross-dressed Hamlet is the movie's strategy of appropriating 'familiar and popular film codes rather than stage per-formance codes for the cinematic transformation of Shakespeare's material' (Guntner, in Drexler and Guntner, 1995, 54). As Lawrence Guntner has argued, despite receiving a mixed critical response, what made *Hamlet: The Drama of Vengeance* the popular box office success of 1921 was primarily two things: its drawing on and reproducing Nielsen's identity as a popular film icon, and its employment of German Expressionist film techniques, designations Guntner calls *film codes*, discussed at length in this book as *film genre conventions*.

Just as the film audience would later be drawn to see Zeffirelli's 1990 film because for them it meant 'Mel Gibson's Hamlet', so was it 'Asta Nielsen's Hamlet' they wanted to see in 1921 – the first time a movie icon had been used to 'sell' a Shakespeare film adaptation. Nielsen's enchanted fans would already be drawn by her low key but effective naturalistic acting style, so geared to the needs of the camera rather than the stage. Many **close** and **medium shots** of her in this film would also frequently display the pallid beauty of her face and large, glowing dark eyes, as well as a figure known for showing off trend-set-ting fashions. Her ability to convey a character divided between inner female and outer male personas is cleverly supported by the tech-niques of film expressionism, most pervasively in the use of shadows and shadowy **chiaroscuro lighting** effects that create a sense of unease, mystery or even evil. Most of these elements feature in other expres-sionist classics of this historical moment in film, for example Robert Wiene's *The Cabinet of Dr Caligari* (1920), Paul Wegener's *The Golem* (1920) and Friedrich Murnau's *Nosferatu* (1922).

2

The Thirties: Hollywood Shakespeare

We have seen that in the silent era, some film-makers were (to refer again to Rothwell's general formula) finding 'the best available means to replace the verbal with the visual imagination'. When Hollywood sound films became established by the early 1930s, the visual certainly became a preoccupation, but principally through a compulsion to create lavish visual *spectacle*. The 'verbal' was not so much getting transformed imaginatively into film imagery; rather, it was being uneasily adapted for a film audience not accustomed to listening attentively to Shakespearean dramatic dialogue (continuing the tradition of spectacular late-Victorian/Edwardian theatre). Since Hollywood cinema was in transition from silent to sound film, the film-makers were primarily focused on two tasks: 'establishing the first principles of matching sight and sound, while at the same time rebuilding an impregnable star system after the silent era in order to sustain the very costly medium which the sound films had become' (Manvell, 1971, 35).

Sam Taylor's *The Taming of the Shrew* (1929) illustrates the challenges of the transition well. Initially released as a silent film (not all cinemas were equipped with sound in 1929), dialogue was shortly after dubbed in and a sound version released, making it the first ever feature-length Shakespeare talkie to be made. As Manvell has observed, the text of this early play of Shakespeare's 'is not normally treated with much respect in the theatre; the spoken word is often severely cut, while the stage business between Katherine and Petruccio is stretched out to win more laughs. This is precisely what Sam Taylor's production did; the struggle was developed into a farcical battle between Douglas Fairbanks and Mary Pickford' (Manvell, 1971, 23–24). In the silent version, the resulting slapstick comedy style was no doubt perfectly acceptable to a silent cinema audience. But in the sound version the verbal delivery was problematic, as Laurence Irving, designer for the film reports: 'Whenever dialogue that could not be cut tended to lag or was reckoned incomprehensible to the ninepennies ... two gagmen ... with an inexhaustible fund of practical comicalities in the Mack Sennett tradition ... were called upon for a diversion. And here and there Sam [Taylor], who was a secret dramatist, interpolated a line or two in the vernacular' (Manvell, 1971, 24). Taylor's enhancing of the dialogue led him to include an opening credit that was to make the film notorious: 'Written by William Shakespeare with additional dialogue by Sam Taylor.' 'Well, I did the stuff, didn't I?' said Taylor, according to Irving, when the latter tried to dissuade him from including the credit. Mary Pickford spoke Shakespeare's and Taylor's lines effectively, Irving finding her Katherine 'engagingly shrewish', but Fairbanks's voice he thought 'too thin to match his robust action'. Perhaps his frequent screen braggadocio posturing together with the insertion of Taylor's modern 'vernacular' and the reliance on knockabout slapstick gags reveals this first attempt at filming Shakespeare with sound more as Hollywood entertainment than as 'Shakespeare'. But Rothwell is also surely right that the Hollywood film-makers were already highly skilled in their visual art, the story line in this film surviving through 'clever exploitation of visual **metonymy**'; a good example being when 'Multiple analytical close-ups and **reaction shot**s spliced in from several different camera set-ups clinically document the Minola family's dysfunctionality' (Rothwell, 31).

Many critics have admired **Reinhardt and Dieterle's *A Midsummer Night's Dream* (1935)**, Kenneth Rothwell still regarding it in 1999 as 'the best Hollywood Shakespeare movie'. Although the film failed at the box office, it was nevertheless a most spectacular effort in dramatising Shakespeare for the screen; this spectacle being mainly achieved by the ambitious, lavish and highly effective use of choreography and special effects, all shot on a massive sound stage of over 38,000 square feet. One of the reasons for its critical success derived from Max Reinhardt's long-standing interest in and experience of staging the play, beginning with a 1905 Berlin production, followed over the years by productions in Salzburg, Oxford, and finally a fabulous version at the Hollywood Bowl in 1934. This was impressive enough for the Warner Brothers to invest $1.5 million on an extravagant Hollywood film version of the play. The large cast of gossamer-winged fairies, emerging from a mysterious forest set in a swirling mist, is expertly choreographed, as they seem to spiral up into the sky to music based on Mendelssohn's thrilling *Overture to a Midsummer Night's Dream*, the use of which echoes the atmosphere of a romantic nineteenth-century production. The remarkable artiness of the gothic lighting effects is balanced by the studio casting famous Hollywood actors in the main parts in the hope that a mass audience would bring hefty financial returns – a ploy used repeatedly since when casting Shakespeare films. A brilliant 11-year-old Mickey Rooney as Puck mimics the calling voices of Hermia (voluptuous Olivia de Havilland) and Lysander (chirpy Dick Powell) as they lose their way in the forest, while in the mechanicals' *Pyramus and Thisbe* rehearsal (3.1), James Cagney brings his own special brand of swagger to the playing of Bottom, until, that is, Puck comes along to make an ass of him. But this is a play with a dark side too, and Victor Jory's gruff, black-costumed Oberon produces a certain Dracula-like malevolence (his costume is very reminiscent of the one used by Henry Irving for his late-Victorian stage performance of Mephistopheles).

Like Reinhardt and Dieterle's *A Midsummer Night's Dream*, **George Cukor and Irving Thalberg's *Romeo and Juliet* (1936)** was a Hollywood extravaganza, this film costing $2 m and aiming, like its predecessor, to provide romantic grandeur, spectacle and sparkle – despite the fact that in genre terms the play was a tragedy. MGM's choice of *Romeo and Juliet* to follow up the Warner Brothers' critical success was well calculated since their themes bounce off each other. The inset *Pyramus and Thisbe* play bumblingly played before their Athenian masters by the 'rude mechanicals' not only self-referentially spoofs the antics of the four lovers of the frame play, but it is also a kind of parody of the tragic climax of *Romeo and Juliet*, in which Romeo, thinking that his lover Juliet is dead, commits suicide, where-upon Juliet stabs herself; just as Thisbe despairingly does when she finds Pyramus dead.

The MGM *Romeo and Juliet* fails for a number of reasons. Firstly, it did not emerge from any previous stage production. In the history of Shakespeare on film it often happens that a prior stage production helps to supply the artistic vision and vitality necessary to make a film dramatically successful. Rather, the business-orientated yet over-reverential MGM producer Thalburg still cherished the earlier silent movie ambition to make movies with 'class' for 'classier audiences', and, in a coinage worthy of George W. Bush, saw what he called the 'picturisation' of a Shakespeare play 'as the fulfilment of a long-cherished dream', regarding the English playwright as a writer whose 'dramatic form is practically that of a scenario'. An insight of sorts, this, but it did not extend to other matters. In a kind of quest for English 'authenticity', the deadly decision was made to cast established, middle-aged expatriate British actors for most of the main roles. There had been a long stage tradition of mature actors playing Romeo and Juliet, but casting 43-year-old Leslie Howard as Romeo and 35-year-old American Norma Shearer (Thalberg's wife) as Juliet, was surely a disastrous one. When Juliet's Nurse comes looking for Romeo in 2.3, encounters Mercutio, Benvolio and Romeo, and enquires, 'Gentlemen, can any of you tell me where I may find the young Romeo?', there is a pause until the mature and confident Howard as Romeo steps forward in response; the viewer is bound to feel nonplussed, if not cheated.

3

The Forties: Olivier and Welles

A fourth major Shakespeare film of the 1930s made in Britain was **Paul Czinner's *As You Like It* (1936)**, made for $1m by Twentieth Century Fox. Like the previous three Hollywood sound films, this production was (as Manvell says) 'again a victim of the star system'. Czinner conceived the film as a vehicle for the talents of his wife Elizabeth Bergner, who in the event was unsuitable for Rosalind, the character upon whom the film and play centres. The charm of her screen character according to Manvell was in depicting 'an ageless, kittenish quality, a kind of self-destructive femininity', an image foreign to that of Shakespeare's Rosalind, who is written as 'a forthright woman, capable, provocative and determined beneath her surface diffidence and charm', as he says (Manvell, 1971, 30, 31). Co-starring with Bergner as Orlando was 28-year-old Laurence Olivier. This was Olivier's first role in a Shakespeare film, for he had turned down an offer the same year to play Romeo in Cukor's *Romeo and Juliet*, on the grounds that 'Shakespeare could not be filmed'.

By the early 1940s Olivier's prejudice was a distant memory, his filming experience having helped him by then to gain a vital insight concerning the difference between Shakespeare for the stage and Shakespeare on film: 'audiences in the theatre swallow dialogue and acting conventions that on screen would draw howls of derisive laughter'. **Laurence Olivier's *Henry V* (1944)** was filmically innovative in many ways, this actor-director being the first to reveal 'the true potentialities of Shakespeare on screen' (Manvell). In meeting the challenge of screen adaptation, he discovered how to structure the play as a film and also found ways to explore the questions about theatrical style and conventions that so interested him. (Olivier's grasp of the differing *conventions* required for stage and film productions cannot be stressed enough for the breakthrough he made. I explore this and other significant films given only brief treatment in this history, in Part IV.) An inspired decision was to frame the film within an 'authentic' reconstructed Elizabethan performance of the play, using a live audience. This 'framing' approach to filming *Henry V* permitted Olivier to ' "play" with style in a Shakespearean way, to shift and blend styles scene by scene, matching Shakespeare's **metadrama** with **metacinema**' (Jorgens, 1991, 133).

With the success of *Henry V*, work soon began on **Olivier's *Hamlet* (1948)** another British Shakespeare film that would this time gain four Academy Awards: Best Picture, Best Actor, Best Art Direction and Set Decoration, and Best Costume Design – a record for this genre which has yet to be surpassed. As with *Henry V*, Olivier made many textual cuts, ruthlessly so in this case, since *Hamlet* is the longest of Shakespeare's plays. The film was attacked by some critics on this score at the time, but it is important to remember that any *popular* film adaptation of Shakespeare will always be contingent on various factors, the primary one being that the movie should appeal to cinema audiences accustomed to two-hour entertainment films.

Olivier's film was again innovative in that it drew heavily on the styles and techniques used in the then popular genre of American 'film noir' and also the earlier styles of German Expressionist cinema. Developed at a time in the 1940s when totalitarian regimes and technology-led mass markets were creating societies of individuals feeling increasingly anxious and powerless, the film noir style typically created darkly oppressive settings inhabited by characters struggling heroically against forces seemingly beyond their control. Classic examples of the genre are Billy Wilder's *Double Indemnity* (1944) and Howard Hawks's *The Big Sleep* (1946).

Although Olivier's *Hamlet* was the more skilfully finished artistic production, winning all the honours, the film artistry used for **Orson Welles's *Macbeth* (1948)** pares back fidelity to the Shakespeare text even more than Olivier does, in order that fidelity to Welles's *own* vision, sometimes extravagant, can be brought forward and expressed. Like Olivier, Welles was an actor-director familiar with the acting and production conventions of both stage and film, and was able and willing to mix these together effectively in his Shakespeare films. Yet Welles's facility for finding visually symbolic equivalents for Shakespeare's meanings (**metonymy**) brings him closer to the visionary Shakespeare adaptations of Kurosawa and Kozintsev.

4

The Fifties: Post-war Diversity

Just as the material economies of America and Europe grew with the pursuit of wealth and consumerism from the late 1940s into the 1950s following a half-century of world wars, so did the cultural economies expand too, and this expansion included an increase in the number and kind of Shakespeare film adaptations. (The growth in TV ownership and programming both sides of the Atlantic spawned an ever-increasing production of televised Shakespeare, discussed in Part V.) Interestingly, as Shakespeare became more and more of an international theatrical phenomenon in the post-war years with faster and easier communications across the world, so were those film adaptations being produced that emerged from a more diverse range of countries and cultures, beyond Britain and the USA. This is evident when we take note of the most significant films of the decade: Welles's *Othello* (Morocco/Italy, 1952), Joseph Mankiewicz's *Julius Caesar* (USA, 1953), Renato Castellani's *Romeo and Juliet* (UK/Italy, 1954), Olivier's *Richard III* (UK, 1955), Yutkevitch's *Othello* (Russia, 1955) and Kurosawa's *Kumonosu-Jô* (Japan, 1957).

Orson Welles's *Othello* (1952) takes the essential elements of a Shakespeare play and, as with *Macbeth*, Welles moulds a cinematic creation embodying his own unmistakeable vision and style. The film opens with a version of the play's ending, as had Olivier's *Hamlet*, so we see the bodies of Othello and Desdemona being carried in a funeral cortege on the ramparts of the 'Cyprus' fort. As well as evoking a sombrely tragic atmosphere with the dirge-like sounds of a pounding percussive piano and a wailing choir in the four-minute pre-titles opening sequence, Welles creates a striking ensemble of visual and aural effects capturing a number of the play's key themes, especially that of entrapment. After being bustled along like an animal on a rope, Iago is hoisted up against high walls in a cage, displayed to all as the deadly conspirator and enemy to the Venetian state that he is. As with Welles's *Macbeth*, images of Christian good (the cross) and demonic evil (the animalistic) are strikingly set one against another. In announcing this *Othello* as 'A Motion Picture **Adaptation** of the play by **William Shakespeare**', Welles proclaims by the equal emboldening of the words 'Adaptation' and 'William Shakespeare' in the titles that his approach will embody as much of his own authorial imprint as that of the originating playwright. His comments on the matter of adaptation, which may be thought to serve as a kind of credo for many of the 'filmic' adaptations of Shakespeare to come, was that

> *Othello*, whether successful or not, is about as close to Shakespeare's play as was Verdi's opera [i.e. *Otello*, 1887]. I think Verdi and Boito were perfectly entitled to change Shakespeare in adapting him to another art form; and, assuming that the film is an art form, I took the line that you can adapt a classic freely and vigorously for the cinema.   (Manvell, 1971, 61)

Joseph Mankiewicz's *Julius Caesar* (1953). It would not be difficult to characterise *Macbeth, Hamlet* and *Richard III* as plays revolving around the theme of political usurpation. In 1948 the politically conscious Welles was producing *Macbeth* at a time when the regicide and Macbeth's ultimate defeat could easily be read in the context of the rise and defeat of a Hitler whose fanatical ambitions had been focused on absolute (German) political supremacy, to the exclusion of all else. *Julius Caesar* is also a play in which the successful efforts of Cassius, Brutus and their supporters to remove (murder) the vainglorious Caesar only for him to be replaced by another dictator in the shape of Caesar's friend Octavius, can be interpreted as demonstrating the tendency for demagogues to triumph over easily led populations. With the return of Hollywood to Shakespeare in the shape of Mankiewicz's film we know that such an 'anti-fascist' interpretation of the play was what the producer John Houseman had in mind, for he says that

> While never deliberately exploiting the historic parallels, there are certain emotional patterns arising from political events of the immediate past that we were prepared to invoke ... Hitler at Nuremburg and Compiegne, and later in the Berlin rubble; Mussolini on his balcony with that same docile mob massed below which later watched him hanging by his feet, dead.
> (Jorgens, 1991, 96)

Much of the film's impact stems from the fine playing of well-cast actors allowed to speak their parts with what are, for a Hollywood film, surprisingly few textual cuts. Yet some of the cuts made, given that this is an overtly 'political' play posing questions about how the *polis* might be best governed, may well be significant in relation to the politics of the period from which Mankiewicz's production emerged. Including the scene of the senseless mob murder of Cinna the poet would seem to fit in well with the film-makers' desire to drive home their 'antifascist' perspective on the play. But although this scene was scripted and filmed, it was finally cut out of the released movie. It may be that the climactic scene preceding this one in the play, where Antony stirs up the Roman plebeians to mutiny, was thought to have provided a sufficient indictment of the mob's gullibility when addressed by a clever orator; movie newcomer Marlon Brando, deploying his own brilliant acting skills in the part – supplemented by tips provided by his on-set coach John Gielgud – certainly portrays a powerful manipulator of the crowd's emotions.

But it is also worth noting that in January of 1953, the year in which this *Julius Caesar* was released, Senator Joseph McCarthy became chairman of the 'un-American activities' Permanent Subcommittee on Investigations in the United States, instituting a kind of official political inquisition in which the careers of many artists and writers working in Hollywood were destroyed by the innuendo-laden anti-communist charges made against them. It is therefore possible that the depiction of Cinna the Poet being murdered by a mob who mindlessly mistake him for Cinna the conspiring politician, was excised because those who had made the film were fearful of including a scene that could be read as an innocent (Hollywood) artist being attacked by forces stirred up to hate those who would dare to challenge the political status quo.

Renato Castellani's *Romeo and Juliet* (1954) has been widely viewed as a critical failure through its poor casting and because of the director's approach of adapting (cutting) the connected rhythms of Shakespeare's poetic language and story into a 'realistic' (prosaic) version of speech patterns that would not distract the audience from their visual enjoyment of this *cinema verité*-influenced film. The costumes, settings and locations were lovingly created and photographed (by Robert Krasker, cinematographer on Olivier's *Henry V*) in order to persuade them that they were gazing into everyday scenes of old Italy. Castellani certainly brought a new dimension to the Shakespeare adaptation by shooting on location in old Italian towns like Verona, Sienna, Venice and Florence, newer and more portable types of film-making equipment having liberated film-makers from Hollywood-style sound stages. He innovated too by casting young actors for the roles of Juliet and Romeo. But whereas Zeffirelli was later to use young actors who played naturally and convincingly, English actor Laurence Harvey delivered a highly mannered Romeo whose fruity diction to twenty-first century ears seems laughable, while Susan Shentall, untrained and in her first acting role, played the notoriously difficult part of Juliet in an equally stilted fashion. Castellani's choice of Shentall for Juliet was emblematic of the priority Castellani gave to the 'Renaissance look' he wanted his film to have: she could easily have passed muster as a young female Italian figure in any of the famous Renaissance paintings he drew on for the creation of many of the costumes, properties and camera set-ups. Of the numerous visual elements modelled on Italian artistic sources, Juliet's dress for the Capulet Ball came from Botticelli's 'Wedding of Nostagio degli Onesti', while Capulet in his study follows Raphael's portrait of the Pope. Castellani must therefore be credited with initiating 'the vogue for "authentic" Renaissance settings in Shakespeare movies and teleplays' (Rothwell, 125), an approach Jonathan Miller rediscovered nearly 30 years later, using it to style the adaptations he produced or influenced in the BBC-TV Shakespeare series.

It is tempting and possibly legitimate to read **Olivier's *Richard III* (1955)** as another post-war commentary on the fearful dynamics of political dictatorship which had been deranging the world for so long by the mid-fifties. As noted above, Welles's *Macbeth* and Mankiewicz's *Julius Caesar* were self-consciously addressing the issue of usurpation in contemporary power politics, and it is feasible to read the ultra-usurping figure of Richard III also in the context of obsessive tyrants like Hitler or Stalin. But Olivier's use of Technicolor for his third Shakespearean dramatisation shows he is primarily interested in returning to a display of mediaeval visual pageantry. Whereas Welles's *Othello* gained a good deal of its impact from being shot on location – Olivier was content in his third and final Shakespeare movie to maintain the careful balance of theatrical and filmic techniques which had already worked for him in *Henry V* and *Hamlet*. Even though *Richard III* formally speaking is a history play, Olivier is able to satisfy both his theatrical inclinations and the needs of the Hollywood film by making a movie that, like *Hamlet*, focuses on the experiences and progress of a single character. Furthermore, with the opportunity of some 18 direct addresses to the audience in this play, Olivier deploys the 'intrusive' camera used so effectively in *Hamlet* to make Richard's nastily cynical point of view ours for the first half of the film.

Like Castellani's film, **Sergei Yutkevich's** *Othello* **(1955)** reveals a desire to utilise exterior settings, the director claiming he had 'broadened the frame of the tragedy by introducing a new element: nature, which can play a much bigger role on the screen than in theatre' (quoted in Davies and Wells, 202). Natural settings and textures are therefore used throughout the movie to register the play's changing dramatic intensities. An example is the low **mid shot** of Desdemona's hands being grasped by Othello on the citadel steps against a bright blue sky on his arrival in Cyprus, helping to signal the joy and optimism of re-united lovers – though an ominous presence stands above them immobile in the shape of Iago. Then there is the film's sombre closing shot showing the ship that carries their dead bodies towards a cloud-darkened sunset over a vast sea, movingly conveying the film's tragic denouement. But Yutkevich's romanticism also created emphases on the personality of characters in their own right, the 'pure' nobility of the Moor being sharply contrasted with the treacherous duplicity of Iago. For in Russia, as Jan Kott observed, 'The tragedy of jealousy there became a tragedy of betrayed confidence, in which Othello fell victim not only to Iago's intrigues but to the envy of the Doge and the entire Venetian senate' (Kott, 1974, 102). Some may feel that having a seemingly innocent and noble Othello being brought down solely by the betrayal of Iago without the Moor's own weaknesses being part of the tragic equation, is a simplification; but neither does the visual 'expansiveness' of Yutkevich's film help it to capture the essentially claustrophobic nature of the character relationships and spatial confinements of Shakespeare's play, something that Welles's more visually experimental production certainly does achieve.

Following Yutkevich's Russian *Othello*, a number of Shakespeare adaptations appeared by moviemakers in non-Anglophone countries. Apart from Kozintsev's Russian films of *Hamlet* and *King Lear*, none has received wider acclaim than the Japanese version of *Macbeth* by **Akira Kurosawa,** *Kumonosu-Jô* **(*The Castle of the Spider's Web*, 1957)**, distributed in the West as ***Throne of Blood***. It has been argued that Kurosawa's film is 'a transmutation, a distillation of the *Macbeth* theme, not an adaptation' (Manvell, 1971, 107). But as my analysis of the film in Part III shows, despite little or nothing of Shakespeare's text being drawn on verbally, a film drama is produced as dramatically nuanced and humanly complex – as Shakespearean, we might just as well say – as the Jacobean play. This is no doubt why Shakespearean director Peter Hall said in 1969 that Kurosawa's was 'perhaps the most successful Shakespeare film ever made', even though it 'had hardly any words, and none of them by Shakespeare' (Manvell, 1971, 113, n.5). Kurosawa's film stands alone as the only powerful sound film adaptation of a Shakespeare play not to use actors speaking his text, relying instead almost wholly on cinematic means to convey the drama.

5

The Sixties and Seventies: Cultural Revolution, Filmic Innovation

In 1960 Kurosawa released *The Bad Sleep Well*, a study of corruption and revenge set in the corporate business world of modern Japan and conveyed in the form of a *film noir* thriller, though also drawing loosely on a complex of themes to be found in *Hamlet*. The setting of his 1985 film *Ran* returns to the Japanese mediaeval civil war period, the social power conflicts of this screen drama again being mediated by the samurai warrior codes so effectively deployed for *Kumonosu-Jô*. Kurosawa stated that Shakespeare was not the inspiration for *Ran*, yet many echoes of *King Lear*, especially its dramatically bitter rivalries, are to be found in it. The film is about what happens when three sons turn on the great warlord father who has decided to divide his king-dom among them in order to seek a peaceful retirement: a kind of Japanese mediaeval hell on earth ensues. Both films are fine artistic achievements, and are certainly worthy of further discussion and analysis. But since neither of them are Shakespeare adaptations within the parameters of this book (or in Kurosawa's own terms either), they are beyond its scope.

If some critics have seen fit to pronounce Kurosawa's *Kumonosu-Jô* a 'masterpiece', many have also come to regard **Grigori Kozintsev's Hamlet (1964)** an artistic triumph of film Shakespeare. This was the first major Shakespeare movie of the 1960s, and like Olivier's 1948 version of the play (from which it partly borrows), it was shot in black and white. 'In *Don Quixote* I used colour because I wanted to capture the quality, the ambience of the warm South', said Kozintsev, 'for *Hamlet* I want the cool greys of the North' (Manvell, 1971, 80). The influence of Olivier's *Hamlet* is revealed mainly in the attempt to create an oppressively prison-like Elsinore setting, full of stony halls and mysterious staircases, and also in symbolically linking the danger-ous life of the castle under the usurper Claudius to a tumultuous sea far below. This Hamlet (played by Innokenti Smoktounovski) is nordically blonde-headed, as Olivier's hero was, and as Branagh's would be in his marathon 1996 version.

But there the similarities between Kozintsev's film and Olivier's end, since the 'entrapping' forces that drive along the Russian Dane are dominantly political, as opposed to the psychological obsessions affecting Olivier's neurotic prince. Kozintsev reinstates Rosencrantz and Guildenstern, and also young Fortinbras, the son of Norway whose mettle, like that of the son of Denmark, is being tested. Kozintsev's political sensibilities had been shaped in the murderous Stalin era, his film deriving from a stage production at the Pushkin Academic Theatre of Drama in Leningrad in 1954, the moment Stalin had died and the Soviet state began its slow political 'thaw' under Kruszchev. Yet there is no evidence of a thaw in Kozintsev's film. Stating that Hamlet was 'a man of our time', he evidently regarded the one-party state of Russia in the same way Hamlet regards Denmark as 'a prison' (2.2.239). This is graphically revealed in the opening sequence when Hamlet, arriving at Elsinore, gallops through the gates of the castle, the giant teeth of the portcullis closing down behind him to meet the rising drawbridge as if set in huge jaws, a terrifying image of entrapment.

This visual **metonymic** is merely one small example of Kozintsev's imaginative approach to adaptation. His primary intention for *Hamlet* (according to Manvell) was to 'emphasize man's essential dignity in a world representing his indignity, and his desire to "make visible" the poetic atmosphere of the play'. This is captured well in the distinctive methods the director uses to represent Hamlet's and Ophelia's rela-tionship to the royal court around them. Given that Hamlet refers to Denmark as a 'prison', it could be tempting to convey his sense of 'entrapment' in too literal a way by playing the action in a dungeon-like setting. But as Kozintsev argues, in reality 'court life is comfort-able', so that 'for a person of ideas and feelings' like Hamlet the stifling conventions that go with this can themselves 'constitute a *prison*'. The film therefore shows Hamlet being treated 'royally' and respectfully by courtiers, many of his acid insights being spoken in **voice-over** as he struts gravely among his bowing and scraping inferiors around the castle. Just as he wanted to get away from the long-established practice of 'Hamletism' – presenting an enfeebled intellectual unable to act – Kozintsev also wanted to avoid the melodramatic style of showing Ophelia in Act IV as a jilted and demented headcase vacantly gathering flowers – pretty much how she appeared in Olivier's version. Instead, she is shown as the 'single happy person' walking about 'a palace that is paralyzed by alarm', her pathetic madness being conveyed so much more emphatically by allowing us to understand that 'To be out of one's mind here is to be happy' (Kozintsev, 1972, 191).

Kozintsev's thoughtful approach to visualising *Hamlet* for the screen was applied just as effectively when he came to film ***King Lear* (1970)**. Once again, the starting point was the 'here and now' of his own country's one-party state. His concern was to convey the essential meanings of the play both in the context of his perception of Russian social struggles and in an articulation which owed much to a distinctly 'Russian' cultural and artistic tradition. Working from Boris Pasternak's translation, as he had for *Hamlet*, and again deploying a powerful musical score specially written by the brilliant Dmitri Shostakovich, Kozintsev creates for his *King Lear* a range of visual **motifs** and an **image system** aiming to show 'certain aspects' of the play 'which the theatre cannot manage'. To 'read Shakespeare in the light of the present day' for this director in the late 1960s was to emphasise the suffering of the world's dispossessed, those socially disenfranchised by the force and meanness of powerful political regimes. In Shakespeare's play, the man who possesses most at the beginning – Lear – is by the end deprived of most, having lost all his property, his favourite daughter, and having plunged his country into the strife of war and division. But before Cordelia is killed and he himself dies, there is reconciliation between them even as they stand surrounded by Edmund's heavily armed forces. This is shown in an image Kozintsev describes as 'goodness encircled by iron, weapons of murder – people gripped by a mania for destruction, by hatred'. It is by the power of such images as this and by the sight and sound of Lear's ragged 'Fool-musician' playing on his hand-made wooden pipe, the plaintive sound of which opens and closes the film, that, in Kozintsev's words, 'the voice of human suffering is accorded more significance than the roar of thunder' (1972, 198).

Another Shakespeare film of this moment that carved an artistic triumph out of a tragic conception was **Orson Welles's *Chimes at Midnight* (1966)**, *Campanadas a media noche* in Spanish, for it was filmed on locations in Spain, and eventually emerged as a Spanish/Swiss production (in the USA it is known simply as **Falstaff**). Leaving behind the virtuoso cinematic productions of *Macbeth* and *Othello*, Welles's relatively orthodox conception for this film grew out of his conviction that 'Falstaff is the best role that Shakespeare ever wrote'. His aims were to 'isolate the story of Falstaff's friendship with Prince Hal – their strange friendship in the taverns and streets of London and the tragedy of Hal's final rejection of the old man once he had become king', regarding the outcome as a 'lament for Merrie England', a comedy 'viewed all in dark colour' (Manvell, 1971, 64).

In focusing on a kind of triangular relationship in which Hal is caught between his love for Falstaff and the low-life freedoms he represents, and his need to be mindful that one day he will become king, Welles manages to achieve a remarkable balance of contrary energies in the film. An enormous amount was inevitably cut from each of the plays he draws on (*Richard II*, *1* and *2 Henry IV*, *Henry V*, *The Merry Wives of Windsor*) in order to focus on his key characters. Yet he not only manages to 'render powerfully the personal, political and mythical dimensions of the original plays', but also succeeds 'as few interpreter-adapters have in preserving Shakespeare's double perspective, the tensions, contrasts, and discontinuities which give the drama life' (Jorgens, 1991, 109).

The film starts in winter with a close-up of the gigantic Falstaff (played by an immensely fat Welles) as he sits in reminiscent mood by the fire enduring good-humouredly the piping chatter of his senile friend Justice Shallow, whose guest he is in Gloucestershire, and to whom he utters the words from which the film's title comes: 'We have heard the chimes at midnight, Master Shallow' (*2 Henry IV*, 3.2.197–8). The film's action then alternates between the high intrigues and happenings of the court of Henry IV (played by John Gielgud), typically shot in the grand and sober loftiness of Cordoba cathedral, and the comic bawdiness of the Boar's Head tavern and whorehouse. Here the king's son Prince Hal both partakes in and studies the antics of the characters who compose a lowlife 'court' presided over by the witty, cunning and benignly dissolute Sir John Falstaff. The **low-angle** shot, Welles's cinematic signature, is used a great deal, often to contrast the power struggle that the austere and aloof figure of the king on his high throne is engaged in, with the discontented nobility. Shafts and pools of bright light from high windows are also frequently used (an idea Welles perhaps borrowed from shots in Kozintsev's *Hamlet*) to pick out favoured individuals like the king, and Prince Hal when he inherits the throne. But tilted-up shots are also used to lend dignity to Falstaff's bulky influence – over Hal in particular.

A hilarious and brilliantly executed sequence of burlesque is achieved in the Boar's Head when Falstaff and Hal take turns at imitating Henry IV on a makeshift 'throne' set on a tavern table. The audience of customers and Mistress Quickly's whores roar with justified laughter at the performance. But, for the knowing spectator of Shakespeare's drama it also turns into a poignant spectacle, when Hal with a cooking pot for a crown chides Falstaff (as Hal) for associating with 'a devil [...] in the likeness of a fat old man', the camera for once tilting *down* on the man whom we know one day will necessarily be rejected by the successor to Henry IV. The film also has very serious elements, such as its widely admired ten-minute battle sequence. This is shot with a gruesome realism in which the *sounds* of the battle – constantly clashing metal, death-dealing thuds from heavy clubs, the shrieks and groans of the wounded whom we see squirming in mud – pain our ears mercilessly. At times speeded up to convey the high energy of opposing first encounters between combatants, and slowed down to emphasise their sheer physical exhaustion later, the sequence has been compared by film-maker Peter Bogdanovich (as against the charming 'pageantry' of Olivier's *Henry V* battle sequence) to 'the war paintings of Goya'. If, as Leonardo da Vinci said, it is the job of an artist 'to breathe life into a two-dimensional plane', then *Chimes at Midnight* breathes life into the two-dimensional form of film art with an authority and a faithfulness to Shakespeare's subtle and all-embracing artistic vision that has rarely been equalled on screen.

If in 1966 Welles had created a near-masterpiece as the culmination of a series of films now dubbed 'Shakespeare for the art houses' (Rothwell), then this moment was also when Shakespeare for the mass cinema audience was being born in earnest, by way of **Franco Zeffirelli's** adaptations of ***The Taming of the Shrew* (1966)** and *Romeo and Juliet* (1968). Although television at this time was providing a seriously diverting entertainment alternative to the hitherto unchallenged supremacy of the big screen, the glamour of film was still a crowd puller, few stars of the period being more glamorous than the 'reigning king and queen of the movies', Richard Burton and Elizabeth Taylor. Alert to the fact that film audiences were increasingly 'gender aware', Zeffirelli sidestepped possible controversy by turning the play into a carnivalesque farce resembling an opera, a form more often than not impervious to questions of inequality and other such social issues. Manipulating and radically cutting Shakespeare's text to create a boisterous vehicle for the notoriously stormy pairing of Burton and Taylor, Zeffirelli excised a good deal of the Bianca and Lucentio love-plot and much else besides in order to foreground Petruccio's spirited pursuit and conquest of the explosive Katherine.

The focus is on colourful display and knockabout humour. The pre-wedding sequence, and the wedding scene itself – only reported by Gremio in the play but played out here for over ten minutes – both reveal Zeffirelli's preference for 'display' over fidelity to Shakespeare's text. Sourly noting how the movie is 'loaded with pleasant but syrupy melodies in the best Hollywood tradition', Jack Jorgens nevertheless persuasively argues (following C. L. Barber's perceptive analyses of Shakespeare's 'festive comedies' (1972)) that Zeffirelli cleverly replaces Shakespeare's frame story of Christopher Sly with his own frame story of Saturnalian revels, Petruccio and Kate functioning as a Lord and Lady of Misrule offering a 'good-natured but thorough assault … on Padua and Paduan values' (1991, 72).

Zeffirelli's *Romeo and Juliet* (1968) has been one of the most popular and commercially successful Shakespeare films of all time: originally funded by Paramount with only $800,000, the film would eventually gross $48 million at the box office. The reasons for its success were many, and I will touch on only a few here. A factor that must not be underestimated (especially by the 'purists' who regard him as a butcher of Shakespeare's verse) is the extent to which Zeffirelli had by 1968 developed immense skills for both staging and filming Shakespeare. He had produced the wildly successful *The Taming of the Shrew*, and now planned to follow up his energetic and highly praised 1960 staging of *Romeo and Juliet* at London's Old Vic with a film loosely based on that production. But he had also learned much from studying previous Shakespeare films, in particular never forgetting Olivier's *Henry V*. Not only is the panoramic opening shot of his *Romeo and Juliet* a tribute to the opening of Olivier's film, but he had Olivier reading both Prologue and Epilogue in voice-over, and used him to dub the voice of Lord Montague as well as for smaller parts and crowd noises: in his last Shakespeare movie, Zeffirelli would also follow closely Olivier's 1948 *Hamlet* interpretation.

The Royal Shakespeare Company Influence: Hall and Brook

Zeffirelli's films were visually lush, engagingly vivacious and hugely popular at the box office – the price to be paid for such success often being a ruthless cutting, manipulating and ultimately underplaying of

Shakespeare's verse in favour of spectacle and sentimental song. Yet there were new and brilliant British theatre directors also working in the sixties who not only gave primacy to Shakespeare's language, but by the end of the decade were eager to translate their thoroughly researched and rehearsed theatrical successes into films, often in very experimental ways. Furthermore, with the exception of Olivier's films, by far the greater number of Anglophone Shakespeare film adaptations to appear by the beginning of the 1960s had tended to star actors more experienced in the cinema than on the stage. By the late sixties this situation had changed, as, along with the new breed of Shakespearean directors came a whole cadre of energetic, highly skilled and articulate Shakespearean actors. Most of these had passed through the rigorous training ground of the Royal Shakespeare Company (RSC) founded by John Barton and Trevor Nunn at Stratford-upon-Avon, where the art of verse-speaking was a mandatory skill, and then often going on to the new National Theatre, led at first by Olivier himself until Peter Hall took over in the mid-seventies. The two most prominent examples of films benefiting from these new talents were Peter Hall's *A Midsummer Night's Dream* (1969) and Peter Brook's *King Lear* (1970).

Peter Hall's *A Midsummer Night's Dream* (1969). This was filmed on location in a country house park near Stratford-upon-Avon in the autumn, Hall's prime concern being to use high calibre RSC-trained actors in order 'to bend the medium of film to reveal the full quality of the text' (Manvell, 126). Most of the movie was filmed **close-up** in one, **two** or three **shots** because this approach seemed to him 'the only way to scrutinise coolly the marked ambiguity of the text', something he thought the cinema can do 'better than the theatre'. The result was a complete vindication of his approach, the superb cast of actors bringing out the nuances of Shakespeare's clever multi-levelled text brilliantly. Hall managed to preserve what he calls the 'lightness and precision' of the actors' spoken words by using **ADR** (automated dialogue replacement). As well as enabling us to hear clearly every word spoken by the likes of Ian Richardson (Oberon), Judi Dench (Titania), Diana Rigg (Helena) and David Warner (Lysander), this technique also helps to promote the dream-like anti-realism of a play Hall thinks of as 'artificial', and 'not a natural one requiring natural sound'. As with the 1909 Vitagraph silent, Hall deploys trick camerawork to make Puck (Ian Holm) and all the other characters of the fairy world magically appear and disappear at various points. But this is the nearest the production gets to any earlier versions of the *Dream*,

Hall once again relying on the text of the play in order to deliver an approach diametrically opposed to the kind of glittering and sentimentally romantic spectacle found in Reinhardt and Dieterle's film. Drawing on the full text of the play allows Hall to make apparent how the contriving magical powers of Oberon and Puck are a key dynamic of it. But using the full text also enables him to show how the quarrelling king and queen of the fairies 'have upset the balance of nature'. As Hall says, 'This is what the play is all about. It is not a pretty, balletic affair, but erotic, physical, down to earth'. His decision to film the play in a wet out-of-doors autumn setting in Warwickshire thus derives from the text, where it is made clear that the play concerns 'an English summer in which the seasons have gone wrong'. The relationships between the lovers have 'gone wrong' too, until 'sweet peace' is finally brought to them by the magical interventions of Oberon and Puck. The film shows that the play is actually 'darker' than the prettifying post-romantic versions which most people had come to expect up until this moment. But as well as the magical and human malevolence on display in the drama, Hall points out how there is also 'great charm and humour as well'. This charm and humour is so successfully brought to the screen by Hall that it offers an object lesson in how it is possible, with the help of a uniquely talented cast of actors, to use the whole text of a Shakespeare play in order to communicate the fullest range of meanings it suggests; always providing that the viewing audience is able to follow the Shakespearean English that is being conveyed.

Peter Brook's *King Lear* (1970). We have already noted how Kozintsev brought a particular kind of cinematic quality to his versions of *Hamlet* and *King Lear*. Through expressive landscape settings and scenes which build toward big dramatic moments frequently driven by Shostakovich's orchestral score, effects are created that may be thought of as romantically epic. Brook's *Lear* could not be more different. Employing no music whatever, and shot in the freezing North Danish wastes of Jutland in deep winter, he pares back the text of the play to its essentials, focusing closely on characters either perpetrating or suffering cruelty in a hostile nature and hopeless world where death feels inevitable. Jack Jorgens aptly contrasts these two *Lear*s by describing Kozintsev's as 'a Christian-Marxist story of redemption and social renewal', while Brook's is a 'a bleak existential tale of meaningless violence in a cold, empty universe' (Jorgens, 1991, 237, 236). The reasons for this remarkable variance in approach and effect lie in the strikingly different cultural experiences shaping the directorial vision of each film-maker. As has already been mentioned,

Kozintsev worked in the politically pressurised context of a totalitarian dictatorship. By contrast, in Brook's de-historicized adaptation, no 'positives' are allowed to enter the film's bleak vision.

The reason for excluding all notions of redemption seems to be because Brook's 'take' on *King Lear* is very much in the 'existential' mould rendered by Jan Kott's pessimistic interpretation of the play in his influential book *Shakespeare our Contemporary* (1964). The little humour Brook introduces is very much of the 'absurdist' kind, a dark wit that plays with or even relishes the prospect of scrutinising, dissecting and imaging a world in which human meaning and value have all but vanished. We often find such worlds conveyed in the 1950s and 1960s drama of playwrights like Eugene Ionesco and Antonin Artaud in France, and in England by the plays of Harold Pinter and Samuel Beckett. There is a definite cultural logic to Brook's reading *King Lear* in this 'Beckettian' way in late-60s Britain, where highly conformist and traditional notions of history and nature were being radically challenged. Although 'History' and 'Nature' were not concepts readily applicable in Shakespeare's period, 'divine-right' monarchy was an institution under threat from an increasingly secularised society, *King Lear* offering prime evidence that the thoughts and actions of 'Machiavellian monsters' are chillingly in evidence. Writing and working in the wake of monumentally destructive World Wars undertaken by power-fixated political regimes that in 1940s Germany had led to the obscenity of the Holocaust, and in the 1950s and 1960s to the Vietnam war, it is therefore not surprising to find many artists and intellectuals by the 1960s feeling that human value had drained out of the world, and that it was time for decades of rigid cultural conformity to be exposed and countered.

Brook counters such conformity by imaging for us a comfortless tragicomedy in which power is thoughtlessly ceded to ruthless Machiavels who destroy themselves as well as others by their own nasty deficiencies of insight. This comfortless imaging is managed by making much of the play's great and central metaphor, sight itself. Lear himself starts out by issuing the dark commands that will lead to disintegration and death, wilfully brushing aside Kent's injunction to 'See better, Lear' (1.1.157). Stripped of power and its delusions, he meets his final end in the brutally blinding light of Brook's Dover beach, where he is shown slowly and literally falling away into death through the bottom of the film frame. In between, seeing and not-seeing are ideas constantly played with, most innovatively by Brook's camera lens often blurring or going to black, to show the distorted or limited point of view of characters who – like Lear himself – cannot see too well when their minds are disturbed. Perhaps Brook's cleverest exploration of the sight metaphor – in which he also toys with the viewer's own perceptions – is in the famous 'fall that isn't a fall' of blind Gloucester. We as well as Gloucester are persuaded by the darkly comic machinations of his son Edgar in close-up shots of them both, that the despairing father is about to tumble to his death from a cliff. In the middle of the climactic moment of tumbling, we cut from a **medium-close shot** of Gloucester to a high **crane shot** that reveals him taking what Jorgens calls a 'silent pratfall on a barren stretch of sand'. Soon after, Lear will say to him, 'You see how this world goes', to which Gloucester replies, 'I see it feelingly'. Curiously, despite the relentless withdrawal of sentiment and feeling in Brook's film, this is how we too are finally encouraged to reflect on what he has shown us.

Tony Richardson's *Hamlet* **(1969)** was staged and filmed at the Round House in London because the space allowed the director to shoot in **close** and **medium-close shots**. Nicol Williamson's angry Hamlet emerges very much as a product of his time, the video publicity blurb's report that he is 'not the conventional poet and scholar', but rather 'the anti-establishment drop-out, rough, sensual, impulsive', for once being correct. The late-sixties ethos of rebelliousness and sensuality in the film does not end with Hamlet either. Before his departure from Elsinore, the warning that Laertes (Michael Pennington) gives to his sister Ophelia (Marianne Faithfull) to stay away from Hamlet seems curiously at odds with her smiling willingness to receive deep and repeated kisses on the mouth from him that suggest an incestuous relationship. This suggestiveness is all of a piece with the sixties' flouting of social convention, as are the flaunted sensual displays toward each other shown by Claudius (Anthony Hopkins) and Gertrude (Judy Parfitt), who choose to receive Polonius (Mark Dignam) while they sup, drink and cavort in the royal bed of Denmark.

Two of the three remaining films to be mentioned in this highly prolific era of screen Shakespeare adaptations were productions in which the American actor Charlton Heston figured large. **Stuart Burge's** *Julius Caesar* **(1970)** had an Anglo-American cast that included Heston as Mark Antony and Jason Robards Jr as Brutus, while English actors John Gielgud played Caesar, Diana Rigg was Portia and Richard Johnson played Cassius. The film was not without credit, Richard Johnson's brilliant portrayal of Cassius realising the 'mean and hungry look' and rebelliously resentful personality of the character in ways that have yet to be surpassed on film. What undoubtedly damaged the unevenly cast production was the flat, lustreless and utterly uninflected performance of Robards as Brutus, one critic commenting that he appeared 'to be receiving his lines by concealed radio transmitter, and delivering them as part of the responsive reading in a Sunday sermon' (Quoted by Rothwell, 161). In **Charlton Heston's** *Antony and Cleopatra* **(1972)**, Heston again plays Antony, casting the South African actress Hildegard Neil as the Egyptian Queen. By no means an inexperienced Shakespearean actor, Heston is nevertheless held back by a modern equivalent of the over-respectful 1930s method, approaching Shakespeare 'deferentially, taking the high road, without a jot of Brook's or Polanski's bitter irony' (Rothwell, 163). This brings us to the last major Shakespeare film of this period, Roman Polanski's accomplished *Macbeth* (1971).

If the Shakespearean adaptations of Hall and Brook had been dyed in Kott's tincture of existential darkness to one degree or another, purist critics feeling these directors had profaned their Bard, **Roman Polanski's** *Macbeth* **(1971)** created even more shock. Polanski's film is realistic, but the way he fulfils his aim of making *Macbeth* 'quite realistic' (his words) is by tapping into the cynicism, political assassinations and terrors abroad at a time of violent political upheaval across the world. The assassinations of politically progressive leaders (John Kennedy, Martin Luther King), America's deadly anti-communist war in Vietnam, and the brutal invasion of a liberalising Czechoslovakia by the Soviet Union – to name only three globally significant phenomena – had produced a wholly justified cynicism about international power politics. Polanski and his co-screenplay writer the distinguished Shakespeare critic and National Theatre dramaturge Kenneth Tynan, were both of this critical and highly articulate generation. Such articulation emerges in the consummate filmic techniques and effects deployed by Polanski to expose the violent and bloody process of political usurpation, and how its outcome diseases and engulfs almost the whole fabric of society as well as its obsessive instigators.

6

The Nineties: Branagh's Renaissance and the Shakespeare on Film Revival

On its release, much critical attention was given to Polanski's *Macbeth*, which is still frequently taught in schools and universities as a comparison text with Welles's movie and is regarded by many as one of the most artistically successful Shakespeare film adaptations ever made. Yet it did badly at the cinema box office, its commercial failure on release prompting some to feel this could be a factor in the virtual disappearance of large-budget adaptations of Shakespeare for the big screen over the following two decades, until Kenneth Branagh's *Henry V* revived the genre in 1989. However, other and more significant factors contributed to this decline. The explosive cultural energies released in Western Europe and the USA by the sixties had created numerous lines of fresh cultural enterprise, especially in Britain. In the area of British Shakespeare performance, once the challenge of exploring how plays could be creatively translated into the film medium had been met by innovative directors like Peter Hall and Peter Brook, they moved on to other drama projects: for them Shakespeare on film had been one cultural project to pursue among many others. Then there was the competition from television, which for a time seduced filmgoers away from the cinema. And as domestic television audiences across the increasingly prosperous 'First World' enlarged dramatically, so did interest in making Shakespeare accessible to big audiences via the small screen. When in the late 1970s the BBC-TV project began of dramatising, recording and broadcasting all 37 of Shakespeare's plays, the initiative channelled a good deal of British Shakespearean theatrical energies into these small-screen productions, a process that continued well into 1985.

But by 1985 two other key transformations had taken place, one being that in the USA multiplex cinemas had taken off in a big way, multi-screen cinemas boosting movie production that in turn provided a greater choice of movies to tempt bored TV channel-hoppers out into public viewing spaces again. This phenomenon soon came to Britain too, intimately linked as the UK has been to the consumption of US popular culture trends since the 1950s. By the mid-1980s the other key transformation – Thatcherite popular capitalism – was also well established and picking up on that part of the sixties' British cultural revolution which old-style socialism could not comprehend or exploit. Popular cultural enterprise had been moving on apace in Britain too. Shakespeare and his company at the Globe had always relied on a paying audience to keep their popular dramatic enterprise going. 400 years later in the mid-1980s the mass movie audience, its collective visual expectations shaped by the inventiveness of film-makers like Coppola, Scorsese and Spielberg to want more and more sophisticated film 'product', were primed and ready to pay to see artistically challenging movies – always assuming that these would also be accessible and entertaining.

Branagh's Renaissance, its approach and influence

The young actor Kenneth Branagh was both a beneficiary of, and shaped by, these shifts toward a new entrepreneurially minded British cultural climate and marketplace. Although trained at the prestigious Royal Academy of Dramatic Art (RADA) in London, his personality and values were indelibly influenced by being raised in a large, lively and character-filled working class Belfast family, his cultural imagination moulded by TV and popular film rather than by the theatre. In fact, he performed as many of his earliest professional acting roles in front of TV and film cameras as he did in the live theatre. Having played the title role of *Henry V* for the entire time he worked in the Royal Shakespeare Company at Stratford and London (1984–85), this was to be the play he felt compelled to adapt and star in on film for his independent Renaissance Films plc. Stifled by the increasingly bureaucratic repertory system of the RSC, he yearned to offer productions of Shakespeare's plays to the public directed by seasoned actors eager to make them accessible to a popular audience, as they had been in Shakespeare's own day. He had therefore founded the distinctly un-bureaucratic Renaissance Theatre Company (RTC) along

with his friend David Parfitt in 1987 for just such a purpose, to promote a drama of (as he puts it) 'life-enhancing populism'. By mid-
1988, with a company of like-minded actor-directors that included
Derek Jacobi, Judi Dench and Geraldine McEwan, RTC had been
achieving just this kind of success with sold-out productions throughout the UK of *Hamlet, Much Ado About Nothing* and *As You Like It*.
His gamble of having seasoned players directing Shakespeare to
smallish theatre audiences (Jacobi/*Hamlet*; Dench/*Much Ado About
Nothing*; McEwan/*As You Like It*) was thus vindicated.

So far, so good, but 'How is intimate acting in Shakespeare shared
by lots of people?' was Branagh's next question. Answer: 'By making
a film of *Henry V*' (Branagh, 1991, 205). By the time everything was
ready and in place for him to direct and star in this film – independ-
ently funded by City finance in London – he was persuaded that
he had 'the gritty realistic approach that was necessary to make it the
truly popular film I had in mind' (Branagh, 1991, 220). His gamble
paid off. Within a few months of its release not only was it apparent
he and his Renaissance team had made a popular film success of a
Shakespeare play mainly about mediaeval warfare, *Henry V* going on
to gain Academy and other awards, but as Rothwell has observed, 'by
a shrewd merger of art and commerce' Branagh had also 'magically
resuscitated the Shakespeare movie just when everyone was announcing
its death at the hands of television' (Rothwell, 246).

What was it about Branagh's method of delivering Shakespeare on
film that produced this first success? Three key aspects of his
approach have not only brought him success in the popular cinema
marketplace, but have also given his Shakespeare films (he has made
others) a distinctive signature and identity. Firstly, he has been determined to make the performance of Shakespeare's text as clear and
understandable to the audience as possible, summed up in his credo
that 'Words and thoughts and actions must always be linked to provide the correct clarity and tone of sound' (Branagh, 1991, 140).
Beyond this, he has also sought for 'an absolute clarity that would
enable a modern audience to respond to Shakespeare on film, in the
same way that they would respond to any other movie' (Branagh,
1993, viii). This aim was ambitious and has involved Branagh in
embracing a range of techniques and requirements to make his films
as popular as others consumed internationally. In all of his movies to
date, he has for the most part created screen characters whom the
audience cares about, mainly by casting talented actors able to
provide strong characters whom we become acquainted with through

the sustained use of **close-up** shots. We get to know and care about most of the characters in Branagh's *Henry V* because we are repeatedly brought up close to them and their intimate actions, by the camera. The same cannot be said of Olivier's film, where most of the characters are kept at a distance. A second and crucial move by Branagh has been to provide accessible screen worlds for his audience through his own familiarity with various influential genre movies that he draws on to create the world of each Shakespeare film story. Each of his films to date has been invested with an ambience and visual references appropriated from an established Hollywood genre. A third and continuing feature of Branagh's Shakespeare films from *Much Ado* onwards has been to use a mixed cast of actors, including famous Hollywood faces previously unknown for playing Shakespeare.

In many ways Branagh's populist approach can be seen to have benefited from the examples provided by **Franco Zeffirelli**. The latter's Shakespeare films had already demonstrated that using the conventions of narrative realism and naturalistic acting were the way to attract a mass audience to a genre the film financiers usually preferred to avoid. In approaching his *Much Ado* Branagh seems also to have taken a tip from **Zeffirelli's *Hamlet* (1990)** and used a mix of American and English actors. But there the similarities end, naturalistic as the acting may be in the films of both directors. For whereas Zeffirelli has often been content in the interests of effortless audience comprehension to drastically cut and paste the Shakespearean text in the registers and rhythms of ordinary speech, Branagh has always encouraged his actors to 'speak the speech' in the poetic rhythms that are embedded in the dramatic scripts Shakespeare actually wrote. Furthermore, where Branagh generally deploys genre film styles to help make the Shakespeare play text 'more available' to a popular audience, Zeffirelli's decision to play *Hamlet* as an action movie was dictated by his choice of a particular actor to play Hamlet – Mel Gibson. In 1990 Gibson was known by film audiences for his roles in the *Mad Max* and *Lethal Weapon* action films. In a further bid to draw large audiences, Zeffirelli cast Glenn Close, fresh from prominent Hollywood performances in *Fatal Attraction* (1987) and *Dangerous Liaisons* (1988), to play Hamlet's mother, Gertrude. Since Zeffirelli was determined to adopt Olivier's 'oedipal' interpretation of Hamlet, it was almost inevitable that foregrounding such sexually charismatic and volatile actors as Gibson and Close would produce a film where 'lethal weapon meets fatal attraction in what turns out to be a dangerous liaison' – as one critic has quipped. The explosive mix of this family melodrama almost detonates in the film's pivotally central closet scene. Here, Hamlet seems only prevented from having sex with Gertrude as they writhe together on the royal bed of Denmark through being interrupted by Old Hamlet's ghost (his only appearance, the Ghost having been excised completely from the opening scenes of the film). For Gibson's Hamlet, the scene is clearly cathartic. From here on he assumes the action-hero persona denied to previous Hamlets, routinely condemned as they had been to playing the inconveniently complicating textual elements that produce the Prince's melancholy irresolution, most of which Zeffirelli removes so that the action-mould of his film is not disturbed.

Christine Edzard had worked with Zeffirelli on his 1968 hit movie *Romeo and Juliet*. But the low-budget adaptation of *As You Like It* **(1992)** she made from her small studios at Rotherhithe, in the run-down docklands district of East London, had little hope of attracting a popular audience. Previously best known for an award-winning dramatisation of *Little Dorrit* (1988), Dickens's novelistic exploration of the impoverishment visited on mid-Victorian London lives both high and low by raw capitalist greed, Edzard now bravely sought to deliver a comparable illustration of the social effects of 1980s Thatcherite 'greed is good' economics using Shakespeare's comedy as a vehicle. For the most part, the substitution of an urban for a wooded pastoral sits neither comfortably nor convincingly with this Shakespearean comedy. It is possible Edzard hoped we would 'see her Arden as a spatial metaphor – a symbolic landscape of the imagination, not some slice of the Warwickshire countryside' (Crowl, 160). But the conventions of narrative cinema in the realist mode dictate that what we see on film will be read 'as if' it is 'real': cinema audiences do not understand the settings of stories they see on screen as 'symbolic' landscapes, but rather as real ones (see my discussion of Edzard's as the first 'periodising' Shakespeare adaptation in Part III).

By contrast **Kenneth Branagh's** *Much Ado About Nothing* **(1993)** is such a well-wrought Shakespeare film comedy that it has become famous for the 'feelgood' effect it invariably produces in its viewers. Branagh had sought for 'a certain fairy tale quality to emerge' in his adaptation of this comedy, and without doubt he secured it by filming in the kind of the pastoral setting that was so wanting in Edzard's film. By shooting his movie at a hilltop villa in the golden summer warmth of Italy's Tuscany amid 'a magical landscape of vines and olives … untouched by much of modern life', Branagh provided a setting to project a festive atmosphere for a comic drama much of which is a festival of witty wordplay. All the elements for assembling one of the most popular and entertaining Shakespeare films ever to have emerged came together for this *Much Ado About Nothing*, triggering in earnest the Nineties boom in this genre: only Luhrmann's *Romeo and Juliet* surpassed its box office success that decade. In a post-feminist world, the spirited playing of Emma Thompson's Beatrice, who speaks her mind intelligently while addressing men in a defiant manner, proved very attractive, the resulting 'war' between her and Benedick evidently appealing to the new generation whose entertainment needs were geared to the kind of witty comic banter exchanged between sophisticated young men and women in the soon to appear worldwide hit TV sitcom series, 'Friends'. It seems exceedingly unlikely that the six major Shakespeare film adaptations that appeared in the years 1995–96 would have made it to the screen without the prior success of Branagh's comedy.

Indeed, **Trevor Nunn's *Twelfth Night* (1996)** could not have emerged without the prior commercial success of Branagh's *Henry V* and *Much Ado*, according to its director. This Renaissance Films production was one of the four films of 1996 – the others being Branagh's *Hamlet*, Luhrmann's *Romeo and Juliet*, and Adrian Noble's *A Midsummer Night's Dream* – that together make that year the *annus mirabilis* for modern Shakespeare movie adaptations. The imaginative quality of Nunn's film derives from his long experience of directing Shakespeare in the theatre, but his approach also benefited from having produced popular musicals like *Cats, Starlight Express* and *Les Misérables* in London's West End. Its music has often been seen as important to achieving a certain tone for *Twelfth Night* in perform-ance, and of the various interlocking elements of this brilliantly crafted play that Nunn realises for the screen so effectively, perhaps none of these is drawn on so cleverly as the play's songs. Branagh had used the song 'Sigh no more' to give 'a strong sense of the interpretive line' of *Much Ado*, and here Nunn deploys both 'O Mistress Mine' and 'The Wind and the Rain' to invest his version of *Twelfth Night* with the bitter-sweet quality that is so defining of this melancholy 'comedy'. His film has appropriately been called Chekhovian, both for its thoughtful tone and for its setting in the Edwardian period. It also has a visual style and atmosphere benefiting from being shot on loca-tion on St Michael's Mount at the geographical extremity of West Cornwall, near Land's End, where the natural light which gives a cer-tain quality to the objects it illuminates for Nunn's exteriors makes it every bit as special as that of Tuscany.

The other Shakespeare comedy released on film that year, **Adrian Noble's *A Midsummer Night's Dream* (1996)**, does not make location setting a feature in the way that Branagh's and Nunn's films do. In fact, limited finance dictated that the film be shot in five weeks on a soundstage at Bray, near London. But Noble's vividly colourful film adaptation uses the entirely new device of a dreaming child to convey this most metatheatrically magical of Shakespeare's plays. We are shown the young boy dreaming, waking, and then silently observing, and sometimes participating in the *Dream* being filmed in a kind of *Alice in Wonderland* fashion. While these elements work effectively for the most part – including a bicycle-across-the-moon shot quoted from Spielberg's *ET* 'childhood fiction' – at certain points the low budget forced Noble into adopting devices from his stage production that did not entirely work on film.

Strange to note then, that despite money being in plentiful supply for the Hollywood-financed and widely released *A Midsummer Night's Dream* by **Michael Hoffman (1999)**, all the forest scenes were shot on what have been called 'unconvincing sets' in a 'disappointingly cramped and sanitized studio woodland'. But it is Hoffman's decision to have Bottom as the centrepiece of his film that makes this *Dream* so different from previous adaptations. Kevin Kline is a brilliant actor, and the performance that turns this *Dream* into 'Bottom's Dream' is accomplished and often very moving. Yet in the same way that Crowl notices how the brilliantly moving acting achieved by Sam Rockwell as Flute's Thisbe nevertheless 'runs against the grain of the comedy' in the play-within-the-play sequence, so does the idea of extending the character of Bottom from a hempen homespun fond of declaiming, to a dandyish, extrovert, but pensive dreamer.

Although drawing on earlier film versions of the play, **Oliver Parker's *Othello* (1995)** also benefited from the input of Kenneth Branagh in two major ways: Branagh plays the part of Iago in the film, and the movie was designed by Tim Harvey, designer on all of Branagh's own films. Beyond this, Parker's clever adaptation seems uniquely his own, and goes well beyond his expressed aim of adapting the play as 'an erotic thriller'. The movie is in no way pornographic, but Hollywood star Laurence Fishburne certainly supplies a physically powerful and erotic presence as Othello. The theme of sexual jealousy is also effectively portrayed by interpolated 'mind's eye' sequences in which Othello fantasises the sexual coupling of Cassio and Desdemona put into his head by Iago's psychological manipulation. But it is the way Parker uses film language to convey such manipulation that counts here, this manipulation stemming from an Iago whose own sexual jealousy of 'the Moor' – 'it is thought abroad that twixt my sheets / He has done my office' (1.3.369–70) – seems as powerful in its fiendish racism as the hatred he feels for his master. Parker's filmic strategies come into their own when the action shifts to Cyprus. Both the 'monstrous birth' (1.3.386) of Iago's plan to destroy Othello and a device to visualise his strategy on film is 'engendered' when Parker has Iago observe Cassio and Desdemona whispering together in the reflected image of his knife blade as he cuts into a fruit on the ramparts of the citadel in Cyprus, just before Othello's triumphant arrival. This device is borrowed from the moment in Yutkevitch's *Othello* (1955) when Iago watches in reflection the same innocent exchange in the bright hilt of his sword.

But Parker takes the idea of what the blurred image could *seem* to suggest – a guilty rather than innocent dalliance of friends – much further by having Iago resolved to implant this blurred 'image' of a torrid affair between Cassio and Desdemona as a reality in Othello's mind. Until the moment that Iago's devilish activities are finally discovered, Parker not only makes Iago the shaper of Othello's perceptions, as he is in the play, but also, as Judith Buchanan has explained, he displays and 'identifies him as the film's internal cinematographer' (Buchanan, in Burnett and Wray, 2000, 186). Besides manipulating Othello into seeing only what he wants him to see, Iago is also constantly telling us where to look, Parker often 'allowing' him to produce images through the camera lens that reveal his mastery over Cassio, Othello, Roderigo, Desdemona and others. In stage performances of *Othello*, audiences are frequently made complicit with the dreadful machinations of Iago by way of his soliloquy at the end of 1.3 and other asides, sharing his scheming ideas with us. By seeming to give actor/director Branagh's Iago 'virtual use' of the camera to convey his demonic powers (a partial echo of Olivier's techniques in *Richard III*), Parker found a subtle filmic device to extend this engrossing but uncomfortable relationship to a screen context.

If Parker brought a subtle expertise to his camerawork in creating a cinematically sophisticated *Othello*, then the collaboration of **Ian McKellen and Richard Loncraine** that produced ***Richard III* (1995)** was in conception and effects nothing short of stunning. It is the *visual context* in which McKellen's clever ability to make the crookback 'humanely' charming and witty as he schemes and murders his way to the English throne, that makes the film so audaciously effective. The London theatre production had reset the play's action from a 1480s to a 1930s Britain where Richard gains the throne using murderous totalitarian techniques, and this setting was now to be translated into cinema. Faced by the familiar problem of how to make a complex Shakespeare play with many characters attractive to a popular film audience, McKellen turned to award-winning film director Loncraine, responsible for making hundreds of successful film commercials as well as feature films. Loncraine 'knew how to appeal to wide segments of an audience in record time', so that within the first ten minutes of the film, using a predominantly visual story-telling mode, they were able 'to draw in fans of action films, period drama, musicals, and even, with the entrance of Robert Downey Jr, light comedy' (Freedman, in Jackson ed., 2000, 66). If there is a test case for the issue of whether Shakespeare's text or cinematic images should take primacy in film adaptations of the plays, *Richard III* probably provides this.

Where the McKellen/Loncraine film ends with a sensational image of manic antihero Richard being engulfed in the inferno of war, the opening sequence of **Baz Luhrmann's *Romeo + Juliet* (1996)**, packed with references to John Woo and Clint Eastwood action movies, climaxes with a gas station exploding into flames after a gun battle between youths of the feuding 'Latino' Capulet and 'Anglo' Montague family clans. Aiming to make his movie 'rambunctious, sexy, violent and entertaining the way that Shakespeare might have if he had been a filmmaker', Luhrmann wanted to attract as wide an audience as possible for his film. This meant appealing to American and other youth audiences around the world whose grasp of their own music, fashion and visually orientated pop culture was so sophisticated that any *Romeo and Juliet* appealing to them would require more edge and irony than a film about young idealistic lovers caught in a painful 'generation gap' – although the play in many ways will for modern audiences always revolve around that situation. Breaking all box office records to date when *William Shakespeare's Romeo + Juliet* 'opened wide' at 1276 screens across the United States in early November 1996, the film evidently found its audience very quickly. Analysis shows that it achieved this by exploiting and exploring what cultural theory has come to call the 'hyperreal' – a world in which 'the real' has in many ways been displaced by media images. In the process Luhrmann has produced a complex Shakespeare adaptation that, among all the later adaptations making media history and media transition a part of their message, can perhaps be said to be the most 'postmodern' of them all.

Although lavish funds supported the production of **Julie Taymor's *Titus* (1999)**, as with Hoffman's *A Midsummer's Night's Dream*, poor box office returns brought commercial failure. But whereas Hoffman's version of Shakespeare's comedy may have failed partly because of the director's wayward decision to make Bottom the film's hero, Taymor's adaptation of *Titus Andronicus* did not find a big audience perhaps because it was difficult for viewers to connect with the characters of the movie, or with the seriously ideological purposes she embedded in it. The decision to cast Anthony Hopkins as Titus Andronicus was shrewd, in a story that culminates with fallen Roman military hero Titus as a chef overseeing the 'cannibal' consumption of Tamora's two sons Demetrius and Chiron in steaming crusty pies, a sickly act of revenge for their rape and horrific mutilation of his daughter Lavinia. And the many inspired cinematic moments and sequences that successfully translate Shakespeare's play text into filmic imagery clearly derive from the major talent for creating visual spectacle that made her staging of Disney's *The Lion King* such a world-wide hit. Furthermore, as Stephen Buhler has said, the words of the play text were spoken in 'a variety of accents' but delivered 'with a sure sense of metrical power and range', Stratford's voice coach Cicely Berry having provided guidance on the production. So there is nothing amiss either with the film's cinematic visions or with the acting.

Rather, the problem seems to lie in Taymor's attempt to make her film accomplish more than this early revenge tragedy is capable of delivering. She casts Osheen Jones, the young actor used by Adrian Noble as the 'framing dreamer' of his *Midsummer Night's Dream*, this time as young Lucius, a 'framing witness' to the unfolding violent events of *Titus*. This is done to indict the violently masculinist military machine that not only makes possible the ancient Rome of the play, but which was also integral to fascist rule in 1930s Italy, brought out in the film by representing Saturninus, to whom Titus has disastrously ceded the imperial crown, as a petulant, Fascist playboy. As Taymor has said, 'The development of the child from innocence through knowledge to compassion is, to me, the essentially most important theme [of the film]' (Quoted by Crowl, 206). The crowning moment of this 'development' comes in the final frames when Aaron's black baby son is carried cradled in the arms of young Lucius out of the Roman 'arena where cruelty, racial difference, piety and entertainment had merged' (Buhler, 2002, 192). Following him through a Roman archway, the camera moves him and us toward the dawning of a new day, the scene shot in slow motion while we are engulfed by hypnotically repeated waves of orchestral sound. This superadded feature was to suggest the possibility that a new generation may learn from the

Blockbuster Video store, or Sam Shepard's chillingly real Ghost dissolving into a Pepsi machine, Almereyda is using these visual constructions to create 'something more than casual irony. It's another way to touch the core of Hamlet's anguish, to recognise the frailty of spiritual value in a material[ist] world.'

Kenneth Branagh's *Love's Labour's Lost* **(2000)** was the director's fourth Shakespeare film, an ambitious attempt to deliver this infrequently performed early comedy in the form of a Hollywood musical. The movie is ambitious because Branagh's idea of replacing most of the play's competitive verbal quipping, obscene punning and rhetorical complexity with song and dance sequences modelled on 1930s Hollywood film musicals not only trades Shakespeare's verbal wit (in the one drama Shakespeare was at pains to display it most) for the lyrics of Broadway 'standards' by Gershwin, Porter, Berlin and Kern, but it does so without sufficient attention being paid to whether the paying cinema audience might like it or not. Low box office returns for both US and UK releases reveal that not many cinemagoers did like it.

Conveying a plot even slighter than *Much Ado*, the enthusiastic cast of *Love's Labour's Lost* sing and dance themselves out on a small number of studio sets – library, quadrangle, riverside, garden – offering the kinds of 'stage frame' indispensable for the effective performance of comedies and musicals (see Introductory note to *Comedies*, Part IV). Branagh certainly captures the luminous 'look' of the classic Technicolor film musical, and in terms of content, part of the production's charm undoubtedly comes from what a *New York Times* critic called its 'gee-whiz amateurism'. The difficulty is that the impact of the singing and dancing becomes compromised by this amateurism – that, and the fact that the film communicates itself in too many generic registers to attract a favourable audience response. Reacting to negative test screenings in which audiences did not know how to 'read' the film (are we engaging with a Shakespeare play adaptation, or watching a Hollywood style musical? – can it really be both?), Branagh's insertion of black and white Pathé-like period newsreel sequences using the voice of a 'cheeky chappy' English male commentator to firm up the plot for viewers, unfortunately only makes matters worse. This is because, not only do we have to deal with radically different shifts of communicative register as between sequences of Shakespearean dialogue, song and dance, and comedy routines, but the World War II perspective (via the Movietone news sequences) evoking a nostalgically British tone of 'togetherness in adversity' is at complete variance with the all-American tone of the Hollywood film musical so emphatically at the core of the movie's semiotic system. *Love's Labour's Lost* is an interesting hybrid experiment, but it is a hybrid that failed to find an audience enthusiastic to enjoy Shakespeare filtered through a Hollywood musical in the same way as Kenneth Branagh and his cast evidently did.

Christine Edzard's *The Children's Midsummer Night's Dream* (2001) is also an experiment of sorts, but if it was a risky move for Branagh to foreground the efforts of amateur singers and dancers for his movie, then offering a film of 'William Shakespeare's play performed by children' of between 8 and 12 years, with no dramatic experience whatever, is bound to be even more fraught with risk. As Samuel Crowl has rightly said, Edzard's film is 'cleverly structured, handsomely costumed, sweetly scored, and often a delight to hear'. But he is even more right to say that Edzard is less interested in popularising Shakespeare for the world of mass entertainment 'than using his art to make, or make a statement about, community.' As an attempt at community theatre, the film is thoroughly worthy, and one can understand the impulse to offer a range of young schoolkids local to Edzard's Rotherhithe Sands Studios the chance to act out a complete Shakespeare play, given the energy, enthusiasm and natural acting ability so often evident in children of primary age. These elements are present in this production to some extent, and there are plenty of delightful moments in the woodland scenes – such as when the fairies giggle with delight at Bottom's appetite for hay and dried peas. There is also an interesting conclusion when the schoolchild audience, engrossed in the performance of *Pyramus and Thisbe* before them, irritatingly quieten the interrupting stage aristocrats (marionettes of Theseus, Hippolyta and Philostrate who are voiced by Derek Jacobi, Samantha Bond and Richard Clifford), their applause frequently drowning out the voices of the Shakespearean professionals. (It is hard to avoid the community 'political' point being made that the child audience prefer to listen to local 'hempen homespun' performers from their own community than to professional actors speaking 'received pronunciation' – as the adult actors rather exaggeratedly do.) Some of the performances also stand out: Oberon performs sturdily and has real screen presence, Bottom is energetic and entertaining, while both Hermia and Helena can be very engaging when agitated and annoyed. But generally the charm and novelty of watching so many young children concentratedly repeating their lines in flat and toneless voices soon wears thin. Despite a clever filmic structure of having a child audience who watch a puppet version of the play enter it and take it over to become the characters themselves, and carrying this through in ways that the cinematography sometimes makes magical, the child performers are not capable of conveying with any depth the richness of Shakespeare's characters and language. One requires the experience and nuanced judgements of adult actors to make the most of these: *A Midsummer Night's Dream* may be a play in which some characters become enchantingly infantilised by magical means, but the delight and comedy of the resulting drama lies in the fact that they are *adult* characters becoming so muddled, and adult characters so reduced need the skills of adult actors to entertainingly persuade us of it all.

Michael Radford's *The Merchant of Venice* (2004) is the first cinematic adaptation of this play since the silent era, and by its attractive use of subdued painterly textures and Venetian location shooting shares some similarities with the beautifully tinted *Il mercante di Venezia* made by Film d'Arte Italiana in 1910 (included in the BFI *Silent Shakespeare* DVD anthology). Film-makers must always have found difficulty in finding ways of delivering a drama that so provokingly presents conflicting issues of race, religion, commerce and justice, and which has the additional challenge of interleaving these with the love and comic elements of a Shakespearean comedy. In Shakespeare's time, Shylock was probably viewed as a scapegoat figure of fun whose intransigence over the defaulted bond with Antonio was a device to dramatically expose the hypocrisy of Christian commercial society's hostility to a usury it nonetheless required to function effectively. In a post-Holocaust world, Shylock is regarded more as a tragic figure whose persecution as a Jew can be read as representative of the treatment of any ethnic group, alienated, viciously attacked or 'ethnically cleansed' by others who claim racial, religious or ethnic superiority over them. Perhaps by 2004, in a post-Cold War world in which race, class and gender are firmly and openly established as serious issues both in educational practice and social policies, it has become slightly easier to tackle on film a play like *The Merchant of Venice*. Yet given the attempt to posthumously collaborate with a playwright whose poetic facility with words is such that his text constantly and mischievously bristles with possibilities and which cannot resist a paradox, a joke or a pun, what is the twenty-first-century adapter to do with Shylock's challenge to Antonio, 'I say, / To buy his favour I extend this friendship. / If he will take it, so. If not, adieu' (1.3.163–5), in which the last word spoken can easily be heard as punning jokily about 'a Jew'?

Attention is deflected away from the punning joke in Radford's film when Al Pacino as Shylock chooses to pronounce the word 'ado', perhaps part of a strategy to speak his lines with a Yiddish-inflected accent the gutturally staccato style of which is only occasionally broken in on by his native New Yorkishness. (As the film progresses, Pacino occasionally lets his 'mafia-style' anger get the better of him, cutting across the more contained character design he perhaps started out with.) Cuts there are aplenty of course to meet the needs of a cinema audience (it runs 131 minutes). But whereas the supposedly comic Gobbo scenes add little value to the movie and could have been excised, Portia's lines are cut when she rejoices at her black Moroccan suitor's failure to choose the correct casket (as does Nunn's 2000 TV adaptation) – 'Let all of his complexion choose me so' (2.7.79). However liberal the world has become, it would still perhaps be too shocking to admit that the charming, wily, but (in this movie) ravishingly beautiful princess-like figure is also a racist, something deeply unpalatable to a modern film audience who like an attractive, strong and independent heroine to prevail.

According to Benoît Delhomme, the film's cinematographer, Radford and he resolve the problem of 'tone' presented by the play's substantially conflicting elements by structuring their movie as a thriller. The film is set and costumed in the year commonly thought to be the one in which Shakespeare wrote the play, 1596, and it is framed by visual devices indicating that although Venice was the most liberal city state in Europe, allowing Jews to practise their religion openly (which they were not in Britain), and to trade as moneylenders and pawnbrokers, they were nevertheless socially separated from the Gentile community, confined to an island called 'the ghetto' (not so evident either in the play or the film, however) and compelled to wear distinctive garb. The predominant image emerging in Radford's scene-setting written preamble and opening is of *exclusion* – a bolt being shut on the door of the Jewish community, separating them from city life. At the end too we see the door of the synagogue being bolted against Shylock, now forced by Antonio and the Duke's decree following his failure to exact the pound of flesh demanded in his 'merry bond', to become a Christian. Within this structure, an accumulating series of thriller-like episodes are built, the frequent shifting of locations in the play affording Radford the opportunity of some slick and stylish cross-cutting between Venice and Belmont, Shylock's painful and strained world, and the gentlemanly Gentile world of commerce and pleasure.

From the first, an operative and equivocal theme of 'flesh' and Christian hypocrisy is established: the shot **montage** that evokes the jostling commercial life of the Venetian Rialto includes naked-breasted prostitutes flaunting their wares; in a series of **two-shots** where Bassanio and Shylock debate Antonio's credit-worthiness, the flesh of freshly killed goat is being weighed in the scales for Shylock; and as Bassanio follows Shylock through bustling crowds his wayward eyes are drawn by flesh of another kind for sale, the bare breasts of a touting whore. In this frank depiction of a society where sex is a trade like any other, Radford is also bold enough to weave a strong thread of homoeroticism – both male and female – into the film. Quite apart from the frolics of courtesans and the cross-dressing of Portia and Nerissa, there is no attempt to disguise the eroticism of Antonio's and Bassanio's relationship: the kiss and stroke of the cheek that Bassanio (Joseph Fiennes) gives to Antonio (Jeremy Irons) is the sign of a homoerotic bond that no heterosexual marriage is likely to alter – as Bassanio makes explicit in the court scene by swearing he would sacrifice the lives of his wife and himself to Shylock if Antonio's could be saved (4.1.276–82).

The movie was bound to be primarily perceived, evaluated and marketed as a star vehicle for Pacino, but the film's strong ensemble playing has the effect of foregrounding many of the play's ethical complexities, the stylishly shot and edited **medium-close** and **close shots** of the principals drawing us into the tangled web of the story's suspenseful plotting. At the same time, while Delhomme states that 'We don't have many landscapes in the film, partly because we didn't have time; the faces are our landscapes' – achieving a filmically stylish 'look' seems to have been a major concern for Radford. Both this look and the counter-tenor voice of the soundtrack help to create a melancholy atmospheric smoothing away of some of the text's prickly conflicts, yet visual style also creates meanings and effects that resonate with us. For instance, the impressive **shot/reverse shot** hand-held camera sequence in which Shylock delivers his 'Hath not a Jew eyes?' speech against an early morning cool blue light also produces a coolly dramatic atmosphere. When the spare sombreness of colour and mood soon give way to the richer and more finely textured colours of Belmont, we are encouraged to feel that fairytale solutions seem possible, such upbeat oversimplification cleverly signalled by the fairytale-like **digitally composited images** of Belmont isle often used to introduce us to it.

One has to say 'seem possible', for although Portia mischievously carries the day in the trial scene and will lead off a meek Bassanio to

her marriage bed, the final frames of the film return us to the melancholy blue tones which had lit Shylock's lament over his lost ducats
and his eloped daughter, Jessica. It is Jessica's sadness that fills the
final frames, which show her gazing toward archers spearing fish in the
lagoon with their arrows, a reminder of that part of Bassanio's early
speech to Antonio concerning the 'hazard' and 'adventuring' (not
heard in the film) of arrows (investments). Her pain leaves us with an
aptly melancholy question mark over what has really been won and
lost in the preceding ad-ventures. Most Shakespearean comedies in
which court or city alternate with a 'green world' of mystery and
promise, usually end with marriages in the court or city setting. By not
returning us to Venice at the end of this play, Shakespeare is perhaps
hinting that the real, mixed-up world of commerce and desire is more
intractable to negotiate than a charmed fictional world, raising difficult questions of a kind he will return to in the later so-called problem
comedies. By producing this film, Radford offers a courageous, if
muted, attempt at raising the profile of one of Shakespeare's more
controversial plays in the world of popular film.

At the time of writing, the Shakespeare on film boom that began in
1989 shows no sign of abating. Whether Branagh's next two Shakespeare
film projects of *As You Like It* (2007) and *Macbeth* are likely to fatten
the spark of interest that keeps Shakespeare on film alive in the
twenty-first century, only time – and the requirements of the movie
industry and its audience – will tell.

Part III

Communicating Shakespeare on Film: Modes, Styles, Genres

Introductory note, Sections 1–4

In the first chapter of his book *Shakespeare on Film*, Jack Jorgens offered a valuable method of approaching the artistic and dramatic potential of film for communicating adaptations of Shakespeare's plays via the big screen, by analysing and discussing such adaptations in terms of three modes of representation: the *theatrical*, the *realistic* and the *filmic* (Jorgens, 1991, 7–12). Since this typology of Shakespearean film adaptation has yet to be bettered for surveying the range of films produced, I rehearse below my understanding of Jorgens's categories with illustrative examples (all quotations are from Jorgens's book, unless otherwise stated). But I also add a further mode, the *periodising*, citing and briefly discussing some recent adaptations which dramatise a play by transposing it to the culture and society of a distinct historical period.

1

The Theatrical Mode

For Jorgens the *theatrical* mode of filming Shakespeare has 'the look and feel of a performance worked out for a static theatrical space and a live audience' (7). Since the aim of this mode was (it having all but died out by the twenty-first century – but see below) to capture as accurately as possible the 'look and feel' of a stage performance, the tendency has been to use the film frame as if it were a theatrical **proscenium arch**. Thus dramatic meaning is conveyed mainly by the words and gestures of the actors, whose performance is captured by **medium** or **long shot** in lengthy **takes** that stress the durational quality of time. The style of this mode derives largely from the style of the performances, which tend to be 'of a distinctly theatrical cast – more demonstrative, articulate and continuous than actors are usually permitted in films' (8). The camera is consequently deployed primarily as a device to record a theatre-like performance, by-passing its capacities to refashion the visual representation of a Shakespeare play using the more elaborate pictorial techniques of other modes.

With its concern for retaining the communicative manner and means of the theatre, the theatrical mode's potency lies in its capacity for preserving the performance of a minimally cut Shakespeare text with the potential to convey the full range of Shakespeare's verbal and dramatic styles, 'from stark naturalism to **metatheatrical** playfulness' (8). The stylistic effects of this mode will also be influenced by the manner of staging, but whatever theatrical space is used, the aim of such screen productions is usually to give maximum exposure to the performance of Shakespeare's verbal text. Although the number of live stage performances filmed skilfully enough to hold the interest of a screen audience is tiny, they do exist, a fascinating example being the *King Lear* recorded on camera during the summer of 1974 as part of the New York Shakespeare Festival held in New York City's Central Park, produced by Joseph Papp and directed by Edwin Sherin. The evening performance was shot under arc lights and captured on four cameras in a lively range of one, **two**, three and **wide shots**, with (more often than not) expertly managed **shot/reverse shot** sequences catching some of the best dramatic exchanges. One argument for making such films is to record exceptional stage performances, and the King Lear given here by accomplished black American actor James Earl Jones has many high points, though the **close shots** of Jones's Lear frequently reveal a vitality and business of movement unconvincing for an 'old and reverend' man meant to be 'four score and upward' in age, something an audience watching at some distance from the stage is less likely to notice. Although other performances vary from the unremarkable ('the women were disappointedly wooden', one critic states with accuracy) to the scintillatingly witty and well-timed (Lear and the Fool of Tom Aldredge in 1.4), the great virtue of the DVD is that it conveys the excitement and atmosphere of a live stage performance being enjoyed by a live audience, who sometimes even clap the entrances and exits of actors.

Two films which both provide 'the look and feel of a performance worked out for a static theatrical space and a live audience', but which are filmed without an audience and had been played in very different theatrical settings are **Stuart Burge's** *Othello* **(1965)**, starring Laurence Olivier, and **Tony Richardson's** *Hamlet* **(1969)**, starring Nicol Williamson. I shall spend a little time discussing these highly contrasting filmed theatrical pieces.

Originally directed by John Dexter on the stage of the National Theatre of Great Britain in 1964, the performance of **Stuart Burge's** *Othello* **(1965)** was captured on Technicolor film running in three Panavision cameras at Shepperton Studios. The stylised studio sets closely followed the design of the stage sets used for the proscenium stage arrangement of the National production, the aim being (in the words of the producer Anthony Havelock-Allan) 'to recreate completely the atmosphere, effect and immediacy of the theatre performance', which would enable 'millions of people throughout the world, who would not have had the remotest chance of seeing Sir Laurence on the stage, to share the experience' (Manvell, 1971, 117). Olivier's stage performance as Othello had been widely acclaimed, and the film version without doubt also reveals something that the 'director-ridden art of film seldom permits: an unfettered actor-generated performance' (194).

Certainly, as one watches the film, which retains the actors, design and **blocking** of Dexter's original, if we keep in mind that what we are seeing is a *record* of Olivier's highly demonstrative style of acting put on for the entertainment of a large theatre audience, then it is possible to become highly engrossed in that performance.

However, it is hard at times to ignore the fact that it is the very commanding physicality of Olivier's sometimes overpowering performance filmed in **medium** and **close shot** that makes for intenseness and exaggeration, the very same gestures and movements which no doubt had communicated to a theatre audience Othello's pain and bewilderment – sitting much further away from the stage than we are from the screen – feeling too expansive and melodramatic for a movie-viewer. This is especially noticeable when Olivier reaches crescendos in certain speeches. For example: once Iago has planted his poisonous lies in Othello's susceptible mind, at 'Farewell the tranquil mind' (3.3.353–62), and at 'Damn her, lewd minx!' (3.3.478–81). Interestingly, Frank Finlay's performance of Iago succeeds better for the filmed version than it did for the stage production. Whereas the swelling speech climaxes of Olivier's Othello that so impressed in the theatre can feel overdone on film, the cool and calculating playing of Finlay's Iago, which was often thought to be too restrained for the stage performance, is perfectly matched for the medium and close shots of film. Although Olivier knew well enough from making his own three Shakespeare films the importance of 'scaling down' his performance from the proximities of theatrical to film space so as not to overwhelm the cinema audience, it seems that the 'heritage' aim of this film to provide a historical record of Olivier's bravura style of Shakespearean acting took priority over more filmic considerations. (The question of Olivier's willingness to play Othello 'blacked-up', a matter of repugnance to many, is beyond the scope of our discussion here.)

Tony Richardson's *Hamlet* (1969). Richardson was among the directors to bring to 1960s British theatre and film a radically realistic 'edge' that was poles apart from Olivier's more self-conscious, 'actorly' style of playing and production. The priority Richardson brought to the staging and filming of *Hamlet* was for the actors to communicate with the audience more directly and closely than had been possible in traditional theatres. The place which enabled him to create this more intimate kind of contact was one of the leading avant-garde venues of the period, a converted brick-built circular Victorian railway engineering shed, the Round House, at Chalk Farm, north London. It is a setting which he felt would

> put the actors into immediate contact with the audience instead of being stuck behind the picture-frame of a proscenium. It does away with that terrible formality, and lets actors speak in a room instead of up on an artificial platform … The most vital thing is space, and at the Round House we have that.   (Quoted by Manvell, 1971, 127–8)

The closeness to the audience that Richardson was able to achieve for the live theatrical performances was emphasised even more for his filming of the same production. His statement that 'it will be a real film, not a photographed version of the stage production' meant in practice using a mobile camera and microphones which constantly strove to catch every gesture and word of the performance. From the beginning, when Francisco brushes past the camera into shot *from behind it* to challenge Barnardo as he emerges from the shadows – the dank and dimly lit Round House interior providing a convincing atmosphere for the Elsinore castle ramparts – we are brought very close to the actors. The reactions on their faces and the speaking of their lines are thus clearly caught, despite an ambient background drone caused by exterior traffic noise, another reason perhaps for filming the actors so close up. This focus on the faces of the characters in one, two and three shots is very apparent throughout the film, the first example being when the terror-struck faces of Horatio, Marcellus and Barnardo are lit by a blinding light representing the Ghost, whose arrival is also announced by solemn, gong-like reverberations. The text is severely cut back here in order to emphasise the shocking impact of this presence on the observers.

In contrast to what is often played as a formal banquet and filmed in **medium** and **medium-close** shot (e.g. in the films of Olivier and Branagh), we here see the succeeding scenes of Claudius and Gertrude celebrating their marriage (1.2) played in **close shot** as a carefree party, a wine-swilling Claudius being followed around by the camera as he pokes fun at 'impotent and bed-rid' old Fortinbras, much to the hilarity of his courtiers jostling together carelessly at his elbow. The party atmosphere caught by this fashion of shooting has immediacy and registers well the contemporary values of 1960s' 'permissive' sexual freedom fast-emerging at this time. Similarly, the close-seeing camera of the following scene when Hamlet speaks his first soliloquy

('O that this too too sullied flesh would melt ...', 1.2.129) allows us to observe and to absorb every nuance of his mood, as he moves between an angry direct address to us, a reflective speaking obliquely focused on some point near the camera, and a more bitter knuckling of his brow in rage at the thought of his mother's hurrying with 'such dexterity to incestuous sheets!' (1.2.167). At all times, both here in Williamson's intense, quick and nasal delivery, and throughout the movie from all the other speaking characters, we are given a level of naturalistic performance that is matched to the intimate requirements of the screen, and not to the spacious acoustic of the traditional theatre.

What Richardson gained by adopting this more intimate style of performance for his filmed *Hamlet* is a form of production that is clearly more accessible to a movie audience than the Dexter/Burge *Othello* is likely to be, since the latter can be rather too revealing of the self-consciously stylised 'artifice' used by Olivier to create what are essentially performance effects designed for a large theatrical acoustic. But in creating such a naturalistically intimate form of playing for the camera, Richardson also either consciously or inadvertently generated the kind of performance that works very well for TV, suited as the small screen is for delivering dramatic material on a more 'domestic' scale. In many ways, the theatrical mode of presenting Shakespeare on screen has worked best when the plays are dramatised for television (see Part V for more discussion and illustration of such productions).

2

The Realistic Mode

The *realistic* mode of conveying Shakespeare on film makes for 'the most popular kind of Shakespeare film', according to Jorgens, 'not merely because film-makers are most familiar with it and mass audiences enjoy the spectacle of historical recreations, but because everyone senses that at bottom Shakespeare is a realist'. He elaborates:

> If realism in film implies something more than a visual style or authentic costumes and settings, it seems to many that this playwright – who filled his Globe with duels, battles, shipwrecks, tortures, assassinations, storms, coronations, trials, suicides, feasts, and funerals, who juxtaposed the ugly with the sublime, the base with the noble, everyday with holiday, who ruthlessly explored both the need for and the dangers of centralised power, the conflicts of young and old, the rocking of order and tradition by frightening, invigorating forces of change – virtually demands screen realism.

Shakespeare's play texts obviously do produce a vast range of dramatic events, contrasts and situations. It is because these are conveyed by convincing characters whose speaking lines describe, suggest or imply a multitude of *recognisably human experiences in particular social settings or locations which impress us as being 'just like life'* that film, with its capacity to 'realise' such settings, locations and situations on screen, can come into its own. If, as Hamlet states in his advice to the players, it is the purpose of theatrical playing 'to hold as 'twere the mirror up to nature', then many film directors adapting Shakespeare to the big screen have seen fit to enhance such playing by positioning it in a variety of realistic 'local habitations' designed to enlarge the scope of the 'nature' being mirrored. However, the way such attempts at screen realism are communicated to us has been as diverse as the stylistic approaches brought to the task by each individual film-maker, inevitably perhaps, since movies are by definition almost always 'director-led'.

Jorgens has noted the approach of various directors using this mode. Zeffirelli's *The Taming of the Shrew* and *Romeo and Juliet* he regards as being of the 'decorative, spectacular, orchestrally accompanied variety ... a descendant of the elaborate productions of the nineteenth century'. Fine as this description probably is for his first two films, it does not really hold so well for the later *Hamlet*, although, as Crowl has observed, that movie does reveal Zeffirelli's 'romantic and grandly operatic' sensibility by projecting Glenn Close's Gertrude as a 'tragic diva' figure. Peter Brook's *King Lear* Jorgens regards as having a 'harsh documentary style'. Shot in black and white in an inhospitably cold northern European setting, it is certainly bleak and unadorned in its approach. Yet I will argue later that it has as many or more 'filmic' qualities in its screen rendering of the play as it has 'realist' elements. According to Jorgens, a 'mixed style' is used for Polanski's 'gory, twilight *Macbeth*', the 'fortress and tangled forest of Kurosawa's *Throne of Blood*', and for 'the silences and wintery empty spaces of Welles's *Chimes at Midnight*'. It could be argued that to do justice to any version of *Macbeth* – or *Hamlet*, indeed – ensuring that the supernatural element in each is communicated effectively will of necessity mean that a 'mixed style' of cinematic delivery is required, the mix being composed of realist and non-realist techniques.

In the post-1989 era of Shakespeare on film, it is Kenneth Branagh who epitomises the use of the realistic mode, his *Henry V, Much Ado About Nothing* and *Hamlet* all employing realistic strategies of cinematic communication. *Love's Labour's Lost*, though realistic in its acting style, remains predominantly what the opening credits of that film announce it to be: a 'romantic musical'. Where Branagh from *Henry V* forward has led, most other film-makers of the 1990s Shakespeare film genre revival have tended to follow, almost all of them shooting their films in the realistic mode. There is a very good reason for this. Apart from the fact that the theatrical mode on film has virtually disappeared, it is Branagh's own particular *style* of employing the realistic mode on film that has set the pattern for so many others. One key feature of this is his frequent and strategic quoting from earlier Hollywood movies to help convey in a vivid and impactful way the *story* of the Shakespeare play he is working to adapt at any one time.

Thus, our first glimpse of his Henry V shows him in becloaked trian-gular silhouette closely resembling the sinister figure of Darth Vader (*Star Wars*); or near the opening of the hugely successful *Much Ado About Nothing* Don Pedro and his men are shown galloping toward Messina side by side, in (as Branagh himself puts it) 'a nod to *The Magnificent Seven*' (Branagh, 1993, viii). Another key element of Branagh's approach to gaining a larger, international audience for his Shakespeare films from *Much Ado* onward was to add high profile American movie stars to his core British cast: a key pattern for the nineties realistic Shakespeare adaptation had been established.

Whatever the kind of realism deployed by a film-maker, we can see that film has the capacity to *show* an immense variety of images which may complement and enhance key elements of the text. But what about that text? Despite the strengths of the realist mode to provide some version of verisimilitude to the realistic elements implied by a play text, there is a danger that if such realism is conceived too nar-rowly, focusing on lavish settings and a mass of 'authentic' detail (for instance) at the expense of conveying the essential meanings of the play text in an accessible way, the audience will not be engaged. Several examples spring to mind. Reinhardt and Dieterle's 1935 *A Midsummer Night's Dream* was in many ways a cinematically innova-tive film, a kind of culmination of Max Reinhardt's interest in using extravagant expressionist styles to animate his dramas. The problem is that the expensive sets, props and costumes developed for this glitter-ing Warner Brothers movie were so extravagant as often to be dis-tracting, distorting the shape of the picture more toward its 'look' than its overall effect as a comedy. One obviously does not expect a non-realist play like *Dream* to be conveyed as a realistic drama, yet in many ways by focusing his efforts on a clear, actor-led performance of the text, as well as employing some visual tricks to convey 'the magic', Peter Hall's 1968 film version of the play is dramatically more effective.

3

The Filmic Mode

Peter Brook has observed how the 'reality of the image gives to film its power and its limitation' (1987, 192), his suggestion being that the film's capacity to articulate images so very emphatically means there is a danger that a *single level of meaning* only might be conveyed to the viewer. Jorgens therefore argues that to be true to the effect of what is invariably a whole *play of meanings* carried by Shakespeare's verbal text, such realistic emphasis must be subordinated to an overall design in which 'the aural has been made visual'. This is a phrase used by Grigori Kozintsev, whose approach to Shakespeare on film exemplifies for Jorgens the advantages of the *filmic* mode. He sees this approach as being that of the 'film poet', whose works 'bear the same relation to the surfaces of reality that poems do to ordinary conversation' (10).

Everyday language can be transformed in poetry by poetic invention to create powerful meanings, images, emotions and other effects in us. But for such poetry to be brought into being, the various literary techniques available (rhythm, rhyme, 'voice', word-patterning, simile, metaphor, etc.) need to be drawn on to make such a transformation effective. In transforming a Shakespeare text often already saturated with poetic imagery and rhythms to the screen, the various techniques and approaches of film language (discussed in Part I) must therefore be embraced and creatively manipulated, if the characters, themes, situations and insights are to be communicated in a resonant way to the screen audience. As Peter Holland has said in discussing the filmic mode, 'filmic films' of this type 'accept the peculiar intensity of the visual over the aural, of sight over sound, that is fundamental to the cinema' (Holland, 1994, 56). In getting into focus the particular problem facing Shakespeare film-makers, Holland, like Jorgens and other writers on this vital translation issue, offers a much-quoted passage from Kozintsev's essay '*Hamlet* and *King Lear*: Stage and Film':

> The problem is not one of finding means to speak the verse in front of the camera, in realistic circumstances ranging from long-shot to close-up. The aural has to be made visual. The poetic texture has itself to be transformed into a visual poetry, into the dynamic organisation of film imagery.
>
> (Kozintsev, 1972, 191)

In seeking to go beyond both theatrical and realistic modes Kozintsev would no doubt be as scornful of the crassly literal film image mentioned below as the critic who cites it, Peter Holland:

> There is a film of *Macbeth* in which, when Macbeth speaks of 'pity, like a new-born babe, / Striding the blast, or heaven's cherubin, horsed / Upon the sightless couriers of the air' (1.7.21–23), the film showed, through a window, a ghastly little cherub on a horse riding on the wind.   (Holland, 1994, 56)

If this sort of literalism is to be avoided and Kozintsev's problem answered productively, 'there must be an imaginative recreation of the language of the play into the terms of the film', as Holland says. Kozintsev achieves this imaginative recreation in a range of ways in his *Hamlet* and *King Lear*, as do other directors whose impulse is to use the language of film to translate the essential meanings and moods of the text of Shakespeare's play into a text of cinema. In the middle era of Shakespeare on film up to 1971, these directors are principally Laurence Olivier, Orson Welles, Akira Kurosawa, Kozintsev and Peter Brook; in the Branagh era, it is Michael Almereyda and Julie Taymor who create the most interesting attempts at 'making the aural visual'.

Most film-makers will acknowledge the import of Peter Brook's statement that in the world of film 'space and time are loose and meaningless terms'. But since the communicative currency of that world has (for understandable commercial reasons) favoured the realistic mode, few adapters of Shakespeare to the movie medium have been prepared to experiment very radically with it in their works of 'translation', well understanding the British film director Alex Cox's observation that 'ambiguity is great, but in the cinema it's almost *verboten*'. Yet non- or anti-realist film techniques have been used from the earliest days to put across significant aspects of some Shakespeare films: trick photographic effects to make delightful magic in the silent

1908 *Tempest* for instance; a darker magic evoked by the fantastic sets and romantic choreography of Reinhardt and Dieterle's *Dream*. Critics preoccupied with stressing the 'patriotic propagandist' elements of Olivier's *Henry V* are perhaps inclined to miss his use of cinematic devices and settings to accentuate this play's own exploration of drama as artifice; all of Olivier's films in fact avoid straightforwardly realistic forms of representation. Welles's approach to screening Shakespeare exemplifies the filmic mode at its most experimental – perhaps one would expect no less from the maker of *Citizen Kane*. *Othello* is the film where his manipulation of a whole range of film techniques is at its most pronounced, most 'Wellesian'. Skewed camera angles, deep focus, dissolves, powerfully graphic compositions, long tracking shots, surrealistic reflections – all serve to pictorialise the unstable and claustrophobic world of destructive emotions and behaviours set in motion by devilish Iago. Welles's enthusiasm for creating a multiplicity of stunningly lit architectural shots or adventurously tilted portraits, when delivered in quick succession (as they often are), can sometimes fragment the **montage**, diluting the dramatic effect aimed at, with aesthetic excess. Yet his mastery of filmic techniques and effects also enables Welles to translate much of Shakespeare's poetic text on to celluloid in memorably filmic ways: the early shot of Iago trapped in a cage swinging high above the Cyprus fortress; an **image system** of iron bars or barred verticals that, together with repeated images of stony vaults or high walls, conveys with emphatic visual power the forces of entrapment that relentlessly develop in the play text.

The aims of Kurosawa, Kozintsev and Brook in their adaptations are also to 'make visible' the poetic atmosphere of each of the Shakespeare tragedies they film for the screen, investing what is photographed with *metaphoric*, rather than realistic value, thus multiplying meanings and effects. Kurosawa's *Kumonosu-Jô* makes no attempt to verbalise Shakespeare's original text of *Macbeth*, but instead shifts the essential structure, themes and characters of his play to a Japanese mediaeval setting, creating a highly filmic version of the play that is rich in visual metaphor. Its mysterious forest scenes, its fort settings, its use of wood as an elemental **motif**, its use of Noh drama methods for the ritually stylised performances, all contribute in conveying powerful dramatic meanings through cleverly wrought cinematic imageries. The elemental forces and textures of nature are self-consciously deployed by Kozintsev in his *Hamlet* and *King Lear* as metaphors for the various powerful forces, situations or qualities that condition and animate the characters of each play. For *Hamlet*, Kozintsev explains the visual codings:

Stone: the walls of Elsinore, the firmly built government prison

Iron: weapons, the inhuman forces of oppression, the ugly steel faces of war

Fire: anxiety, revolt, movement; raging fiery tongues

Sea: waves, crashing against the bastions, ceaseless movement, the change of the tides, the boiling of chaos ... the silent endless surface of glass

Earth: the world beyond Elsinore, amid stones – a bit of field tilled by a ploughman, the sand pouring out of Yorick's skull, and the handful of dust in the palm of the wanderer-heir to the throne of Denmark.

(Kozintsev, 1967, 266)

The stylistic and pictorial values of Brook's fine film of *King Lear* are also informed by a focus on nature, for as Brook sees it, 'One real element that emerges from the plot is the notion of nature as something hostile, against which man has to battle.' As he says, the play revolves around the storm, but since from a psychological point of view what counts is 'the contrast between the safe, enclosed spaces and the wild, unprotected places', this logically led to 'two denominators of security: fire and fur'. The movie was therefore shot in the appropriately inhospitable location of North Jutland, Denmark, in the winter, the brilliant playing of this adaptation's focus on the drama's essential themes of power and powerlessness being informed and shaped by the material conditions of life in a cold, primitive setting. Brook's manipulation of the *mis-en-scène* is metaphoric almost at every turn because of the focus on what one might think of as 'who has the fire and the fur, and who hasn't'. He takes his filmic approach even further when stressing the other key themes of the play – blindness and insight – by manipulating the camera lens to give us Lear's blurred, black and sometimes blank subjective viewpoint in the turbulent scenes of his madness during the storm. This is a bleak film, bleakly executed in an attempt to evolve what Brook calls 'an impressionistic movie technique, cutting language and incident to the bone, so that the total effect of all things heard and seen could capture in different terms Shakespeare's rough, uneven, jagged and disconcerting vision' (Brook, 1987, 204, 206). This is a Shakespeare adaptation of great filmic power, yet because its power derives from what is a densely concentrated use of the filmic mode, it may not be assimilated so easily by those accustomed to the less demanding methods of the realistic mode.

It is probably the onset of the more 'commercially populist' Shakespeare film genre revival of the 1990s so favouring a Hollywood-style realistic mode, which explains the reluctance of film-makers to adopt the more 'poetic' filmic approaches, appealing as these traditionally have to the less commercial and thus smaller **art house** audiences. Michael Almereyda's *Hamlet* is an exception in this trend, as his film, coming 30 years after Brook's *King Lear* can easily be seen as employing 'an impressionistic movie technique, cutting language and incident to the bone'. The camerawork and frame imagery of Almereyda's movie uses surfaces in the *mis-en-scène* in a way that recalls the metaphoric imagery of Welles's adaptations, impressionistically 'showing' far more than 'telling' us about the dilemmas of a young, disenchanted Hamlet and a lonely Ophelia as they struggle to make sense of the slick, manipulative business world of AD 2000 Manhatten. In the case of Julie Taymor's *Titus*, the movie is so eclectic as to be drawing on the 'widest mixture of film and acting styles' in the history of Shakespeare on film (according to Crowl) and in doing so various elements of her movie frequently convey themselves with meanings and effects which communicate in an essentially filmic style. As well as including the remarkable dream sequences she calls 'Penny Arcade Nightmares' in 'dreamlike and mythic' counterpoint to the realistic events of her film narrative, Taymor can also create what may be thought of as filmic epiphanies of great power. Such an epiphany comes with the pivotal crossroads scene (3.1) when the camera shows the Andronici family members, ruined and sunk to their lowest moral ebb, gazing together at their images in a puddle. As Titus quietly enjoins them to 'Plot some device of further misery, / To make us wondered at in time to come', rain begins to fall, blurring the watery reflections we gaze at, until, in an inspired visual transformation the image **dissolves** to that of the saint-like face of young Lucius gazing out at the rain from a window, the transformation somehow suggesting that a resurrection of the family fortunes may well be possible. It is the 'somehow' of such effects which the filmic mode can sometimes produce, offering moments of poetic intensity as moving as the effects created in fine stage performances of Shakespeare's poetic drama.

4

The Periodising Mode

The primary feature of the *periodising* mode is taking the story and characters of a Shakespeare play and transporting them wholesale into the cultural trappings and social dynamic of a distinctly recognisable historical period. An approach familiar in stage productions for many years, this mode only really took off in film adaptations as the Shakespeare film revival of the 1990s got under way. Directors of 'updating' stage productions had long employed special costuming, sets, props, lighting and sound effects to 'periodise' them into evocative cultural or political settings aimed at making the drama more alive and relevant to a modern popular audience. Such productions frequently used these techniques to evoke and critically allude to the way people are manipulated and put under pressure in the cultures of modern political regimes or business empires – the modern analogues, as modern directors might see it, of the Machiavellian structures of courtly and mercantile power prevailing in Shakespeare's time. In *Hamlet* the prince instructs Polonius to see that the visiting players 'be well used', warning him that 'After your death, you were better have a bad epitaph than their ill report while you live' (2.2.503–6). If many of us take Hamlet's stern words to Polonius as suggestive of Shakespeare's own sense of the cultural, social and political value of the public theatre, and if these players (among whose number he would no doubt include himself) really 'are the abstracts and brief chronicles of the time', might there not even be an *obligation* on those who present his dramas to the public to make them as relevant as possible to 'the time' in which we ourselves happen to be living?

Even if the answer to this is a resounding 'yes', what matters of course is how well the historical transpositions facilitate effective dramatic communication with an audience. Within the transposed settings of the periodising mode for the big screen, there is scope for both realistic and filmic modes to be used, as can be seen in the small number of Shakespeare adaptations to have embraced the periodising approach thus far. Taymor's *Titus* is an interesting experiment in filming *Titus Andronicus* across a variety of period settings, dominantly those of ancient Rome and 1930s Italy. Strictly speaking however, only four movies stand out as attempts to convey Shakespeare plays wholesale through the cultural optic and social dynamic of a distinct historical period. These are Christine Edzard's *As You Like It* (1992), Richard Loncraine's *Richard III* (1995), Baz Luhrmann's *William Shakespeare's Romeo + Juliet* (1996) and Michael Almereyda's *Hamlet* (2000). I will now consider briefly how each of these films makes use of the periodising mode, noting the audiences targeted in each case, and the extent to which the transpositions are effective. It is important to mention at once that two of the four films share features that make them somewhat distinct from the other two. Both *As You Like It* and *Hamlet* were low-budget movies aimed at a specialist or arthouse audience, each film seeming to take it for granted that these audiences will have a prior familiarity with each play. Another way of putting the point is to say that without a familiarity with these two plays, it would probably be difficult for a viewer to follow the storyline of each simply on the basis of the verbal and visual signals being supplied. The difficulties may be less with *Hamlet*, a play whose famous lines and characters resonate to a degree within popular culture and the target teenage audience: like Romeo and Juliet, Hamlet and Ophelia already exist perhaps as familiar icons of popular culture.

Yet the periodising settings can create problems, and this becomes particularly noticeable with **Christine Edzard's *As You Like It* (1992)**. The original comedy draws on the pastoral tradition to set up competing value systems of court and country, creating opportunities for the 'outlaw' forest exiles to satirise the world of corrupt courtly values. Edzard opens her film with one of these exiles, Jaques (Edward Fox) giving his 'Seven Ages of Man' speech ('All the world's a stage …') as a way of getting the film audience's attention, for this is the one speech which might be recognised. Familiar as it may be, the cynical and world-weary perspective of Jaques is not necessarily the most inviting or dramatic introduction to a Shakespearean festive comedy. Yet it does ease us into Edzard's modern urban setting, where rebellious and disenchanted Orlando and banished Rosalind desert the grand edifice of a large London corporate enterprise ('the court') for a riverside wasteland where Duke Senior and the rest of his banished followers scratch a living like down-and-outs on the bleak and rubbish-strewn foreshore ('the forest'). Though it quickly becomes clear that this modern period setting is being used to show how capitalist economics creates a deprived underclass, it is hard to see how those unfamiliar with the play could (as Michael Hattaway puts it) 'match the heightened speech of the text to the naturalistic décor'. All too often, the gap between the Elizabethan text and the modern film setting is unbridgeable. This is especially noticeable when words or phrases are heard that make no sense in such a setting – such references to killing venison, or Corin's claim that 'good pasture makes fat sheep' (a jumbo jet is heard passing close overhead as he speaks). Elsewhere, I have referred to the fact that most Shakespearean comedies thrive on the presence of a live theatrical audience (Introductory note to Comedies, Part IV). In this play too, there are many lines which ache for direct audience complicity in order to bring the comedy alive, as with Touchstone's semi-aside to Audrey during his 'wooing' of her, 'Sluttishness may come hereafter' (3.3.32–3), a line inevitably falling flat for a film audience which merely 'overhears' it.

If there is a mismatch in Edzard's adaptation between Shakespearean text and setting, the other three films fare better in integrating the language of their scripts into the chosen periodised settings. *Hamlet, Romeo and Juliet* and *Richard III* all have strongly defined, exciting plots, memorable leading characters and the suggestion of specific settings, so that together these features offer the potential for an engaging identification between character and viewer in a realistic setting. With **Michael Almereyda's *Hamlet* (2000)** the text of the play – much reduced – has been integrated successfully into the periodised postmodern Manhattan setting. It succeeds largely because there is such a strong congruency between the power structures of the Denmark Corporation empire represented and the Machiavellian structures of courtly and mercantile power prevailing in Shakespeare's time. This is not to say that certain elements of the translation of the action from 1600 renaissance court to 2000 New York City business culture do not produce occasional oddities. The duel scene with rapiers between Hamlet and Laertes held on a balcony of Denmark Corp's headquarters in the Elsinore Hotel high up among the vertiginous heights of the Manhattan skyline might seem a little out of key with what has gone before.

Baz Luhrmann's *Romeo + Juliet* **(1996)** is also aimed at a young movie audience of course. But instead of Almereyda's sophisticated camerawork and use of reflective surfaces to convey meaning, Luhrmann's phenomenal commercial success with this group comes from a rather different approach. The periodised socio-cultural setting he constructs for the adaptation is designed so that the audience can be grippingly entertained by the many flashy, loud and sophisticated elements of popular culture he uses to tell the story of the play, while the integration of its leading characters into this popular cultural texture enables them to identify with such characters. Partly shot on location in Mexico City, the film's constructed locations also suggest contemporary (mid-1990s) cityscapes of southern US states like Los Angeles or Miami. Brilliantly capturing the macho posturing of the feud that lies at the heart of the play, the story of the trigger-happy rival 'Anglo' Montague and 'Latino' Capulet youth gangs offers a seductively exciting and violent context with which a modern audience can connect. Luhrmann's movie communicates with and convinces its sophisticated street-savvy Generation X audience best when it puts the tragic story (as opposed to text) of Shakespeare's play across using a brash MTV visual style and soundtrack. This is a dimension of 'periodising' style that teenage audiences recognise and like, so when the action of the film is visually extended by dressing it with the types of designer clothes, cars, movie film references and witty allusions to the world of advertising they encounter from their everyday lives, this provides a cinematically convincing semiotic that is richly satisfying.

Richard Loncraine's *Richard III* **(1995)** is the only one of the periodising films considered here to have been based on a (highly successful) stage production, which itself had been designed to convey the action of the play in a 1930s British political setting. Richard Eyre's production already projected Richard Duke of Gloucester (Ian McKellen) as a political opportunist who becomes monarch using the murderous methods of the totalitarian tyrant, and his private army were seen (after 3.4) dressed in Blackshirt uniforms, the whole design of his dictatorship increasingly using Nazi-like displays. Skilfully building on the 30% of the lines Ian McKellen had retained from the play for the draft screenplay, Loncraine's film takes the décor and design process much further, evoking the fascistic style of Richard's fear regime with far more elaborate visual detail than was seen in the stage production. But it is not only that almost every detail of the film's *mis-en-scène* makes the period setting realistic and believable.

Compared with other adaptations undertaken in the periodising mode, many of the elements that go toward recreating an 'authentic 1930s look' here have the deeper and more vital function of dynamically informing character identity and the development of the story's action. McKellen has observed how important it is for theatre or cinema audiences to be enabled 'to recognise who is royalty, aristocrat, commoner and who is politician, civil servant, military' among such a multitude of characters. Says McKellen, 'By their clothes, you shall know them (McKellen, 1996, 12)', repeating a formula that applies not only to a recreation of 1930s Britain, but which resonates even more for Shakespeare's period, when the lives of those playing and watching stage dramas in Elizabethan England were contained by rigid social hierarchies and severe legal sanctions. Comparing some of the changes made between stage and screen versions reveals the importance Loncraine and McKellen attached to considering the different ways a film needs to communicate with world cinema audiences rather than theatregoing audiences of Europe or the United States of America. Here it must suffice to focus on two changes.

In the stage version of what was turned into a banquet scene (1.3), not only were Elizabeth's sons Dorset and Gray as well as her brother Lord Rivers present, but so was old Queen Margaret, dominating the action so much that this took the focus off Richard for much of the time. (Generally speaking, as was discussed in Part II, it is important for film audiences to be able to focus on and identify with the progress of a single protagonist.) Not only this, but since Rivers and the others also partly *supported* Richard in expressing his animus against Margaret, there is little doubting the difficulty a cinema audience would have in following the lines of dramatic action and interaction of this scene, conducted among so many players. In the film therefore, not only is the character of Margaret omitted, but so are Dorset and Gray, leaving only Elizabeth and her brother Rivers to 'represent' the Woodville faction. Since Lady Anne, Richard's new 'conquest' from the Lancastrian regime he has defeated, is also introduced at his side, the opposition between Yorkist and Woodville factions now becomes very apparent to us. What makes this factional opposition even more distinctive for a cinema audience is having Queen Elizabeth and Rivers played by American actors whose accents and social manner identify them as commoner 'arrivistes' in the court, as compared with the marked aristocratic drawl and cool behaviour of Richard and his traditionally English Yorkist followers. Another very notable change between stage and film centres around the character of Richard himself. When Richard rows with his mother the Duchess of York in the stage version (4.4), he reveals no sense of vulnerability to her insults and curses. In the film however, Richard is visibly shaken by his mother's attack, providing evidence of a Richard whose character has been coded differently for a film audience. As explained in the essay on this film in Part IV, McKellen's notion that Richard's wickedness 'is an outcome of other people's disaffection with his physique' is used by Loncraine to turn Richard into the kind of mentally twisted criminal type whose rise and fall is familiar from various gangster films from the 1930s onward, with the result that the dramatic curve of this movie becomes very influenced by gangster film and political thriller genres. Noticing this leads us neatly into the all-important subject of film genres, and the conventions and codes they use to communicate with the film audience.

5

Film Genre: Conventions and Codes

How at any one time do we choose which movie to see in theatrical release at the cinema, or by rental DVD/video at home? With a world-wide movie industry fiercely competing for the attention and money of filmgoers wanting to be entertained in a variety of ways, this is a question filmmakers (as well as viewers) have always had to consider from the outset, since they need not only to entertain effectively, but also to avoid making a loss, moviemaking being an expensive business. Almost from the beginning of movies being commercially screened in cinemas, the process of choosing what to see for viewers has been made easier by most films being conceived, made, marketed and consumed according to type or *genre*. Some people may be dismissive of 'genre films' because the less imaginative products brought out can seem formulaic and predictable. Yet the world of film cannot do without generic categories, since most of us have preferences for one particular genre or another, be it action pictures, romantic comedies, horror movies, musicals, gangster or science fiction thrillers, 'European' or 'foreign' movies – or even perhaps movies of the Shakespeare genre. Furthermore, as the fiction entertainment film grows in popularity, it can be more and more difficult for browsers to make their choices as they trawl the aisles of the DVD/video store, since movies increasingly mix one genre with another. This makes film genres – such as the 'thriller' – harder and harder to contain or define in a single category. The thriller has changed in style a good deal over the years, and can embrace elements taken from horror, erotic, detective, political, gangster (or other) films, creating the need for more and more genre-mix labels in order that particular films can be identified and marketed with some success.

Yet this situation is not new, as Shakespeare himself wittily illustrated around 1600 when he parodied the classifications of contemporary dramatic theorists by having Polonius in *Hamlet* refer to plays of 'tragedy, comedy, history, pastoral, pastoral-comical, historical-pastoral, tragical-historical, tragical-comical-historical-pastoral ...' (2.2.379–81). In fact, Shakespeare is the exemplary case of a dramatist who wrote scripts of a generically 'mixed' style, creating and mingling together in the same play sophisticated and low-life characters, juxtaposing serious themes and episodes with comic ones. Numerous instances of such juxtaposition exist in all his plays, one of the most famous being the gravediggers' scene in *Hamlet*, where dark comedy sits cheek by jowl with tragedy. One very good reason why Shakespeare repeatedly produced plays in this generically mixed style was a commercial one: more money could be made at the Globe playhouse if the drama being played appealed to the widest possible paying audience, an audience ranging from university-trained wits and the professional orders, to tradespeople and labourers. Whoever they might be, it was also important for the audience to know in general terms what kind of play they might expect to see if they went along one afternoon to a Globe performance, whether they would be expected to laugh, or to cry. This is why Shakespeare did not call his essentially serious and questioning play *Hamlet*, but rather *The Tragicall Historie of Hamlet, Prince of Denmarke* (1603), and why he provided titles like *Much adoe about Nothing* (1600) to signal an appropriate expectation to playgoers who were looking for a comedy to entertain them.

Providing suitably descriptive titles for posters and playbills advertising the play performances would therefore have set up a particular psychological and emotional expectation – a *genre* expectation – which the audience would look to have satisfied by the actual performance if they turned up. This is what the jargon of marketing nowadays calls 'positioning the audience', a process we commonly see at work in the advertisement and marketing campaigns on billboards and TV for numerous large-budget Hollywood movies. What makes one film succeed more than another will of course depend on many factors, not the least of which are the ways in which the audience are persuaded to continue watching, entranced and entertained, for the two hours or so that they sit gazing at the large or small screen. Part of how they become engaged by the film may well be determined by the way their *genre expectations* are fulfilled, and the extent to which the demands behind what has been called 'the contract between filmmaker and audience, the promise of something new based on something familiar', are met (Bordwell and Thompson, 2001, 99). The elements that provide this 'something new based on something familiar', applies to the majority of popular narrative fiction entertainment films written, marketed and watched around the world, and almost always sponsored by the major film distributors. These elements are usually called *genre conventions* (sometimes *film codes*) and, surprising though it may seem at first glance, for most Shakespeare on film makers who have wanted to attract and to connect with a larger movie audience, such genre conventions have also been woven into filmed Shakespeare adaptations.

6

Genre Conventions and the Shakespeare Film Adaptation

To see how all this may apply to Shakespeare adaptations on film, we first need to explore what genre conventions consist of, the areas where films resemble each other in certain ways, given that film-makers, audiences and reviewers do share a kind of community of expectation concerning the distinct film genre identities that have developed and prevail in the world of film. Film genre conventions may be considered under four main headings: ***Plot elements, Themes, Film techniques*** and ***Iconography***. By recognising the conventions that give a film genre its identity, a viewer is provided with a pathway into that genre, an approximate guide to what to expect in approaching and 'reading' the film. Makers of the most popular, 'mainstream' Shakespeare film adaptations have certainly attended to the need to communicate effectively with a popular cinema audience, manipulating genre conventions in order to grab the attention of the viewer, and having engaged it, working to sustain that attention. After briefly exploring what the major genre conventions are, I illustrate below in each case how some of the Shakespeare films have deployed these genre conventions.

Plot elements

We expect certain plot elements to shape films in the various genres. *Westerns* often embody a revenge plot, and frequently involve family conflicts/vendettas or the competition over land or livelihood. (As a 'pure' genre, the Western has now all but disappeared, yet was extraordinarily popular during most of the twentieth century up to the 1980s). In a *detective* or *mystery* film, we expect some kind of systematic and progressive investigation to take place. *Gangster* film plots often focus on the rise and fall of a central gangster figure struggling against rival gangs and the law. *Musicals* will manipulate plot to provide situations allowing the actors to sing or dance. *War films* tend to focus on the fortunes of a heroic individual courageously facing the dangers of combat, and emerging a battered survivor who has lost one or more close friends or 'buddies' along the way. The plots of *action* films are like those of war films, but instead of a war between nations, the ingenious and usually strong hero is an 'outsider' or 'vigilante' figure pitting his wits against an evil gang or organisation intent on some form of large-scale domination. The *epic film* is a movie in which the plot is often vast, meandering, and peopled by a large cast, many of whom may be famous actors playing 'cameo' parts: the issues at stake in the plot are usually large scale, as are the settings, pacing and scope of the movie, which is also often shot on 70 mm gauge film.

Quite obviously, the plot elements contained in any Shakespeare play already pre-exist in the play text that has come down to us. Filmmakers adapting a play for the screen may choose to cut or restructure parts of that text in various ways to make the movie more acceptable to the viewing audience. But if the translation to film is to be a *Shakespearean* adaptation of the play and not something else, then the film must carry the plot elements that the lines of the original Shakespearean text invariably produce. This does not mean to say that these 'fixed' plot elements cannot be *conveyed* in ways that may draw on modern genre conventions in order to increase audience accessibility, appeal and involvement. As we have seen already above in 'The Periodising Mode', Loncraine's *Richard III* uses a 1930s British cultural setting to deliver Shakespeare's play on screen. Yet the manner in which that film's plot is conveyed is also indebted in many ways to those of the classic 1930s gangster movies, Richard's powermongering career stylistically drawing on the rise and fall pattern of the ruthless and bullying gangster-type. For Kenneth Branagh, the plot of *Love's Labour's Lost* seemed to fit so well with the style and mood of 1930s Hollywood musicals, that his film of the play cuts much of its linguistic wit, substituting instead romantic love song 'standards', thus virtually turning a Shakespeare film into a 1930s Hollywood musical movie.

Again, so alert was Laurence Olivier to the importance of incorporating genre conventions or film codes into *Henry V* to communicate effectively with the popular film audience, that he drew on Western and Robin Hood film conventions of the period, and in doing so created the first really successful Shakespeare play adaptation in English on film. The simplified characterisation Olivier achieved by extensive cutting of the play text was further enhanced for a wartime audience primed for the consumption of patriotic sentiment, by his 'setting up' the invasion of France in the film along the lines of a Western 'revenge' plot: the Dauphin's gift of tennis balls comes across to us (and his boisterously loyal 'ready-made' onscreen Globe audience) as an insult to 'Englishmen', that must surely be avenged – as it will be. In the outdoor scenes involving horsemanship skills (Olivier mounts and rides like a cowboy) and in the battle of Agincourt, all the Western genre conventions come into play for a screen audience already well 'trained' to read them through a regular diet of consuming Western movies at the cinema. A clear sense of the moral superiority of the English is thus solidly established, while the French are conveyed as the 'baddies' (rather than the usual 'Injuns'), while the riders on horseback also suggest the association between man and nature so well established in Westerns. In turn, long shots connected by **tracking shots** and camera **pans** together with the parallel **montage** sequences of the approaching armies (in Westerns it is usually US Cavalry vs. The Indians) all convey the atmosphere, setting and sense of limitless space of the Western.

Branagh's 1989 *Henry V* also incorporated tried and tested genre conventions, but this time the film codes he drew on were from the 1980s Vietnam war movie. Where Olivier draws on the ethos of the Western hero and the frontier range war for his audience, Branagh adapts Oliver Stone's and Stanley Kubrick's **subjective shot** techniques (from Vietnam movies *Platoon* (1986) and *Full Metal Jacket* (1987)) to convey the more personal and painful elements of war. The idealization of male bonding, the *aestheticization of violence*, immersing the viewer in the often complex emotions affecting individuals and their frequently strained relations with one another, are all expressed by way of long and detailed camera **close-ups**. Branagh even deploys Western genre conventions in adapting a Shakespearean comedy for the screen, the arrival of Don Pedro and his comrades on their return from the wars near the opening of his 1993 adaptation of *Much Ado About Nothing* being played with (as Branagh says) 'a nod to *The Magnificent Seven*', John Sturges's popular western movie of 1960.

Branagh's 1996 *Hamlet* bears many of the features of the film epic. The text used is not only the fullest available, from the Folio edition, but this is supplemented by lines from the other main *Hamlet* text, the shorter Q2, so that the film, shot on 'epic gauge' 70 mm, runs to four hours with an intermission. Like many of its predecessors with life and death themes shot on a large canvas with exotic costumes (*Spartacus, Dr Zhivago, Lawrence of Arabia*, etc.), the film takes us through every detail of the play's large variety of incidents and scenes, creating a sweeping epic arc of plot at a pace measured out by a score of symphonic dimensions, shot variously in the magnificent opulence of Blenheim Palace or on enormous sound stages: the end of the first part just before the intermission has Branagh speaking the 'How all occasions do inform against me' soliloquy as an isolated Hamlet stands alone on a vast frozen plateau, just about to be taken to England. The enormous cast includes many 'cameo' appearances from famous American actors like Jack Lemmon, Charlton Heston (himself a veteran of many film epics), Billy Crystal and Robin Williams, whose presence give the film scale, as does the massive commando-style invasion of Elsinore by Fortinbras, his forces toppling the great statue of Old Hamlet, bringing one cycle of Denmark's history to a close.

Themes

Some genre conventions can be *themes* that are produced repeatedly in films to convey broader meanings. Loyalty to one's comrades, often involving immense sacrifice, danger or death in the service of an ideal, is a recurring theme in *war films*. A common theme of *gangster films* is the price to be paid for criminal success, the gangster becoming self-obsessed and cruel in his rise to power, typically enjoyed only briefly before an aloof isolation and neurotic instability ensure his demise. What used to be called the 'battle of the sexes' can be a thematic staple of so-called screwball and *romantic comedies*, where the male and female leads are typically in conflict with each other – and also perhaps with a socially constraining milieu – for most of the movie, before a final reconciliation takes place. *Mystery* or *detective films*, especially those tending toward the 'noirish', may with their meandering and labyrinthine plots involve the theme of the hero-investigator's sanity or mental strength being tested in the face of those hostile to or unsympathetic with the aims of the investigation.

The status of 'theme' as a potential genre convention to be drawn on in the Shakespeare adaptation is similar to that of 'plot element', since the themes in a Shakespeare play are often those produced by the pre-existing play text. It is no surprise to learn that the plots of Shakespeare plays which tend to appeal most to audiences will also generate the themes of greatest audience appeal. Much of the success of Branagh's *Henry V* was due to the way it delivered its themes of loyalty-testing among an army warring on foreign soil, and how a leader against all the odds could inspire his men to follow him in adversity and yet still succeed.

The ability of Loncraine and McKellen to manipulate the already resonant theme of ruthless Elizabethan Machiavellianism in *Richard III* into a form that parallels almost exactly the rise-and-fall themes of the classic gangster film is an achievement of great filmic skill. One thematic convention of this genre is for the gangster anti-hero to feel excluded from society, his writhings of resentment and humiliation often stemming from low or shameful birth. In two famous American gangster films, this feeling of being set apart is caused by a physical problem, Paul Muni being disfigured in *Scarface* (1932) and James Cagney suffering from a mental illness in *White Heat* (1949). Similarly, feeling socially excluded because of his crooked body, Richard is also obsessed in Loncraine's movie by a mother who has rejected him from birth, this lack of maternal affection being the primary motivation for his resentful and ruthless climb to power, rather than any political, racial or military drive, despite the film's overt storyline of the rise and fall of a British fascist-like dictator. Coming from the world of TV ads and commercial films, Loncraine was quite at home both in quoting from a range of genres, from the slasher movie to the 'English heritage' film, and in also deploying the kind of fast editing, upbeat period music and visually stylish design that would appeal to a popular audience.

The 'battle of the sexes' theme, so beloved of screwball and romantic comedies, has been exploited in at least two Shakespeare film adaptations: Zeffirelli's *The Taming of the Shrew* (1966) and Branagh's *Much Ado About Nothing* (1993). Contemporary screen icons Richard Burton and Elizabeth Taylor (see also **Iconography** later) were celebrated in real life for having a love-hate relationship, and this fed easily into the play's theme of reluctant bride pursued by penniless gold-digger, Taylor's ferocious temper and Burton's swaggering nonchalance providing the kind of overblown romantic convention that popular audiences craved. In a similar vein, the lively, real-life and highly public relationship of Kenneth Branagh and Emma Thompson was ready-made to animate the skirmishing antics of Kate and Benedick in Branagh's *Much Ado*. The style of playing in the argumentative exchanges between these two is again and again reminiscent of the many Hollywood screwball romantic comedies which had preceded it, from the 1930s films of Howard Hawks (who initiated the genre), onward.

Film techniques

Film techniques are sometimes associated with specific genre conventions. Lighting that creates sombreness and shadows is characteristic of mystery films (especially *film noir*), of thrillers and (most decidedly) of horror films. The increasingly powerful lighting technology of the 1940s that made **chiaroscuro** techniques and low-key illumination so helpful in creating the mysterious atmosphere of many melodramas of the 1940s and 1950s, also made the cinematographer's technique of **deep focus** a major stylistic option throughout the same period. The technique (also facilitated by faster film and shorter-focal-length lenses) can have a number of effects from the viewer's point of view. By maintaining both near and distant figures and settings in sharp focus, the camera almost forces the viewer to scan the whole of the frame, encouraging us to consider the *relationship* between a near and a more distant figure, both kept in focus, rather than just considering one of them. On the other hand, this refusal to focus on the significance and actions of a single human figure or event can also have the effect of 'dehumanising' the scene in front of us by 'objectifying' (making an object of) all that we see, an effect that is also potentially destabilising and disturbing for the viewer. By seeming to shift the power for effective human agency away from any single protagonist, we can see how the deep focus technique might appeal to film-makers interested in making prominent a powerful non-human presence that is of a threatening or mysteriously alien nature. This is perhaps why deep-focus photography was revived in Steven Spielburg's 1970s films, particularly *Jaws* and *Close Encounters of the Third Kind*.

The chiaroscuro lighting so characteristic of expressionist-influenced film noirs and melodramatic thrillers of the 1940s was used extensively in Olivier's *Hamlet* and also by Welles in his *Macbeth*, both films being released in 1948. For the story of a man who 'could not make up his mind' (Olivier's view, expressed by him in voice-over at the film's beginning), the shadowy passageways of Elsinore created by chiaroscuro effects provided a sombre, haunted look entirely fitting for a Hamlet suffering mental torment and indecision. The guilty unease distinguishing the afflicted mind of Welles's usurping Macbeth is a characterisation also given emphasis by this director's use of light and shadow. Just as Olivier's lighting of a labyrinthine Elsinore images the anxious workings of Hamlet's mind, so does the sinisterly lit setting Welles creates for Macbeth's castle, its dim, dark and dripping cavernous passages functioning as a kind of visual **metonymy** for the 'scorpion-filled' mentality of Macbeth. Deep-focus photography is used extensively by Olivier in *Hamlet* to suggest both the alienation of the Prince in relation to others (especially to Ophelia) and how all at Elsinore seem to be at the mercy of large, impersonal forces (the world of the Ghost). Similarly, in a number of the scenes shot for *Macbeth*, Welles uses deep-focus photography to indicate the controlling mysterious supernatural forces of the witches.

The battle scenes of both Olivier's and Branagh's versions of *Henry V* use rapid cutting techniques in order to convey the atmosphere of violent excitement experienced in battle. The famously powerful ten-minute battle sequence of Welles's *Chimes at Midnight* (the battle at Shrewsbury) is often made more effective through the use of speeded-up shots. These capture in a grimly unsentimental way the suddenness of death in battle; while slowed-down shooting shows the weary ignominy of exhausted men flailing grimly at each other in a waste of death.

Iconography

A film genre can often be identified by the repeated use of visual elements signifying or symbolising meaning in a conventionally iconographic way. Settings, or the objects in them, can supply iconography for a genre. The setting of a battle-torn landscape, for instance, usually tells us that we are in some kind of war film, while a long-shot of a stagecoach snaking its way across a wide open prairie signals we are in an American Western. Machine guns fired from a sleek, fast-moving black 1920s automobile should be enough to tell us we are watching an old gangster movie. A large mansion in semi-darkness or castle with a labyrinth of sombre, shadowy corridors is often the setting for gothic horror, and silver spaceships sliding through the dark vacuum of star-filled space signify that we are caught up in a science fiction film. Even film stars can become iconographic: Arnold Swarzenegger or Mel Gibson for the action adventure film, John Wayne for the Western, Fred Astaire and Ginger Rogers for Hollywood song and dance musicals.

It would be difficult to claim that the Shakespeare film genre displays a specific iconography, except that the most traditional and conventional of film adaptations typically trying for an 'authentic historical look' have created a *mis-en-scène* imitating Elizabethan settings, dressing the actors in Elizabethan costume. Examples of such 'men in tights' adaptations are George Cukor's glittering Hollywood *Romeo and Juliet* of 1936, Olivier's *Hamlet* and *Richard III*, and the *Romeo and Juliet* movies of Castellani (1954) and Zeffirelli (1968). Often in the theatre from the 1960s onward, and certainly since the renaissance of Shakespeare films post-1989, *mis-en-scène*, costuming and overall film design have more and more been dictated by what each film-maker deems is workable and conceptually appropriate in order for their adaptation to communicate successfully with the target audience. In Shakespeare's own time, there seems to have been little concern for getting players to be dressed in anything like the 'authentic' dress of the period of the play being depicted. As the sketch by Henry Peacham of a staging of *Titus Andronicus* by Shakespeare's company in 1595 shows, an attempt at 'period correctness' has been made by dressing Titus in Roman costume, but his soldiers are shown carrying Tudor halberds (see *Norton Shakespeare*, 1997, 3291, where the sketch is reproduced).

Perhaps the most iconographic element of any Shakespeare film adaptation is the frequently bold display of Shakespeare's name itself, given either in or near to the main titles: after all, the name 'William Shakespeare' has for so long maintained 'classic' status, synonymous with 'genius', that no film-maker at work in the 'designer label' conscious marketplace would not want to prominently attach the peerless 'Shakespeare' brand to their movie. When it comes to iconographic film stars for the Shakespeare film, there are of course a good number: Laurence Olivier and Orson Welles for an older generation, Kenneth Branagh for the latest, are all actors who have made and starred in several of their own Shakespeare adaptations. But there are others who also crop up repeatedly in Shakespeare movies for the cinema or TV, and have become iconographic, in particular, John Gielgud, Ian McKellen and Judi Dench. Many famous screen actors have played lead parts in Shakespeare films, but few have done this more than once, so few can be considered to have become iconographic for the Shakespeare adaptation genre.

7

A Cross-cultural Shakespeare Adaptation: Kurosawa's *Kumonosu-Jô*

I conclude this part of the book with an analysis of Kurosawa's version of *Macbeth* not only because many admire *Kumonosu-Jô* as a movie which stands brilliantly alone for conveying Shakespeare's play on film without using one word of the original text. As will be seen, it does this by utilising the most creatively filmic of 'filmic' approaches, drawing on many of the elements of mode, style and convention discussed above. But as well as being a *tour-de-force* of cinematic artistry, the film is also unique in reworking Shakespeare's play for the big screen using a non-Western society's culture and history so radically that the result is unparalleled in the Shakespeare film genre.

Kumonosu-Jô (The Castle of the Spider's Web) [Throne of Blood] (Japan, 1957)

Director: Akira Kurosawa

Adaptation: Akira Kurosawa, Hideo Ognuni, Shinobu Hashimoto, Ryuzo Kikushima

Editing: Akira Kurosawa

Design: Yoshiro Murai

Production company: Toho

Medium: Black and White, 16 mm, 110 minutes

Main actors: Toshiro Mifune (Taketoi Washizu/Macbeth); Isuzu Yamada (Asaji/Lady Macbeth); Minoru Chiaki (Yoshiaki Miki/Banquo); Akira Kobu (Yoshiteru/Fleance); Takamaru Sasaki (Kuniharu Tsuzuki/Duncan); Yoichi Tachikawa (Kunimaru/Malcolm); Chieko Naniwa (Forest Witch).

Photography: Asaichi Nakai

Music: Masaru Sato

Akira Kurosawa's highly acclaimed Japanese samurai films *Seven Samurai* (1954) and *Yojimbo* (1961) became the basis of successful Westerns, the first being the model for *The Magnificent Seven*, while *A Fistful of Dollars*, Sergio Leone's first 'spaghetti Western', drew loosely on the second for its plot. The samurai film genre conventions of swordplay and revenge translate well in many ways to the Western genre, with its frontier town stories of bad blood and shoot-outs. But Kurosawa discovered that the genre for which he had attained fame was also the ideal vehicle for dramatising *The Tragedy of Macbeth* by Shakespeare, as he explains:

> During the period of civil wars in Japan, there are plenty of incidents like those portrayed in *Macbeth*. They are called *ge-koku-jo* [where a supposedly loyal retainer usurps power by murdering his lord]. Therefore the story of Macbeth appealed very much to me, and it was easy for me to adapt it.
>
> (Quoted in Manvell, 1971, 102)

As Thane of Glamis, Macbeth in effect fights as 'warrior retainer' under King Duncan at a time when (in mediaeval Scotland) warring rival kings and their clans battled for supremacy by force of arms in a social, political and military setting, which does obviously parallel the structure of the samurai warrior society of the Japanese mediaeval civil wars. So the parallels of history and of social power structures are authentic and they resonate for us in Kurosawa's film. Another indispensable element from *Macbeth* that Kurosawa also embeds most effectively into the dramatic dynamic of *Kumonosu-Jô* is the supernaturally evil prophecy, which seizes the imaginations of both Macbeth and Washizu (Kurosawa's Macbeth figure) so obsessively. In the Japanese version no occasion ever occurs for Washizu to dismiss his belief in the witches' prophecies in the way that Macbeth does: '... be these juggling fiends no more believed / That palter [equivocate] with us in a double sense', says Macbeth, just before he and Macduff fight to the death (5.10.19–20). Nevertheless, the notion of each protagonist believing in witches, who prophesy the succession to a supreme power ordained by what Banquo calls the 'instruments of darkness' (1.3.122), is one that underpins and animates the narrative flow of both tragic dramas.

The famous opening scene of *Macbeth* has three witches chanting magical rhymes, formulae that signal the play themes to come of paradox and ambiguity: these utterances also establish an important ritualistic framework for the play. As if to demonstrate to us how effective the power of the witchcraft over Macbeth already is, Shakespeare has Macbeth in his very first entrance tell Banquo as they return from battle that 'So foul and fair a day I have not seen' (1.3.36). In Kurosawa's film, ritualistic elements are introduced from the beginning too, the whole being shaped by various formal conventions and visual images that serve as important signifying functions in translating the play into a different culture and into the film medium. Not only are the set design and acting style of the film based on the highly formal Japanese Noh drama that developed over the period of the mediaeval warring samurai factions, but Noh music is drawn on too, the otherworldly sounds of a piercing Noh pipe and hypnotically pounding sticks being played over the opening Japanese titles. The film itself is also formalistically 'framed' at beginning and end by a chorus of deep, droning male voices. As we are shown a bleak and misty landscape containing only a wooden monolith memorialising the site of the once 'mighty fortress' of 'Spiderweb Castle', the sternly chanting chorus tells us (in translation) that this is the story of a 'proud warrior' who was 'murdered by ambition'. Yet his spirit is 'walking still', for 'what once was so now still is true'. What could therefore be construed as a ghost story at one level supplies a chilling moral conveyed in the style of a sung epic tale taking us back to earlier times.

As the obscuring mist clears to reveal a mighty fortress, we see a number of frantic messengers reporting to Tsuzuki (Duncan), Lord of Spiderweb Castle, and his council, on the progress of a rebel attack on their forts. The Noh style of playing is evident from the start as the ruling samurai council sit rigidly immobile on a raised plinth before a horizontal war screen, all staring ahead intently, only occasionally consulting with each other in short, vehement, almost barked exchanges. This is the style of playing – where intense emotion and physical stillness co-exist – that will especially characterise the performance of Mifune's Washizu. When Tsuzuki learns that Washizu and Miki (Banquo) have turned the tide of battle against the rebels, he beams and says that they will be rewarded, at which point the camera shows us Washizu and Miki making their way toward Spiderweb Castle, only approachable through the Spiderweb Forest, which one of Tsuzuki's generals has described as a 'natural labyrinth' functioning as a confusing barrier against enemies of the prevailing order.

The image of the Spiderweb which Kurosawa applies both to the Forest and to the Castle is the film's central visual metaphor. This is because the Forest is really not so much a natural as a *supernatural* labyrinth, a site of mystery and potential threat familiar to anyone attentive to the universal folk mythical warning about the danger of venturing into wooded areas, and captured in the words of the song, 'if you go down to the woods today, you're sure of a big surprise'. Before Washizu and Miki encounter their big surprise in the shape of an androgynous evil forest spirit, we see them at a bewildered stand on their horses in the Forest amidst a strange mixture of lightning, pouring rain and wide beams of sunlight streaming down through the high canopy of trees. 'What weather!' declares Washizu, 'I have never seen anything like it' – the equivalent of Macbeth's 'So fair and foul a day I have not seen.' The camera then gives us repeated glimpses of both samurai behind a screen of trees and thickets galloping along forest paths in an attempt to leave the Forest behind and reach Spiderweb Castle. Even when it is clear they are lost, they laugh this off by telling each other how Spiderweb Forest makes their enemies lose their way, while they are privileged to know every trail. It is only when Washizu's defiant action of firing an arrow high into the trees creates echoing shrieks of unearthly laughter throughout the Forest that he realises 'an evil spirit is blocking our way'. Their curiously compulsive response is to charge off furiously along the selfsame trails, Washizu firing off arrows wildly, while Miki fiercely brandishes his spear at nothing in particular. This pointless activity is finally halted when they (and we, from their point of view (**POV**)) glimpse ahead a white stick hut sitting behind a large tree trunk. What the astonished pair (and we) see behind the white wooden uprights of the hut after dismounting is a kneeling white-haired, white-cloaked figure turning a spinning wheel, whose quavering high-low voice produces a song, warning about the false beliefs that men's minds fabricate when deluded by pride, vanity and ambition. When Washizu finally snaps out of his entrancement with the scene and tears open the door of the fragile, cage-like hut, the witch calmly prophesies that he will become Lord of Spiderweb Castle after taking over the North Castle – it soon becomes clear that his ridiculing response masks Washizu's ambitions as a samurai warrior. It is only after the witch prophesies that Miki's son will eventually become Lord of Spiderweb Castle that she and her spinning wheel unaccountably fly up and vanish into thin air, proving that she is indeed an evil spirit, and not human.

The set made for shooting this scene and the camera and lighting techniques used in it not only produce the various kinds of image required to make such an other-worldly and magical encounter seem convincing, but they also seem to offer **metacinematic** comments on the nature of filmic perception and space. Jorgens suggests that like the witch who sits 'like a spider at the centre of a web', spinning her wheel and toying with the vulnerable minds of Washizu and Miki, Kurosawa as film-maker also 'enmeshes his characters in a formal pattern so rigid that it becomes an aesthetic equivalent of Fate'. The spinning wheels which Jorgens says resemble reels of film at an editing table 'seem to inscribe the circles followed by Washizu and Miki as they ride in circles in the forest, and are caught up in the cycles of war, fear and ambition that give the illusion of movement in this futile form of feudalism' (Jorgens, 1983, 172). The 'illusions of movement' so evidently at the animated core of the cinematic process we typically view are certainly cleverly achieved in this scene, with its flickering light source, the demonstrated insubstantiality of the witch and the hut, made to disappear through trick photography, and the 'screening' effects, used here and elsewhere throughout the film (Donaldson, 1990, 60–91). These all offer perspective and depth, yet ultimately do so only through the flickering images created in front of our eyes by spinning reels of celluloid film.

In complete contrast to the spirit-controlled tangles and enmeshments of the Forest that Kurosawa **metonymically** deploys to convey the tangled emotions of Washizu (while also establishing the seeds of the 'inner' narrative), the Noh interiors inhabited by Washizu and Asaji (Lady Macbeth) we soon see at North Castle are neatly geometric. The worlds of the fortresses and castles throughout the film are in fact largely figured in horizontals and verticals, from the opening shots of the war council sat in a horizontal line, to the last scenes showing Washizu's defeat as he moves ever downward floor by floor in the Spiderweb Forest Castle to final death at the hands of his own men. An affinity with the spatial techniques used by Welles in *Citizen Kane* is shown by Kurosawa's stress on the horizontal when he comments that in order to 'emphasize the psychology of the hero, driven by compulsion, we made the interiors wide with low ceilings and squat pillars to create the effect of oppression' (Richie, 1965, 123). The verticals and horizontals of the man-made forts in effect represent the rigidly hierarchical Japanese feudal order. The contained decorum of this social order is made dramatically emphatic in turn by the Noh choreography and ritual used to play out the scenes when Asaji, using arguments of *realpolitik*, finally convinces Washizu of the need to kill the Lord of Spiderweb Castle, a sequence concluding at the point where Asaji raises the alarm of 'intruder, murderer!' following the assassination of Tsuzuki.

In Shakespeare's *Macbeth*, Lady Macbeth's speeches in 1.5 align her with the malevolent supernatural realm of the witches. Kurosawa creates a similar alignment by providing strong visual identifications between the Forest Witch and Asaji, especially in the scene where Washizu is persuaded by Asaji to kill his lord, which starts with Washizu uneasily mocking her cynical attitude toward 'loyalty' in much the same way that he had earlier laughingly dismissed the Forest Witch's songs. Asaji's calmly seated posture, her position in the right of the frame, and the boldly lit harsh whiteface make-up aimed at recreating the look of a Noh mask, are all strongly reminiscent of the Forest Witch's presentation. 'I firmly believe in that prediction', says Asaji, commenting that 'the stage is set' for him to make it come true, an apt metaphor given the deployment of compelling Noh-choreographed movement that is to follow. The calling of the crows, which Asaji says is telling him 'the throne is yours', marks Asaji's move from stony immobility to initiative-taking, ritual Noh music accompanying her motions of standing up to literally lead Washizu by the hand into a new physical position while she explains what must be done to bring about the fulfilment of the prophecy. It is at this point that Washizu becomes startled by the flickering lights of the servants seen passing along behind the *shoji* screen, the camera moving round to frame him and Asaji in front of it. This shot of them in front of an illuminated screen viewing the opaque flickering lights behind seems once again to be functioning as a **metacinematic** device, this time perhaps suggesting a link between the seductive illusions of the cinematic screen world and the mysteries of the supernatural realm. This link is reinforced when Kurosawa has Asaji eerily disappear through a doorway to fetch drugged wine for the guards by using a fade-to-black, fading her image in again from black on her return with the wine pitcher. This makes her seem like a spirit. She is again made to 'disappear' when her image dissolves to that of the unconscious guards sprawled out legs akimbo, their horizontal line of stability destroyed by the drugged drink. The only sound to be heard after this is that of her swishing kimono as she shuffles purposively along the wooden floors, to the accompaniment of a Noh pipe. In fact, from the moment that Asaji takes the initiative from Washizu, the only significant noise to be heard on the soundtrack is the unsettling Noh sound effect of her swishing kimono as she busily scurries about, performing her otherwise silent, single-minded and deadly business.

We are prepared for the deed to be committed by Washizu by further cinematic techniques of 'showing', rather than 'telling'. While Asaji is busy obtaining the murder weapon from one of the comatose guards, Washizu sits awaiting her return in the bloodstained room earlier 'purified' by his servants. Several times he glances apprehensively toward the bloodstained wall through a rack of vertically stacked arrows, and it is here, in the camera's precise imaging of Washizu against the stain's ugly, irregular outline 'so at variance with the quiet angles and lines of design', that 'prophecy and destiny become irrevocably knit' in this drama (Davies, 1988, 162). For the wood of the deadly arrows links this 'forbidden room' where the traitorous Fujimaki died, both to the tempting prophecies of the Forest Witch (the magic Forest is made of wood), and to Washizu's own vacillation about undertaking the same treasonous action on Tsuzuki. This vacillation lasts only until the swishing reappearance of Asaji, who plants the guard's spear at a diagonal angle into his hands. This diagonal line functions visually as a sign of disruption and treachery, confounding the horizontal lines of feudal power and defence shown in many other sequences of the film. The emotional agitation of Washizu seen before now intensifies as, preparing for murder, Toshiro Mifune gives his panting, animal-like grimace with bared teeth that mimics so well the Noh warrior mask Kurosawa had asked him to imitate. After his departure to kill Tsuzuki, Noh theatricality continues when Asaji, left alone, twice glances round at the arrows and the wall (just as Washizu had) before springing up and, to the accompaniment of hectic Noh syncopation, performs a small but ecstatically vigorous dance between the arrow rack and the wall, as if symbolically acting out the violence which her husband is committing on his Lord at that very moment. (Peter Donaldson may be right that this sequence creates perhaps 'the most remarkable of the many screening effects in the film.') It then only remains for Asaji to purposefully remove the blood-soaked spear from the grip of a returned Washizu who sits panting convulsively after the murder; to put it in the hands of a drugged guard; to ritually wash her hands of the blood; to raise the alarm – and this extraordinary sequence is at an end.

Of course, Asaji is only able to persuade Washizu to murder because, as with Macbeth in the source play, these warriors have a deep need to be 'winners', and are driven by ambition, albeit of a clumsily 'vaulting' variety (1.7.27). In Kurosawa's film the disturbed emotions fuelling Washizu's ambition are revealed in various ways, seen fairly openly in his vain encounter with the Forest Spirit, but conveyed more subtly in other episodes. Eschewing recourse to speech, Kurosawa finds clever visual means to image these powerful emotions as Washizu responds at North Castle to Asaji's first blunt attempts to persuade him to usurp Tsuzuki's power and position by killing him. We watch him pacing around in discomfort as she coolly proposes treason, while in the courtyard stockade just behind we also glimpse and hear a horse being galloped about wildly. This image of powerful instinctive forces under constraint is an exquisite visual **metonymic** of the true emotional ferment churning inside Washizu, and which is at complete variance with the unconvincing hissed remonstrations of loyalty he makes to the sphinx-like Asaji.

We see a similar visual metonymic of Washizu's tense emotional life following Asaji's startling announcement of her pregnancy, news that produces a terrible conflict of loyalty in him, since he has promised to make his friend Miki's son his successor. This is imaged in the careering uncontrollability of Miki's horse that we see next, which Miki's son says is (correctly) an 'ill omen'. The final eruption of animal energies to disturb the cool angularity of the fortress interiors is the one that Washizu mistakenly regards as a lucky omen, but which is once again a visual emblem of his hopelessly self-deceiving emotional impulses. This eruption occurs when Spiderweb Castle is invaded by birds which have lost their home in the Forest that Noriyasu, Kunimaru (Malcolm) and their invading army have partly torn down to create their Forest camouflage (as in Shakespeare's play). This is an action enabling them to defeat Washizu, fulfilling the Forest Witch's prophecy that the only battle he will lose is when the Spiderweb Forest begins to move and approach the Castle (when 'Birnam Wood / Do come toward Dunsinane' (5.5.42–3)).

The chopped-down wood of the enchanted Forest that turns an illusion into reality for the incredulous Washizu also brings him face to face with the realities of retribution and death, a festoon of arrows mortally piercing his body. Yet before this happens, as he staggers down the wooden steps and structure of Forest Castle, we see him somehow seeming to be able to defy death. Mortally porcupined by the arrows of his own men, he yet confronts these soldiers who have turned on him, but who now back away as if terrified by a ghost or demon, as well they might, since the arrow transfixing his neck has arrested the typical warrior grimace into a demonic mask-like rigidity. Death does finally take him, but even in his final collapse he falls attempting to draw his sword, a samurai warrior to the end. This final sequence has been described as 'the very keystone of the film's formal structure', since 'here at last that tense, horizontal alternation between scenes of decentred frenzy and dramatic but static scenes is resolved into a vertical orgasm of on-screen violence' (Burch, 1979, 317).

Kozintsev's comment that he thinks Kurosawa's film 'is the finest of Shakespearean movies'(1967, 29) is no doubt inspired by the fact that Kurosawa had been so successful in achieving Kozintsev's own ambition as a Shakespearean film-maker, that of 'making the aural visual'. As we have already noted, to achieve this Kozintsev says that the 'poetic texture' of a Shakespeare script 'has itself to be transformed into a visual poetry, into the dynamic organisation of film imagery'. Analysing his film shows that the power of Kurosawa's 'visual poetry' derives from a design of delivering the story and inner life of Shakespeare's drama in a structure of images whose meaning and effects draw on a highly formalistic non-Western dramatic tradition (Noh theatre) and film genre (the samurai movie) that are arguably as rich in cultural signification and resonance as the verbal text of the Shakespearean original.

Part IV

Critical Essays

1. Comedies

INTRODUCTORY NOTE

There have been far fewer notable translations of Shakespearean comedies to film than has been the case for the tragedies and histories. The reason for this is summed up well by Michael Hattaway:

> Shakespeare's comedies create relationships with their theatre audiences for which very few directors have managed to find cinematic equivalents (Hattaway, in Jackson ed., 2000, 85; bracketed page-references in the following refer to his essay).

Another way of expressing this is to say that the *stage conventions* for which the comedies were written and which assume the presence of a live audience do not transfer well to film, which has to find ways of involving the audience without requiring their active participation in the same way (see discussion in Part I). The conventions of *film realism*, whereby an **identification** between the actor and their role is created for the audience, who in turn are drawn to *identify* with the characters on screen, are more readily suited for the adaptation of Shakespearean histories and tragedies to film than are the comedies.

It is much more difficult to make such conventions of film realism work for Shakespearean comedies, since the theatrical precondition for creating comic effects relies *not* on an identification between actor and role, but on what Hattaway calls an 'aesthetic estrangement or alienation between actor and role' (90). In other words, there is in comedy a 'distance' established between the role performed and the actor performing it, something readily perceptible to and enjoyed by the audience. Characters in theatrical comedies therefore tend to be person *types* rather than individualised, fully rounded personalities, and they frequently perform within groups or ensembles, with the actors relying on 'audience response in order to conjure the folly of the play, to demonstrate and to exploit the difference between themselves and their roles' (91). Since the performance of film comedy by definition is deprived of the benefits of a live audience, its effectiveness is also likely to be more reliant than the stage is on the screen characters *themselves* functioning as an audience to each other; thus providing responses with which we can in turn identify. Such comedy also works best in a physical 'stage frame' that functions for the audience as a continually visible 'sign of those conventions for game and revelry that govern the action' (86).

In the three comedy adaptations discussed here, I hope the reader will be stimulated to think about the extent to which film directors have found ways of involving the screen audience in their comedies. Kenneth Branagh's *Much Ado About Nothing* works the comedy-producing mechanisms mentioned above with some skill. This is because much of the comic action takes place among the high hedges and numerous walkways of the Tuscan villa location, providing the kind of 'stage frame' needed for the episodes of deception, overhearing and spying that is at the heart of this play's comedy. Also at its heart are the characters of Benedick and Beatrice, and Branagh not only makes the most of their virtuoso flourishes of witty verbal artistry, but also of their love interactions, unusually complex for a Shakespearean comedy and therefore very welcome for a Hollywood audience that thrives on 'true love'. The film is less successful in the scenes involving the exaggerated playing of Dogberry and Verges, for without a live audience to register the highly conventional response required for overblown farce, their grotesquerie tends to fall flat.

Adrian Noble carried over some of the devices he had used in his stage version of *A Midsummer Night's Dream* to his film, but these are sometimes too 'abstract' to work well in the realistic settings needed for film. Yet his creation of the Boy to 'dream the action' of the play works well as a kind of fantastically imaginative equivalent to a 'stage frame', inside which the characters 'play' at love, and are also metatheatrically 'played with' by Noble to conjure up colourful images of dream-like wonder and delight. All Shakespearean comedy revolves around love, 'but for Hollywood, "falling in love", the necessary prelude to bourgeois marriage, is too serious to be treated as a sport or crucial negotiation' (92).

Michael Hoffman's *Dream* does however take its love seriously in this sentimental fashion and modifies the character of Bottom in order to satisfy the romantic fantasy needs of a Hollywood audience. Having little of the theatre about it other than elaborate sound stage sets that outdo its glittering 1935 Warner Brothers predecessor, Hoffman's 'frame' uses operatic song, ensemble comedy and Kevin Kline's skills as a superlative comic actor to create a 'Bottom's Dream' that in some ways has the feel of a sentimental opera rather than a Shakespeare film adaptation.

Kenneth Branagh's *Much Ado About Nothing* (UK, 1993)

Medium: Technicolor, 35 mm, *c*.104 minutes

Main actors: Kenneth Branagh (Benedick); Emma Thompson (Beatrice); Denzel Washington (Don Pedro); Keanu Reeves (Don John); Robert Sean Leonard (Claudio); Richard Briers (Leonato); Brian Blessed (Antonio); Michael Keaton (Dogberry); Ben Elton (Verges); Kate Beckinsale (Hero)

Director: Kenneth Branagh

Screenplay: Kenneth Branagh

Design: Tim Harvey

Producers: Stephen Evans, David Parfitt, Kenneth Branagh

Photography: Roger Lanser

Music: Patrick Doyle

Kenneth Branagh has been described as the 'flamboyant realist' of Shakespeare-on-film (Kael, 1992, 216), and this coining is nowhere more applicable than in the case of his most commercially popular success, *Much Ado About Nothing*. Branagh's basic approach continued that of the ground-breaking *Henry V*, to provide 'an absolute clarity that would enable a modern audience to respond to Shakespeare-on-film, in the same way that they would respond to any other movie'. The 'absolute clarity' required for a movie audience unfamiliar with the play would again be achieved through an 'utter reality of characterisation', and since three-quarters of the play's dialogue is in prose this could help the (especially non-Shakespearean) actors provide an even more accessible conversational tone. Branagh is only too aware that in the absence of a strong plot line the dramatic life of the comedy relies heavily on well-timed use of dialogue, a necessarily ample amount of which (over 50%) is retained for this production. His aim of providing a 'user-friendly' approach to Shakespeare's language right from the beginning includes having the words of Balthasar's song from the play 'Sigh no more, ladies, sigh no more' (2.3.) appear on the screen in time to the rhythmic speaking of the lines by Emma Thompson (Beatrice), a 'determined attempt to show' how the words can be 'dramatic in themselves', and which allows 'the audience to "tune in" to the new language they are about to experience' (Branagh, 1993, xiv).

In this second Shakespeare adaptation, much of the 'flamboyant' element enabling the film audience to respond as they would to 'any other movie' was to be influenced by a new factor – the example and practice of Franco Zeffirelli's Shakespeare moviemaking. Branagh's general approach to directing and performing Shakespeare in theatre and film already possessed the energy of Zeffirelli's work, but to present a Shakespearean comedy of Italian setting there could be no better cinematic models to follow than the vivid, colourful and sunny movies *The Taming of the Shrew* and *Romeo and Juliet*. Furthermore, since the ground-breaking release of what Branagh had called his 'quintessentially English project' (Branagh, 1991, 217) *Henry V* in 1989, Zeffirelli's 1990 *Hamlet* had shown how the casting of internationally famous stars in key roles could make a Shakespeare adaptation reliably bankable. Big box office returns are evidently what Branagh now wanted, for at the moment that he was playing Hamlet for the second time at London's Barbican theatre and also editing his *Much Ado*, he told Crowl in an interview, 'If I can't make Shakespeare live for a broad audience with all the Hollywood that got packed into the film, then I doubt I will be able to raise the financing for a *Hamlet* film' (Crowl, 231, n.8). He need not have worried, for the US teenage audience at which the film was targeted flooded into cinemas to see Keanu Reeves, Robert Sean Leonard, Michael Keaton and Denzel Washington perform their way through a *Much Ado About Nothing* that was to exceed the box office take of Zeffirelli's *Hamlet* by a good margin. The high-profile marriage of Branagh and Oscar-winning actress Thompson was also turning the couple the newspapers dubbed 'Ken and Emm' into a kind of Burton and Taylor for the 1990s, and this factor no doubt helped to make the movie popular too.

Yet there was more to Branagh's remark about 'all the Hollywood that got packed into the film' than the casting of iconographic US film stars to draw in a large movie audience. One aspect of the Hollywood mix he put together may have been drawing on the Zeffirelli film said to have made more money over the years than any other Shakespeare adaptation, the 1968 *Romeo and Juliet*. In framing and suffusing the texture of his *Much Ado* with 'Sigh no more, ladies, sigh no more', Branagh echoes the kind of pervasive use of the Nino Rota song 'What is a youth?' that gives Zeffirelli's film its attractively melancholy tone and mood. Without doubt, the catchy tune of 'Sigh no more', which is spoken, sung or played at the beginning, middle and end of the film *and* over the credits, supplies an infectiously joyous atmosphere, pleasing and uplifting the imagination and feelings of the audience as much as the heat of the Italian sun evidently warmed and energised the cast. It was no doubt an inspiration to set the movie in a Tuscan hilltop villa in high summer, rather than – bearing in mind the needs of a youthful cinema audience – in the potentially more subdued urban setting of Messina, Sicily. There are other elements of the 'Hollywood mix' which are clearly aimed at engaging the screen audience, two in particular drawing on earlier film genre conventions. Firstly, besides the use of accessible upbeat music already mentioned and the verdant, bucolic setting foregrounded at the beginning, there is the exciting approach of Don Pedro and his men thundering ostentatiously toward Leonato's villa on horseback, with a lively cutting between 'the men's sexy arrival' in 'heat haze and dust' (Branagh, 1993, 8) and the women's frenzied excitement as they prepare themselves for the men's closer approaches. For despite being atypical among Shakespeare's earlier romantic comedies in *not* having lover-pairs who are forced to overcome obstacles like parental disapproval or lack of fortune before they can marry, the ultimate conclusion of *Much Ado* will nevertheless be the conventional comedic one of the play's lovers ending up happily married.

   A full nine minutes of screen time is taken up between the opening reading of 'Sigh no more' and the confrontation of Don Pedro's male group with Leonato's predominantly female household, captured in an **overhead shot** where each group faces the other in V formation, the moment punctuated by the climax of Doyle's brassy, boisterous score. From the languid images of Leonato's 'family' responding to Beatrice's incitement to be 'blithe and bonny' in the face of 'men's deceptions', through the rapid **cross cutting** between the bare flesh of male and female bodies as they bathe and frolic in splashing water, until the moment when both groups meet, these opening nine minutes prepare us for the picture's key dramatic themes: sexual attractions and tensions between men and women, their playful delights and intrigues. Even the music of the sequence provides a kind of miniature exposition of the emotional ups and downs to come – though throughout the movie as a whole the predominantly sentimental musical style will be a vital component in manipulating and registering the emotions of the drama (see Appendix 2 for a breakdown of the film's structure of emotional registers and rhythms). The 'battle of the sexes' implied by the initial confrontation between male and female groups then gets played out in the drama of the film proper in the register of the Hollywood 'screwball comedy' (as noted by several critics (e.g. Jackson in Davies and Wells, 1994, 117; Crowl, 66ff).

   This Hollywood film coding is discernible in the episodes of prickly banter between Beatrice and Benedick throughout the film – 'There is a kind of merry war betwixt Signor Benedick and her', says Leonato (1.1.49–50). But it is especially noticeable in their earliest encounter, where a subtle use of the camera gives Beatrice narrative control as the main **focaliser** of the scene. Her **POV** is prioritised in a number of ways by the camera (it had been through her eyes that we observed the approach of the galloping men in the title credit sequence). When Benedick makes a witty remark about Hero's resemblance to her father, a **medium-close reaction shot** of Beatrice shows her observing him with a sceptical look – significantly revealing, since despite her next comment to him that 'nobody marks you', we see her marking him very closely indeed. When they are framed together for the first time, the camera follows her brushing flirtatiously past him, she ending up much nearer the camera than he does, a position which at this point promotes her cause. When their verbal skirmishing starts in earnest, this is captured in a series of **shot/reverse shots** where she only ever looks at him, while he turns away twice to look at the others, as if to gain their support. This gives her narrative control, as does the fact that it is *she* who opens and closes the exchange of gazes. Furthermore, whereas at the end of their exchange in the play text, Beatrice's remark 'You always end with a jade's trick. I know you of old' (1.1.118) would normally be construed as being part of their barbed banter, here Thompson performs the line as a regretful aside, unheard by him, a dramatic manoeuvre suggesting she retains some deep hurt from a past failed relationship with Benedick; we are thus persuaded to sympathise with her.

Before long it will be Benedick's turn to gain the audience's sympathy, when in the villa garden he is gulled into believing Beatrice loves him. Before that there are the various inciting plot incidents to set up which produce the range of contrasting emotional registers and rhythms in the film's structure; key to these varying rhythms are the 'overhearing' scenes so beloved of comedy and farce. Don Pedro's agreement to intercede on Claudio's behalf to win Hero's hand is overheard by Borachio, whose disclosure of this to Don John marks the beginning of the latter's determination to ruin the marriage plans of Claudio and Hero. To make the second phase of his villainy more dramatically effective for the film Branagh moves Don John's agreement to carry out Borachio's plan of 'showing' Hero's supposed sexual betrayal of Claudio at her window in 2.2 (a mere 'talking' with Borachio in the play text) back to a position after 3.3, following the antics of Dogberry, Verges and the Watch on duty. (Appendix 2 shows how these alternations of positive and negative emotional shifts, so valuable for sustaining dramatic suspense, are structured.)

It is in the pivotal outdoor scenes at the heart of the movie where both Benedick and Beatrice are gulled into believing each is passionately in love with the other, that it achieves its most engaging and comically brilliant moments, allowing Thompson and Branagh – especially the latter – to display their natural talents for comic acting. Having heard Benedick confusedly debate with himself – somewhat flamboyantly – the selfsame issues Beatrice had broached at the mask festivities, we are encouraged to sympathise with his dilemmas when he is made to hear the Prince, Leonato and Claudio concocting the story of how Beatrice pines for him. Both gulling scenes are crucially dependent on the split-second timing of intercut camera shots capturing the faces of the scheming gullers and the shocked reactions of the gulled, the latter straining to hear themselves discussed while dodging back and forth for concealment behind the indispensable theatrical-like props of the ornamental high hedges. Of the several brilliantly timed comic moments during and after Benedick's gulling, perhaps none is so cleverly achieved as when with a Cagney-like gesture (and Branagh knows his Cagney inside-out) he beams, cackles, and, as he brings himself to a halt with an upfling of his arms, declares with genuine puzzlement: 'Love me? ... **Why**? – It **must** be requited.' The key pause strategically inserted between the two questions cleverly manipulates the play text's blander 'Love me? Why, it must be requited' (2.3.199), creating an extraordinarily appropriate laugh at the expense of someone unable to comprehend why **any** woman should love him. When in his extended reverie Benedick spots a ferocious Beatrice marching forth under orders to invite him into dinner, *we* see someone bristling with the classic look of the scorned female lead of screwball comedy, while *he* spies 'some marks of love in her'. This leads him to strike a pose and a tone of voice sitting on the edge of the fountain (as the screenplay tells us) 'that reminds one of Tony Curtis as Cary Grant in *Some Like It Hot*' (another Hollywood code). Once Beatrice is also 'limed' into believing Benedick loves her, the garden scenes end with a series of intercut slow motion **dissolves** showing them ecstatically happy at feeling both in love, and beloved, Benedick kicking up the water of the fountain (recalling another classic Hollywood image, Gene Kelly in *Singin' in the Rain*), while Beatrice 'beatifically swings' in a 'fairyish bower'. With Doyle's music swelling to a triumphant crescendo, this is meant to be the film's most romantic moment – but actually becomes its 'cheesiest', simply because the imagery descends, regrettably, to the clichéd quality of a TV chocolate or perfume ad.

It is only after the aborted wedding where Claudio accuses Hero of being an 'approved wanton', that the feelings of Beatrice and Benedick are more fully explored, Beatrice's distress over the slandering of Hero providing the focus for Benedick to finally show emotional maturity and a commitment to the woman for whom he now declares his love. In the chapel scene, after a series of close-up shot/reverse shots of Benedick and Beatrice in which Benedick makes a solemn emotional commitment to her by promising to challenge Claudio, the camera moves close to Benedick when Beatrice leaves, following her in long shot from his **subjective** viewpoint. From that time near the beginning of the film when the camera had forced us to sympathise with the feelings of Beatrice, we are now persuaded to identify our feelings with Benedick, the narrative control of the action switching to him. Although there are 'local' shifts of scene, mood and viewpoint still to take place in the last 35 minutes of film following this, in terms of inciting us to strong sympathy, little further change occurs, Benedick having the last word when he issues the instruction to 'Strike up, pipers'. Would that one could argue strong sympathy is created for the comedy of Dogberry and Verges in the movie; the reverse is rather the case. This is chiefly because the exaggerated gestures, inappropriate mugging and peculiarly 'Oirish' speaking voice adopted by Michael Keaton's Dogberry becomes a baffling obstruction to comedy occurring. His manner of expression is just too writhing and mangled. Dogberry's unintended malapropisms are capable of producing great humour, but Keaton's eccentric vocal delivery makes it impossible for the film audience to figure these out. Branagh ensures all of his other actors speak their lines clearly, knowing that the audience needs to be engaged by the vivacity of this play's verbal wit. The same approach should have been applied for Dogberry, whose antics and mugging may well have succeeded with a stage audience, prepared as they must be to make the highly conventional response required for overblown stage farce; but for a film so dependent on words as *Much Ado* is, Keaton's mumming grotesquerie falls flat.

Branagh states in his screenplay introduction that he wanted 'to give a different kind of space to the Claudio/Hero plot' since 'Beatrice and Benedick are, after all, the subplot'. Claudio and Hero are given a different treatment here in two ways, both of which are meant to provide animation and interest to characters originally written as conventional and colourless. Branagh tells us he and Thompson wanted to suggest Benedick and Beatrice were re-encountering each other as former lovers whose first romantic entanglement and break-up might have occurred ten years before, at the age of twenty, about the age of the young lovers Claudio and Hero are now. Linking the lives of the two pairs of lovers in this way is perhaps meant to make them more significant and interesting, but it is a moot point as to whether this is achieved. What does significantly affect how Claudio is 'read' by the screen audience is the sentimental way he is played by Robert Sean Leonard, and by that actor's having become for the crucially important teenage segment of the audience, an emotional screen icon identified with the persecuted figure of Neal Perry in the movie *Dead Poets Society* (1989). Throughout *Much Ado* Claudio tends to be played as a vulnerable figure whose face registers immediately his internal emotional state, and this becomes no more apparent than when the camera captures in tight close-up his response to being shown (by Don John) Hero's supposed illicit coupling at her window. As Samuel Crowl so acutely observes, this response 'severely skews the audience's reaction'. As an experienced teacher of US undergraduates he is able to explain how this moment in the film

> rarely fails to elicit an audible flow of sympathy – particularly from the teenagers who became the prime market for the film – for Leonard's grief. After all, this was the same actor who, as many in the audience know, had already suffered and died for Shakespeare in his previous film, *Dead Poets Society*. (Crowl, 2003, 77)

Together with the sentimental religious music accompanying the night-time vigil procession to Hero's tomb where Claudio does solemn penance for her 'death', the cumulative effect of Leonard's playing is to manipulate us into sympathising with him as a 'wounded lover', instead of the rather shallow and unthinking fellow of Shakespeare's play. The casting and playing of Claudio to convey these effects suggests Branagh's weakness for what Crowl calls a 'particularly American sentimentality about the precariousness of youthful innocence', a trait which has made deep inroads into the literature of the American high school curriculum.

Despite the fact of this element of the film 'skewing' it in the direction of a more receptive reading of the play than the awkwardness provided by the original text, it does have the effect of making the final reconciliation of Claudio and Hero as fulfilling for the audience as that of Beatrice and Benedick. After the wedding of Claudio and Hero in the presence of the whole ensemble, we get a **long shot** of Benedick calling for Beatrice, followed by an **eyeline match** with her as part of the group. Thereafter, the POV moves from that of the group observing them as a couple in a series of **two-shots** in which they are finally 'united', to that of the remainder of the action, where the whole group is itself observed uniting in celebration. This warming conclusion begins to be captured as the song that began the film is struck up, and everything starts 'rising' to the joyous occasion, including the ubiquitous **Steadicam** operator, who, after following the group round the villa as they sing and dance, steps on to a ramp to be craned up high in a final and continuous two-and-a-half minute shot that literally gives a soaring and uplifting overview of the scene. The full-throated voices of a choir provide an emotionally satisfying ending, very reminiscent of the climaxes of American light comedy musicals of the 1930s and 40s. This is the most popularly successful adaptation of a Shakespearean comedy on film; strange though that Branagh omits to notice how his seeming conviction that the song he chooses to highlight in it – 'Sigh no more, ladies' – as embodying its 'moral' of 'men were deceivers ever', is contradicted by the fact of Benedick's final utter *loyalty* to Beatrice ... .

Adrian Noble's *A Midsummer Night's Dream* (UK, 1996)

Medium: Technicolor, 35 mm, *c*.99 minutes

Main actors: Alex Jennings (Theseus/Oberon); Lindsay Duncan (Hippolyta/Titania); Desmond Barrit (Bottom); Barry Lynch (Puck/Philostrate); Monica Dolan (Hermia); Kevin Doyle (Demetrius); Daniel Evans (Lysander); Emily Raymond (Helena); Osheen Jones (The Boy)

Director: Adrian Noble

Adaptation: Adrian Noble

Production and Costume design: Anthony Ward

Producer: Paul Arnott

Photography: Ian Wilson

Music: Howard Blake

Adrian Noble's film of *A Midsummer Night's Dream* frequently draws on his highly successful 1994 RSC production of the play, which toured both England and the United States to great applause. Many RSC productions of this play have since 1970 been influenced to one degree or another by Peter Brook's groundbreaking 'abstract' version, in which the colourfully costumed actors frequently performed from a trapeze inside a three-sided 'white box' with doors through which they could also enter and exit. Noble's film also uses (free-standing) doors, is brilliantly colourful and employs aerial techniques to suggest the sense of magical and fantastical transformation so essential for this Shakespeare comedy to conjure up. Another element now considered essential for productions, besides the verbal and knockabout humour of the mechanicals (which even the most amateur of productions can get to work well such is the efficacy of Shakespeare's actor-led dialogue), is a sense of darkly sensual eroticism and desire, particularly to be expressed between Titania and the 'translated' Bottom. This movie generates such eroticism at various points – at times overtly – but it is finally mediated through the device of an unusual optic, that of a young boy's dream.

Noble had already wanted the actors in the stage production to 'find the child-like in themselves', arguing that 'the logic of the *Dream* is experienced by the characters in an extraordinarily intense way'. When it came to finding 'an overall camera angle' that would open up the text for cinema audiences, he took the notion of utilising 'the child-like' one radical step further:

> I thought we should look at literally making it a dream – a child's dream;
> someone through whom we could relive the story ... [a dream that would
> allow us] to quote in quite a saucy and playful way a wide range of child-
> hood fictions. And that was joyful too as it seemed quite in keeping with the
> spirit of Shakespeare's text.   (Crowl, 176)

The result is a film which dramatically conveys the *Dream* as if it is
being dreamed by a young boy (The Boy, Osheen Jones), who also
takes part in the action. We approach the start of this action when the
movie begins by the camera moving down through a cloudy night sky
into the open window of the Boy's bedroom (one is reminded a little
of the way Olivier's *Henry V* starts). The music having shifted from a
light, waltz-time romantic violin tune to a sombre, more mysterious
repeated bassoon figure, the camera moves round the room showing
us its contents – various dolls, puppets and teddy bears (one of which
sits on a toy swan), a toy Victorian theatre, a cricket bat, and many
other toy objects and figures: aeroplane, cars, rabbit, harlequin doll, a
rocking-horse, a radio. This is clearly an imaginative child deeply
interested in 'play' and the pretend world of the theatre. A bedside
clock tells us it is midnight, the 'witching hour'. The camera finally
settles on the figure of the sleeping Boy, fallen asleep with the light on
while reading the book at his elbow, an Edwardian edition of
A Midsummer Night's Dream illustrated by Arthur Rackham (1908).
A close-up of the Boy's face reveals flickering eyelid movements,
suggesting he dreams, and since he has been reading *this* book,
Rackham's illustrations are likely to be the stimulant for the pictures
that fill the frame of his dreaming mind's eye. The Rackham edition is
well chosen for this purpose, since many of its illustrations suggest a
dark Otherness: the mysterious woodland world alive with semi-alien
life-forms – snakes, toads, spiders, giant beetles – or images carrying a
strongly erotic implication. For instance, 'Titania lying asleep',
Rackham's first illustration, shows her draped on the ground asleep
in the dark wood, the shapely contours of her 'open' limbs and body
clearly visible beneath a clinging, flimsy garb. And in the stylised line
drawing adorning a margin of the text's first page, two scantily clad
maidens (possibly representing Hermia and Helena) are shown
slumbering on winding tree boughs, one figure revealing the nipple of
a bared breast, while an observant Puck is imaged leering across at
them from the neighbouring margin: a 'saucy' source for the Boy's
dream indeed.

Thus at the beginning of that dream, when we see him peeping goggle-eyed through the keyhole of a door while a receptive Hippolyta is slowly and erotically caressed by Theseus murmuring to her the first words of the play, it is no surprise to see the Boy's voyeuristic impulses so vividly aroused, in a situation plausibly linking a young lad's natural and dreamy curiosity about his parent's sex life (we assume it is this which makes him seek out their bedroom door), to the semi-erotic illustrations of the Rackham *Dream* edition in which he has been so 'innocently' absorbed. Once the vexed Egeus bustles past, angrily interrupting the 'pre-nuptials' of the Duke and his betrothed by flinging Hermia into the room and arguing how Lysander has 'bewitched' her into rebellion, the film's story starts in earnest. The way is clear for the Boy to find himself both observing at close quarters that story, and sometimes to become a close part of it. Inspired by a dreamer's impulsive curiosity to pursue Helena out of the room to the wood, we then see him careering down a whirling vortex into a stove pipe, ending up in the hut where the 'rude mechanicals' are arriving to rehearse *Pyramus and Thisbe*. His terrifying descent echoes elements of two more of Noble's 'childhood fictions': the descent of Alice down the rabbit hole in Lewis Carroll's *Alice's Adventures in Wonderland* (1865) and the account of the tornado in L. Frank Baum's *The Wonderful Wizard of Oz* (1900). In one of the best essays on this *Dream* movie, Mark Thornton Burnett identifies these and many other allusions to literary or film narratives used by it to evoke a child's perceptual world (Burnett, in Burnett and Wray, 2000, 92). Hence the airborne umbrellas facilitating the entrances and exits of the fairies recall P. L. Travers's *Mary Poppins* (1934); when Titania takes away the 'translated' Bottom in her deep-pink upturned umbrella across the wide water toward the giant moon, this is evocative (as Burnett says) of 'Edward Lear's sea-loving and moon-seeking animals, the owl and the pussycat'; while the silhouettes of Bottom riding his motorbike and Peter Quince his bicycle across the same moon is a direct quote from the escape of 'ET' in Steven Spielberg's famous movie. In all these literary and film narratives a child or children typically displace the power of parental figures as key triggers of the action, previous popular films like the *Home Alone* series also cueing film or DVD audiences to embrace Noble's child-mediated design. In this movie too the Boy at times 'makes things happen', and most interestingly when his toy Victorian theatre is incorporated into the scene where, in imitation of Puck's bubble-blowing creation of an image of the Boy dressed as the 'changeling boy', the Boy himself blows bubbles into his toy theatre, whereupon he looks down (as do we) to behold Titania's fairies and finally Titania herself bursting forth from these bubbles to take up their stage roles: when we look up at the Boy's delighted reaction, it is we who are part of his spectacular creation too, a dream-inflected notion that looks forward to the final frames of the movie.

The Boy's controlling hand is also seen at work later on. Following Puck's return with the 'little western flower', he and Oberon crouch as a two-fairy audience before the toy theatre, and we view them and the scene from the Boy's backstage **POV**, he initially being shown drawing aside a back **flat** depicting the wood, as if he has emerged from it. We watch the Boy push forward on to the stage a miniature figure of the 'sweet Athenian lady' (Helena) and Oberon instructs Puck to 'anoint' the eyes of the 'disdainful youth' (Demetrius) so that he may prove 'fond on her'. As Oberon and Puck grasp their 'Mary Poppins' umbrellas to depart, we cut to a shot showing the Boy manipulating their upward movement as if they are marionettes on strings. Both the **shot/reverse shot**s that switch us back and forth between views of the Boy and Oberon and Puck, and this seemingly directorial control of the action by the Boy, are visually suggestive at a number of levels: implying that in dreams anything can happen, 'agency' constantly shifting between controller and controlled; foregrounding the notion that the theatre/performing space is a space of transformation; conveying a 'fairyland' where magical transformations take place. Sequences such as this are thus filmically effective, and there are others too where 'transformation' occurs, best of all perhaps the erotically charged scenes between Titania and Bottom, and those towards the end of the film. Since the Boy's eyes are once again nearly popping out when he views the heaving bosom of a voluptuous Titania lying back to rest in her deep-pink umbrella bower – especially since she seems to shoot an inviting glance at him – it is no surprise to discover that Titania's seduction of Bottom is sexually suggestive in the extreme – and very funny too. The playing of this sequence seems to illustrate both of Freud's observations that 'the word "No" does not seem to exist for a dream', and that dreams 'take the liberty of representing any element whatever by its desired opposite'. The shapely Titania refuses to take 'no' for an answer from an initially timid, pot-bellied Bottom whose tail she caresses suggestively before making him 'bray' by nuzzling her head into his private parts. Conforming to the dream-like logic of his statement that 'reason and love keep little company together these days', Titania follows up her deluded response of 'thou art as wise as thou art beautiful' by rubbing Bottom's crotch with her toes, visibly arousing him. His removal of her foot offering him a glimpse of her genitalia, initial embarrassment is soon overcome by his further arousal, so that her command to 'go with me' (with the emphasis on *go*, in Shakespearean usage meaning to 'come' sexually) is only weakly resisted by Bottom, and later we see him energetically pumping into a Titania abandoned to sexual ecstasy. Although at this point onlooking Oberon seems to approve, telling Puck that 'this falls out better than I could devise', in fact his disapproval is shown by the smile draining from his face, an 'ironic insertion' by Noble at Oberon's expense, if ever there was one.

The screen audience is successfully engaged by erotic sequences like this, or by visually experimental ones that 'toy' with notions of what theatre might be, objectifying it, or by sequences where the playing of witty dialogue does the trick, those, typically, in which Bottom and the 'rude mechanicals' play – even extending to the amusing antics of the latter group who 'double' as Titania's personal fairy entourage. But the attention of the screen audience will tend to wander or be lost in the forest sequences involving the trials and tribulations of the lovers. This is simply because Noble uses the same staging techniques for the film in these sequences as he used in the stage production. For the stage production's depiction of the forest scenes, a set of four free-standing doors in their frames were the means by which the lovers made repeated entrances and exits, their escalating confusions and tempers producing farcical antics that made for truly comical effects. As Peter Holland has said of the stage production, 'The lovers became mechanical creatures in a farce which, like all good farces, depended on doorways' (Holland, 1997, 188). But while such antics can be an enticing delight for stage audiences, who accept and even relish the comic conventions being used as a matter of course, the use of such devices on film fall flat. Despite Noble's use of fast-cutting and many close-up shots of the lovers as they move in and out of their tangles and through the doorways, it is always very obvious to the viewer they are acting on a plain open wooden stage, with the result that the film (as *The Times* of London newspaper review in 1996 put it) is 'lacking in screen presence'. Douglas Lanier generously (and perhaps naively) comments that most of 'the film's *mis-en-scène* actively flaunts its artificiality' (Lanier, in Burt & Boose, 2003, 160). But Noble's later comments on his film make clear that the dramatic shortcomings of the forest scenes were due to financial constraints: 'Everything in the forest was compromised by resources'. Had he known this earlier, he 'would have done everything differently', shooting the scenes outside in order 'to provide another dimension to the multiple layers of reality the text and film represent. All those elements like the lake I could develop more fully ... I'd create a strange world of forest and water' (Crowl, 178). Despite the dramatic shortcomings of the fairy wood scenes, many elements of Noble's film do make an extraordinarily effective impression, drawing us into the **metatheatrical** probings about the meaning and effects of 'dramatic representation' which this play, entertaining 'comedy' though it primarily is, is also concerned to engage us in. The last 20 minutes of the film are especially winning in this sense, partly because the mechanicals' performance of *Pyramus and Thisbe* before the 'onstage audience' of Athenian nobles (here seated as a conventional theatrical audience) allows the movie audience to be simultaneously entertained and metatheatrically challenged by this deployment of an 'inset' play by Shakespeare. Theseus himself provides a thoughtful comment when defending their attempts as novice actors: 'The best in this kind are but shadows, and the worst / Are no worse if imagination amend them', a point not wholly answered by Hippolyta's 'put-down' response of 'It must be your imagination, then, and not theirs' (5.1.208–10). His reference to shadows also has a double resonance these days because the movie characters we watch in the cinema are quite literally illusory shadows made visible on the screen only by an electric light shining through images on moving strips of celluloid. But this last section of the film, following the resolution of the lovers' difficulties and chiefly devoted to the mechanicals' performance and Robin's Epilogue, engages us also because it begins and ends with the movie's imaginative device of the Boy, offering a resolution of sorts, but in such a way that strange queries linger on about the relationships between dream and reality, theatre and performance, performers and audience. A hint as to what the key element in these relationships might be is given when the Boy flings open double-doors to reveal a feasting court, this action causing a momentary quiet in the proceedings and Theseus, Hippolyta and the lovers all turn round to greet the new arrivals – the camera, the Boy, us? – with glad smiles. This creates a strange and estranging moment of relationship between us and the film actors not paralleled in the theatre, an effect repeated in a slightly different way at the film's end, when the Boy's presence is embraced more fully.

The Boy's fuller involvement in the 'theatricals' of the final section begins in earnest with another use of doors. A moment after Philostrate takes the Boy's hand, they run like the wind through a red corridor (recalling the Boy's original dreamy wandering from his bedroom), and for a few seconds we see Philostrate metamorphosed into Puck (Barry Lynch playing both parts), suggesting that their crossing of the threshold into theatre marks a transition from one kind of (real) world into another (fairy-like) world of dreams and magic. As he stands gazing around in wonder at the theatre space, we understand how the Boy is feeling this to be a 'dream come true', his realisation that he has made the shift from toy theatre to real theatre, from childish pretence to grown-up pretence, now galvanising him into the stage-hand activity of hauling on a rope to raise the curtain on the mechanicals' play. After the completion of what is a satisfyingly entertaining and involving play for all concerned – players included, besides the Athenian nobles and the Boy too – the Bergomask dance performed by Bottom and Flute is interrupted by midnight's tolling bell and all stand stock still looking up, entranced. For midnight marks the transition into that entrancing dreamtime which had begun the film, here punctuated by a series of rapidly intercut **slam zoom** shots showing the Boy watching alone from the theatre balcony, the hands of his bedroom clock at midnight, a repeat of his panic-stricken calling for mummy from bed, Oberon roaring like a lion, a large risen moon with howling wind heard behind, the Boy's toy theatre stage with two characters on it, one of whom seems to be a caricature of Shakespeare himself. After Theseus's announcement that the 'iron tongue of midnight' signals fairytime and their need to retire, all disperse, and in a kind of *hommage* to Branagh's *Henry V*, the theatre is closed down to the sound of light switches being clunkily turned off.

And now, (as if) through the magic of cinema, the footlights of the theatre come on again, giving us at the witching hour of that darkness so necessary for moviegoers to view their entertainment, a long shot of Puck from the POV of the Boy up in the balcony (it is his dream we are in, remember). Soon Robin and the Boy are in a misty backstage realm overhung by a firmament of yellow light bulbs, looking out together toward Oberon, Titania and the fairy band advancing in a group across the water on which Titania and Bottom had made love, an enormous moon looming behind them. After Puck's closing speech, he leads the Boy and the fairies back on to the stage to meet Bottom and the other characters. The Boy now becomes their focus of attention as he is hoisted aloft and passed around the group, all holding out hands lovingly toward him before he is finally set down at the front of the colourful assembly, which closes up as if posing for a group photograph, each member of the group gradually and self-consciously shifting their gaze up from the Boy toward us, we who are watching the Dream they have created. It is a memorable and strangely moving tableau, bearing witness both to the magic of theatre and to the peculiar cinematic magic that makes this kind of moment between performer and movie audience possible. If Noble's is not a uniformly successful adaptation, this is the best of many sections of a movie which points toward the way an imaginatively produced account of this play on film could one day be more fully realised.

Michael Hoffman's *A Midsummer Night's Dream* (USA, 1999)

Medium: Technicolor, 35 mm, *c*.115 minutes

Main actors: Rupert Everett (Oberon); Michelle Pfeiffer (Titania); David Strathairn (Theseus); Sophie Marceau (Hippolyta); Kevin Kline (Bottom); Stanley Tucci (Puck); Anna Friel (Hermia); Christian Bale (Demetrius); Dominic West (Lysander); Calista Flockhart (Helena); Roger Rees (Peter Quince); John Sessions (Philostrate); Bernard Hill (Egeus)

Director: Michael Hoffman

Adaptation: Michael Hoffman

Production design: Luciana Arrighi

Costume design: Gabriella Pescucci

Producers: Leslie Urdang, Michael Hoffman

Photography: Oliver Stapleton

Music: Simon Boswell, Robert Urdang

Michael Hoffman's *A Midsummer Night's Dream* did not emerge from a stage production, but instead was influenced in its concepts, design and casting by other films, in particular those of Hollywood, which lavishly funded the movie in pursuit of a popular audience. Much of the lavish funding is spent creating visual spectacle, particularly for Theseus's palace and the fairy wood scenes, as well as for costuming, and in this respect the film echoes the glittering Hollywood Reinhardt/Dieterle *A Midsummer Night's Dream* of 1935, and often creates similar, but updated, effects. In terms of period, setting and casting Hoffman also attempts to follow Branagh's highly successful *Much Ado About Nothing* (1993). His chosen period is similarly late-Victorian, so making the strict social codes of the play plausible – although Theseus's early pronouncement that Hermia should 'prepare to die/For disobedience to your father's will' (1.1.86–7) is here harshly *implausible*, even for the social rigidities of 1900 Italy. The lush and colourful Tuscan setting of fictitious hill town Monte Athena also follows *Much Ado*, offering a version of that film's summery golden glow. What Crowl calls an 'all-star Anglo-American cast' is an idea also borrowed from Branagh, leading Hollywood actors Michelle Pfeiffer (Titania) and Kevin Kline (Bottom) playing romantic leads almost guaranteeing a strong box office allure.

Without the experience of a stage production to help guide him, what shaped Hoffman's dramatic vision for his adaptation? Hoffman explains in the Introduction to his screenplay what he understood to be the key contrasts and elements of the play, 'love and dignity, conditioning and subversion, a rich world of images' – and yet 'still the adaptation lacked a center in terms of character'. The 'character' he creates to give his film the 'emotional spine' he felt it needed is a deepened and modified version of Bottom, in his view someone who 'clings to delusions of grandeur because he has no love in his life'. This signals how Hoffman wants to turn the relatively two-dimensional characters of Shakespeare's comedy into realistic three-dimensional *people* who have 'emotional backstories', his preoccupation seemingly that of the Hollywood screenwriter who requires every character to have a coherent psychological 'motivation'. Hence (he tells us) Egeus has 'an obsessive attachment' to Hermia, who in turn 'is unable to empathise'; Puck has a 'fundamental love of chaos' (it is actually a love of mischief that truly animates him); and, following his discovery that it is 'Nick Bottom the dreamer, the actor, the pretender' who will become the 'emotional spine' of his movie, Hoffman has a corresponding revelation as to how Titania should be presented: 'I suddenly saw her as a woman who wanted to love simply, unconditionally, in a way the politics of her relationship with Oberon made impossible.' For him, it then follows that 'Titania and Bottom's struggle with love and pride, and their simple, if brief, discovery of each other, felt like a gift'. I dwell on Hoffman's explanation of how he came to conceive of Shakespeare's *A Midsummer Night's Dream* for the big screen conveyed almost in the language of a psychotherapist, in the full knowledge that the 'what's my motivation?' approach to dramatic adaptations may and perhaps even does contribute to making some Shakespearean comedies on film 'work'. But this play is not (for instance) *Much Ado About Nothing*, where characters like Beatrice and Benedick provide sufficient textual complexity to justify the addition of little dramatic touches which the 'reality-demanding' Hollywood screen and its audience need. By concentrating so much of his film's emotional intensity in the character of Bottom (Kline is on screen for almost a third of the movie), what makes for one of the film's major strengths – Bottom's Dream – also becomes its weakness. This is because skewing the adaptation toward a kind of character study in melancholia does not really sit well with this – or any other Shakespearean comedy for that matter – they work best when played as *ensemble* pieces.

Despite fundamentally altering the tone and atmosphere of his adaptation by creating a more 'dimensioned' Bottom than the film plausibly requires, there are nevertheless marvellous elements to the completed movie which work well and make it hugely enjoyable. For example, Hoffman makes intelligent, effective and entertaining use of music throughout his film, creating a musical correspondence for the various groups of characters. It opens like its 1935 Hollywood predecessor with the incidental music from Mendelssohn's 'A Midsummer Night's Dream', possibly a tribute but music which provides an appropriately majestic register for establishing the fact of Duke Theseus's imposing rule over Monte Athena. (After the muddle and mayhem of the woodland dream ends and order is restored, the 'Wedding March' from the same composition is fittingly used for the processional entry of the noble Athenian couples to the 'Pyramus and Thisbe' performance at the end.) Mendelssohn's *presto* high violin music fits perfectly the dancing of the Disney-effect fireflies (later identified as fairies) around the frame over the opening titles, until the use of **time-lapse photography** rapidly brings up a dawn, the film title breaking up into fluttering Disneyesque butterflies until the camera takes us into the environs of Theseus's palace. Here we are treated to a **montage** sequence where the mobile camera **cranes** and **pans** around showing the bustle of preparations for the Duke and Duchess's forthcoming marriage, a **Steadicam** nosing through the palace to show mountains of colourful food being prepared amid Italian kitchen clatter and chatter; we also see two dwarf figures (who later turn out to be Titania's fairies) steal silver plate and a gramophone, the latter to figure significantly in the film's central scene between Bottom and Titania in her bower. Near the beginning we also see Hippolyta listening to a record playing on a gramophone, suggesting that the Mendelssohn we thought was only the film's soundtrack is actually part of the film's **diegetic** meaning.

Which is perhaps the appropriate point to say that if Mendelssohn works well to support the opening of the movie at its most serious and 'formal' moments, then the use made of operatic song to reinforce the 'emotional spine' of the film is an inspired one. The gramophone was new as Italy, the film's location, moved into the twentieth century, and just as the 'high culture' of Shakespeare was starting to be adapted for (silent) film in Europe and the USA, so was the 'high culture' of Italian grand opera music beginning to be circulated more widely through gramophone records. The phonograph stolen from Theseus's palace by Titania's fairies figures prominently at this film's emotional epicentre when a newly 'translated' Bottom, sitting under the entranced gaze of Titania in her bower, is offered fruit by Cobweb from a phonograph disc being used as a food tray, which he clears and places on the turntable to play. The sound that ravishes the ears of Titania and her fairy retinue, the beautiful cavatina 'Casta Diva' from Bellini's *Norma*, so enthrals them, astonished at music emerging from thin air, that their cries of 'Hail mortal' convey utter conviction. But the stirring music finally overcomes the evidently unprepared emotions of Bottom too, the song becoming the soundtrack to the 'falling-in-love' moment so treasured by popular movie audiences. Later, when he and Titania make high-spirited love in her bower, the music is heard again, this time played in **non-diegetic** instrumental form. In grand opera, the leading tenor frequently plays the role of heroic lover seeking his female counterpart, the soprano who will fulfil his dreams; Bottom, the (anti) hero of this film, cannot sing, but in his moment of glory he becomes (in his dreams as it were) the heroic tenor finding his soprano in Titania. That the song Norma sings embodying an appeal to the chaste goddess of the moon to give her strength does not really fit the case of Titania, is less important than the ravishing effects of the singing on the susceptible emotions of Bottom, Titania – and us. This outcome is very different from the moments earlier in the film when Bottom had his spirits and his suit dampened by practical jokers pouring *chianti* over him. Then, he had retreated to the misery of what Hoffman calls 'a lousy marriage' and a 'dingy flat', his rejection and loneliness caught well by the non-diegetic use of the cavatina 'Una Furtiva Lagrima' from Donizetti's opera *L'Elisir d'Amore*, an effective aural underlining of Bottom's mood of dejection.

A quite different mood is captured at various points when the film makes use of 'Brindisi', the breezy drinking song from Verdi's *La Traviata* which celebrates the pleasures of living life to the full. It is heard first of all when we are introduced to the bustling town activity of Monte Athena and the spirited optimism of the mechanicals in their enthusiasm to put on a play for the Duke and Duchess. The song is then amusingly reprised when the mechanicals enter the woods for their rehearsal singing the song as part of the **diegesis**, *a capella*. Much later, when Quince and the mechanicals are delighted with the return of Bottom, their star turn, 'Brindisi' is again played extra-diegetically, supporting the upbeat mood that leads into their performance of 'Pyramus and Thisbe'. However, because the 'emotional spine' of Hoffman's movie is provided by a Bottom whom even Kline dubs 'an artist at heart', when he returns home alone following the triumphant entertainment of the Athenian nobility, he finds himself again in a dejected mood, gazing blankly from his window. But as he sighs, revolving in his fingers the miniature crown so resembling a ring that he vaguely identifies with some lost happiness, Hoffman provides him with an image to momentarily lift up his heart. Among the cloud of Disneyesque fairies dancing outside his window, one brighter than the rest seems to be dancing for him alone, the Titania who had caught his heart so completely. But then they are all gone, and Bottom must return to being the unhappy weaver. It is like a fairy tale, not only in the use of Disneyesque digital effects, but also in the deep swathes of sentimental melody conjured up by the film music's writer Simon Boswell, elaborating on music drawn from Mascagni's *Cavalleria Rusticana*.

Those aspects of the film so effectively carried along by music are unfortunately not matched in quality by some of its other key features. In particular, Hoffman's movie often puts spectacle and extravagance of detail ahead of an interest in ensuring that Shakespeare's text is performed more effectively. The film's opening does have visual strength, but as soon as Theseus and Hippolyta begin speaking the gains are quickly lost, partly because Hippolyta's thick foreign accent makes her words hard to understand. It is also because the halting exchange between them excises Theseus's apologies in the text for wooing Hippolyta with his 'sword' and doing her 'injuries', promising to wed her 'in another key'. Presumably, since Hoffman had decided that 'everyone in the play wants to be loved', the implication that Theseus has conquered Hippolyta by raping her would disfigure the anodyne Hollywood romance he seems determined to create. As it is, we are left guessing the reason for the evident discord lingering between them. An unaccountable textual omission is noticeable too when Theseus, responding to Hippolyta's wonderment at the 'strange' reports the lovers have been giving of their night in the woods, is prevented by Hoffman's script from speaking eleven of the most famous lines in the Shakespearean dramatic corpus (and *only* those eleven!). It is from his speech at the beginning of 5.1, starting: 'The lunatic, the lover, and the poet / Are of imagination all compact', and ending '… and gives to airy nothing / A local habitation and a name' (5.1.7–17). I can only assume Hoffman felt the lines might somehow prove distracting – if so, this would be decidedly odd since Theseus is credited with being a 'poet' and a 'lover' on page one of his script.

Hoffman was clearly very taken with the idea of supplying his Tuscan setting with resonant images, but the fairyland wood scenes are often overloaded with elaborate 'Etruscan' scenery, little and large monsters and set-piece tableaux bearing little or no dramatic link to the text, and therefore having only a 'surface' effect. Neither does his drawing on Moreau's 'The Muses Leaving Their Father Apollo' for Oberon's court setting, or on Waterhouse for images of the 'gentle innocent sensuality' of Titania's fairy band, have much impact, conveying instead a static insipidity. At the other extreme, creating a crowded grotto Fairy Bar (based on Jabba the Hut's bar in George Lucas's *Return of the Jedi*) out of which Puck and one of Titania's fairies stagger rolling drunk, is a novel idea, but it hardly fits in with the sense of exorbitant magic that dreams should produce. One clever piece of magic that does 'work' is when Bottom, having gone 'to see a noise that he heard' instead finds a top hat and a walking stick (crowned with an ass head) at a tree stump. Bottom responds to Puck's blowing on to him by slapping his neck (a bit of business virtually copied from the 1935 *Dream*) and when Puck blows again, the tree stump (through **digital imaging**) transforms into a shimmering liquid gold mirror which the vain Bottom cannot resist gazing into: there is a commendable logic to making his vainglorious ambitions the cause of his 'translation' into an ass, and the movie would benefit from having more such insightful devices.

If there is one scene embracing the best elements of the film it would have to be the three-minute one between Bottom and Titania in her bower, culminating in the 'Casta Diva' song from *Norma*. Just as Pfeiffer's Titania is stunned into admiration and love of Bottom for his seemingly magical creation of divine-sounding music, so does Kline's Bottom become quickly bewitched by her beauty and the romantic embrace of the moment. The dawning of some profound realisation is registered so movingly on his face that we have to be persuaded, without Kline's acting gifts, the film would undoubtedly not only lack an 'emotional spine', it would be hopelessly shallow.

2. Histories

INTRODUCTORY NOTE

It is important to remember that the plays listed under the genre heading of 'histories' in the first Folio are just that: 'plays'. To be sure, all their titles give the name of a monarch who had reigned in English history, and each play dramatises the events of that reign, frequently ending with the monarch's death. That is the case with *The Life and Death of Richard the Third*, yet the title of the play as printed in the first Folio is *The Tragedy of King Richard the Third*. So is the play a history or a tragedy? The conventions of comedies dictate that they should end in marriage: The *Life of Henry the Fifth* ends in marriage, so does that make it a comedy? Clearly not, for it is most famous for its portrayal of the battle of Agincourt. Similarly, no one thinks of *Richard III* as a tragedy, as it too is famous for its concluding battle at Bosworth field.

The 'histories' are not *history* in the sense we understand that term in the twenty-first century, that is to say, a discipline based on the sifting and careful evaluation of a wide range of written or other items of primary evidence to reach an impartial account of past events. Shakespeare drew on the limited historical sources at his disposal in the 1590s to give *dramatic shape* to those materials, so that he could produce plays of about two hours in length to entertain and engage an audience who at that time had a great interest in hearing about their English past. His purpose was thus to create a *performable* and *dramatic* representation of English history for the stage, not a 'documentary'. If this meant omitting, inventing or altering historical figures to give dramatic shape or impact to the play, or indeed creating elements of comedy or tragedy to strengthen its entertainment value, then he did not scruple to do so.

What implications do the above observations have for creating film adaptations of the histories? First and foremost, although such plays differ from the tragedies by seeking to dramatize the activities of England's governing royal order, they do nevertheless focus on the fortunes of a single character, their deliberations, anxieties and accomplishments. Where this focus on character is particularly well developed and engaging, as it is in the plays of *Richard III* and *Henry V*, filmmakers are not slow to use the camera to scrutinise in **close-up** and **medium shot** the behaviour and state of mind of central characters, just as they would do for key characters in the tragedies. Though Olivier in his *Henry V* tends to avoid the use of close-shots (his Henry is rarely troubled by doubts), in *Richard III* he does use the close-up more, and neither Loncraine nor Branagh in their movies waste any filming opportunities to explore character in this respect.

Film's capacity for creating spectacle can obviously come into its own when filming histories, since the mobile camera can be used in exterior locations to capture all the clash and excitement of battle to great involving effect. Interestingly, each of the four films discussed here handle their scenes of battle in quite different ways. Little of the anguish, blood and violence of war is to be seen in Olivier's battle scenes; Branagh's Agincourt by contrast is more realistic, full of blood and mud; Loncraine's Bosworth field is set in the environs of London's old Bankside power station in the mid-1930s, aiming for a portrayal of more modern warfare on ground and in air.

Laurence Olivier's *Henry V* (UK, 1944)

Medium: Technicolor, 35 mm, 137 minutes

Main actors: Laurence Olivier (Henry V); Leslie Banks (Chorus); Felix Aylmer (Canterbury); Nicholas Hannen (Exeter); Robert Newton (Pistol); Renée Asherson (Princess Katharine)

Director: Laurence Olivier

Producer: Laurence Olivier

Photography: Robert Krasker

Music: William Walton

One kind of modern critical orthodoxy has been content to conclude that Laurence Olivier's *Henry V* was 'designed as propaganda, or escapist fantasy which glamorises war and boosts morale' (Cartmell, 2000, 100). Judged solely in ideological terms, no doubt the film can be seen this way, but such an evaluation takes no account of those dimensions of the movie that make it a brilliantly innovative *filmic* adaptation of Shakespeare's play, as well as a movie of immense popularity. Instead of dismissing it as a kind of euphoric patriotic hymn, we therefore need to comprehend the film in terms of its *cinematic* achievement, to appreciate why film theorist Andre Bazin should assert, 'there is more cinema, and great cinema at that, in *Henry V* alone than in 90% of original scripts' (quoted in Jorgens, 133).

That Olivier regarded his *Henry V* as part of the war effort in 1944, the film's pre-titles statement makes clear: 'To the Commandos and Airborne Troops of Great Britain, the spirit of whose ancestors it has been humbly attempted to recapture in some ensuing scenes, This Film is Dedicated'. Olivier was a serving pilot in the Fleet Air Arm, and his patriotic motivations for making *Henry V* are very evident in his published account of the film's making. 'There we were', says Olivier, 'a band of artists and technicians, humble in our souls because Hitler was killing our countrymen, imbued with a sense of history ... As I flew over the country in my Walrus [a sea plane] I kept seeing it as Shakespeare's sceptred isle.' (The 'sceptred isle' reference relates to John of Gaunt's apparently 'patriotic' speech in *Richard II* (2.1.40).) A kind of conservatism also colours Olivier's view of Shakespeare and his play: 'We were inspired by the warmth, humanity, wisdom and Britishness just beneath the surface of Shakespeare's brilliant jingoism' (Olivier, 1987, 171, 167–8). One-dimensional as this vision of *Henry V* might seem, it nevertheless supplied Olivier with the vital and clearly focused *vision* that all major film adaptations of Shakespeare require, even if this vision would necessitate many textual cuts to realise it. Olivier was determined to project Henry as the kind of heroic figure wartime audiences would warm to and be inspired by, making it necessary for scriptwriters Olivier and Alan Dent to remove 50% of the play's lines. Much of the cutting turns a complex and some-times equivocal play into a film where the English side is shown as heroic and resolute, led by the valiantly charismatic Henry, while the French are portrayed as vain and dissipated, their leaders concerned more with elegant living than with the gritty challenge of war.

In order for Henry to come across as a benign and goodly king whose reign is relatively trouble free, many lines and passages are edited out. A few examples must suffice. When speaking to the French Ambassador, Henry boldly states that 'We are no tyrant, but a Christian king', omitting to speak the next lines: 'Unto whose grace our passion is as subject/As is our wretches fettered in our prisons' (1.2.241–3). The whole of the Cambridge, Scrope and Grey treason plot is also removed, even though at Southampton Olivier allows Scrope to remonstrate with Henry for pardoning a man who had 'railed against [the King's royal] person' (2.2.41). This excision was presumably made because the episode shows Henry cunningly toying with the courtiers' pretended loyalty to him, prior to the chilling moment when he hands them their death warrants as traitors. Displaying Henry in such a devious mode complicates the positive image of 'Britishness' Olivier wanted to convey for his king. Other cuts serve the same purpose of playing down Henry's violent side. The intimidating message he sends via Exeter to King Charles threatening a 'hungry war' that will consume French 'husbands, fathers, and betrothed lovers', leaving widows, orphans and maidens weeping (2.4.103–8) is missed out. So is Henry's vicious (if rhetorical) speech before the gates of Harfleur in which he conjures up images of daugh-ters defiled, the 'reverend' heads of old men 'dashed to the walls' and 'naked infants spitted on spikes' (3.3.112–15). Other troublesome parts of the text are also removed: Henry's decision to hang Bardolph for stealing; the part of his anguished pre-Agincourt prayer in which he conjures God not to 'think upon the fault / My father made in com-passing the crown' (4.2.275–6) (Henry's father Bolingroke usurped the throne from its rightful possessor, Richard II); and the strategic command to have all the French prisoners' throats cut (4.7.55–7). Finally, Olivier cancels those lines of Chorus's Epilogue that tell the Elizabethan audience what many of them would know from seeing

I *Henry VI* (not many, presumably, in a popular film audience): how King Harry was to die all too soon after his triumph, his successor Henry VI leading a state in which 'so many had the managing / That they lost France and made his England bleed'. Such a climax would hardly be welcomed by a wartime film audience expecting victory without qualification. They did welcome it on release, turning it into an Academy Award winner.

How did the world's first significant Shakespeare adaptation achieve this? How did one make a popular *Shakespeare* film in English, when Shakespeare had for the most part been perceived as poison at the box office? Part of the answer is that the film followed a heavily cut text designed to satisfy the narrative expectations of a cinema audience whose encounter with the struggles of love and war occurred in the relatively uncomplicated screen worlds of Westerns and Romances. Olivier's own answer is that his was 'the first serious attempt to make a truly Shakespearean film' (Olivier, 1984). By 'truly Shakespearean' he seems to mean something as inventive in using the possibilities of cinematic technique as Shakespeare had been in exploring the theatrical possibilities of his own day, when theatre was new. By 1943 had Olivier learned an enormous amount about the techniques of popular film-making, especially from William Wyler, in whose movie *Wuthering Heights* (1939) he had starred as Heathcliff. 'I was amazed,' said Olivier, 'how easily I thought in the language of film: panorama shots, tracking shots, dolly shots, medium short, close-ups, and movement and prying of the camera.' (This 'movement and prying of the camera' was to become a lasting technical signature of his Shakespeare films.) Yet even with a sound grasp of film language, the problem remained for him of finding 'a style which Shakespearean actors could act and yet which would be acceptable to the audience of the time, used to little other than the most obvious propaganda' (Olivier, 1987, 168) (i.e. the 'reverential' approach to Shakespeare that turned so many off).

His solution emerged from the text itself, when he noticed how in *Henry V* more than any other of his plays, 'Shakespeare moans about the confines of his Globe Theatre – "Or may we cram / Within this wooden O the very casques / That did affright the air at Agincourt?" ' Mulling over this key **metatheatrical** issue that Shakespeare has the Chorus raise when speaking of the Globe Theatre's constraints for showing a battle, he realised that 'the goddamn play was telling me the style of the film':

> Dress the Chorus as an Elizabethan actor (which he was), get him – with broad gestures – to challenge the imaginations of the unruly audience in the

pit. Maybe that way the film audience would be challenged. Play the first few scenes on the Globe stage in a highly, absolutely deliberate, theatrical style; get the film audience used to the language, and let them laugh its excesses out of their systems before the story really begins. I was determined to bring in the comics, Falstaff and his friends Nym, Bardolph and Pistol, for without them, it would have been two and a half hours of Henry, Henry, Henry: the film cried out for light relief!' (Olivier, 1987, 169)

At one stroke Olivier had hit upon a brilliant device and structure for delivering *Henry V* on film and for making a movie that could be intriguingly accessible to a popular (wartime) audience. By using an Elizabethan performance of the play to frame the movie – a very Shakespearean 'play within a play' contrivance after all – Olivier overcame the common resistance to Shakespeare among cinema audiences so often repelled by reverential adaptations, by using Shakespeare's own secret weapon – *entertainment*. The artificial style of theatrical presentation he used to do this is completely evident from the outset, when from an overhead **crane shot**, as described in the opening lines of the screenplay:

> We see an aerial view of London, based on Visscher's engraving of 1600. Track back to show the City in long shot, then track in on the Bear Playhouse and then to the Globe Playhouse, where a flag is being hoisted. (Olivier, 1984)

In fact, what we see first of all is a handbill fluttering through the air to the accompaniment of a chortling flute, the handbill announcing a performance to be held of ' "King Henry the Fift, with his battle fought at Agincourt in France" by Will Shakespeare at the Globe Playhouse'. The camera then cranes over a vast model of Elizabethan London, zooming in 'mistakenly' toward the Bear amphitheatre before swerving rightwards to find its goal, the Globe, where the performance of *Henry V* is about to begin. The camera swerve is the film's first **metacinematic** shot, alerting us to the fact that what we see is facilitated by the movement of the recording camera and its lens. A second 'baring of the device' occurs when Leslie Banks's Chorus, having addressed the Globe audience, now strides **downstage** to look into the camera, inciting the film-viewer to 'on your imaginary forces work'. Curiously, it is as if we are being asked to prepare ourselves for the privilege that will be denied to the **diegetic** audience – the privilege of not merely imagining, but of *seeing* the Agincourt battle. We will see it of course, represented for the first time ever through the magic of location film shooting, making the imaginary (cinematically) real.

Before the performance does begin, the hustle and bustle of back-stage (tiring-house) preparations of the actors is shown – including a close-up of Olivier himself coughing nervously prior to his entrance as Henry – then the colourful spectacle of a pseudo-Elizabethan performance commences. This includes the boisterous response of the Globe audience whose noisy delight at the antics of Falstaff-surrogate Pistol helps to establish the kind of sturdy register of 'Britishness' that Olivier was aiming to convey; casting the twinkle-eyed, rough-diamond of a well-liked movie actor Robert Newton in the part of Pistol being a shrewdly effective way to code for popular cinematic success. Yet we never come to feel we are being *enjoined to believe* in what has been called the 'comedy of incompetence' going on between the actors playing churchmen Canterbury and Ely. In fact, this strategically comic opening enables Olivier to achieve just the kind of *distance* between film audience and Globe actors needed in order that his own confident, forceful playing of Henry as heroic king *will* be persuasive and believable. This is achieved by at least three aspects of Olivier's performance. When the French ambassadors have presented the Dauphin's twin insults – his message, 'you savour too much of your youth', and his 'tun of treasure', the tennis balls – Henry's cool, initially amused expression sours rapidly into one of deadly threat, the camera backing away from him as he stands up and increases the Olivierean verbal volume. (This technique – used again for 'once more unto the breach' and St Crispin's day speeches – was introduced by Olivier to manage a Shakespearean vocal 'climax' on film that he noticed had always failed in previous films employing a close-up static camera shot.) This climax sets up the terms of the coming war as much in the tone of a Western hero's menacing threat, as it is the warning offered by a monarch on behalf of his nation. The cowboy style is taken further when, 'relaxing' after the departure of the ambassadors, Henry casually slings his crown on to the back of his throne, just as John Wayne may have done had he been playing the part. The Western style is adopted again much later when, after the triumphant Crispin day speech, he slips effortlessly into the saddle of his waiting horse, in slick contrast to the heavily armoured French knights who need to be winched down on to their horses by block and tackle.

Thus far in the film, Olivier's device of the Elizabethan Globe performance has been achieved in a **metatheatrical** register. But when Chorus pulls across a stage curtain that changes to a kind of gauze through which a **medium-long** shot of Southampton comes into focus, we witness the mingling of filmic and theatrical transitions as one form of scenic artifice moves into another. The artifice of both mediums is thus revealed, compelling the film audience to feel a shift from **metatheatrical** to **metacinematic** forms of visual representation. Moving from the patently Victorian theatrical spectacle of Henry's ship and preparations for war with France at Southampton, Chorus, now speaking in the filmic register of **voice-over**, asks us to 'still be kind, and eke out our performance with your mind'. This firmly engages the film audience, Olivier now employing his 'prying camera' to take us through the upper window of the Boar's Head tavern into a room where Falstaff is dying. Walton's music – scored to brilliantly dramatic effect for many parts of this film – accompanies the camera in this interpolated scene at Falstaff's death bed, creating a strong emotional effect by the use of a short repeated passage in the bass, upon which the main structure of the music is built. Complemented by Mistress Quickly's famous description of his death to Pistol *et al* (2.3.9–23), the loss of this 'loveable rogue' of the English stage is feelingly conveyed in a nostalgically 'British' tone, prior to our encounter with the French court, Harfleur, Agincourt, and finally Henry's wooing and marriage to Princess Katharine, following British victory.

Conducted by our aerial courier Chorus to France through 'royal purple' mists created by conventional trick photography, we move above (a model of) the English armada ploughing through the Channel far below us – more film artifice. After the conquest of Harfleur, we are introduced to a *mis-èn-scene* of the French court modelled after the mediaeval illustrations for the *Calendar of the Book of Hours* of the Duke of Berry, whom we are shown reading his own book, the visual source for the scene in which he is standing. Exeter presents Henry's ultimatum to King Charles in a heavily abridged version of 2.4, and the French king faints into the arms of an exasperated Dauphin. This and other satirical tableaux depict the French as over-refined and vain, utterly ill-prepared for war. Such 'distanced' portrayal of a feeble enemy contrasts strongly with the display of a brave Henry, cleverly depicted in the night scene before Agincourt in what the Chorus calls 'a little touch of Henry in the night'. The full text expressing Williams's animus following Henry's 'I think the King is but a man, as I am' speech, is retained (4.1.130–42), as is his challenge to the disguised king after the ransom discussion. It is perhaps to Olivier's credit that the uncomfortable complaints of Williams and Bates are not cut. Much of the 'Upon the king' speech is included too, Henry reflecting quietly in the dark on the burdens shouldered by a monarch in wartime (though without the reference to Richard II). His ruminations upon the coming battle being coupled with an interpolated view of his commanders at prayer in their tent, offer visual and aural registers that help produce the kind of sentimental mood of sympathetic identification Olivier clearly wished to establish with the screen audience at this crucial centre-point of the movie.

In great contrast to this low-key prelude, is the spectacular and colourful battle of Agincourt itself, arguably the film's really memorable centrepiece. It is a battle all audiences up to now had only been able to imagine, but which is recreated for this movie using location settings in Eire, hundreds of extras, and a mile-long set of tracks permitting the camera to travel with the speeding advance of the French cavalry upon the English. Olivier introduced the French cavalry charge to create 'pace, rhythm and conflict' (Oliver, 1987, 172), the long **tracking shot** following it through from gentle horse-trot to thunderous gallop, and alternating this horizontal tracking by the camera of the galloping French cavalry, with shots of the waiting English army. Lines of archers, bows raised to shoot, anxiously watch for Henry's poised sword to drop as the signal to release both arrows – and tension. As the cloud of hissing arrows sound in a quiet pause from Walton's stirring music it becomes clear that here we have a considerable actor-king (Henry) whose talent for manipulating events is matched by the multiple role-playing figure of Olivier himself: the leading actor, director and producer of a war film inspired by the needs of wartime.

Olivier said that ideally Agincourt should have been enacted on green velvet, in order to fit in with the 'picture book' look of the film (Oliver, 1987, 173). Instead, he made a film which offers a balance of the artificially 'medieval' and the dynamically real. Much of this contrast is achieved on the one hand by aligning 'the artificial' with the slightly ridiculous French, who, along with the relatively anonymous military ranks of the English, we are never really allowed to know. On the other hand, we do come to sympathise with Olivier's heroic, Western-style Henry, who, among all the visual artifice, emerges as the likeable leader whose bluff, 'no-nonsense' and sexually attractive style is successfully adapted to appeal to the cinema audience of the time.

Kenneth Branagh's *Henry V* (UK, 1989)

Medium: Eastmancolour, 35 mm, 132 minutes

Main actors: Kenneth Branagh (Henry V); Derek Jacobi (Chorus); Brian Blessed (Exeter); Ian Holm (Fluellen); Judi Dench (Mistress Quickly); Robert Stephens (Pistol); Richard Briers (Bardolph); Emma Thompson (Princess Katharine); Paul Scofield (French King)

Director: Kenneth Branagh

Producer: Stephen Evans

Photography: Kenneth MacMillan

Music: Pat Doyle

When Branagh adapted *Henry V* for the screen – setting off the great wave of Shakespeare movies of the 1990s – his aim was to 'make a truly popular film' (like Olivier), believing the play could be told as a story 'that would make you laugh, make you cry, and be utterly accessible to anyone of whatever age or background'. But instead of scripting a movie with a 'seemingly nationalistic and militaristic emphasis' – the way he saw Olivier's version – he understood the play as 'a deeply questioning, ever-relevant and compassionate survey of people and war'. This inquiring approach would need quite a different style of acting and presentation, especially in the case of Henry himself. Noticing the play suggested 'an especially young Henry with more than a little of the Hamlet in him', Branagh wanted to convey the king as a more complex figure than Olivier's heroic monarch. A daunting challenge, it was in some ways parallel to the test presented by his own youthful project to lead the new style Renaissance company to triumph and conquest in the realm of Shakespeare performance. In a post-Falklands and post-Vietnam era, part of the complexity would also be delivered by unflinchingly presenting many (but not all) of the more negative and controversial aspects of Shakespeare's play that Olivier's film had left out, while at the same time bringing the film audience closer to the human experiences and dilemmas of the key characters.

   Central to Branagh's modern approach and the film's success was his 'idea of abandoning large-theatre projection and allowing **close-ups** and low-level dialogue to draw the audience deep into the human side of this distant mediaeval world'. This is in marked contrast to Olivier's method, which is to maintain distance between the audience and his characters. Olivier's heroic Henry is aloof (even in the night-time sequence when Henry confides his thoughts in voice-over); the foppish French court and their bumbling king are a laughing-stock; and most of the other main characters, including Henry's followers both high and low, tend to be portrayed as character 'types'. Olivier's use of an identification shot followed by framed long and very long shots positioning Henry as actor-king surrounded by his soldier-cast each doing their bit toward the final English triumph creates this distancing effect. Branagh's key strategy of filming almost throughout using **mid shots** and **close-ups** is to draw the audience into the inner life of his characters: he wants us to identify with the feelings, emotions and anxieties, not only of Henry and his friends, but of the French too.

The close camera work is apparent from the film's opening, when, offering a visual pun on his first line as Chorus, Derek Jacobi wishes for 'a muse of fire' while simultaneously lighting his own face with the flare of a struck match. From here to the end of 1.1, the way light and shadow reveal or hide characters and settings within the frame of the screen provides a clever and teasing commentary on the opening of Olivier's film, while also offering a much more serious and dramatic introduction to the figure of a radically different Henry. Olivier had used the conventions and backstage setting of the Elizabethan theatre to intrigue and engage his film audience. Here, once Jacobi throws a massive light switch, the camera follows him through what we see is a film studio, with all the paraphernalia of movie-making littered about that will be used in making this film: camera, arc lights, scenery, props and so on. We are clearly being told that the 'brightest heaven of invention' (Prologue, 2) these days comprises the full resources of the film studio. Jacobi flings open huge double-doors on to black, and after light streams from the gap behind a cautiously opened door, in **close-up** we see a sinister Canterbury (Charles Kay) looking stealthily out as he whispers conspiratorially with Ely (Alec McCowen): the **metacinematic** point has been made that we are entering the constructed world of – a film.

Henry's entrance, interrupting a series of **shot/reverse shots** of Canterbury and Ely in secret conference, is spectacularly effective. From Henry's **POV**, we briefly see huge double doors again flung open, and then, accompanied by a fanfare of startled strings, we are shown in **long-shot** from his courtiers' viewpoint a small, be-cloaked figure in silhouette isolated in the vast open doorway against brilliantly bright arc lights. For the Star Wars generation, it is therefore a mysterious Darth Vader-like Henry we first see and to whose POV the camera now reverts, viewing in **mid shot** his courtiers bowing to him/us as we move through this avenue of figures toward the throne, where a glimpse of him is caught as he turns to sit down. Only now is it that the camera fully reveals the face and figure of the bareheaded Henry, looking very young, boyish and vulnerable, on his large throne. The remainder of the scene is played in quite a different acting register to that of Olivier's film. Instead of the knockabout humour between the clerics and Henry, there is a deadly seriousness about the young and inexperienced king that proves more than a match for the wiles of Canterbury and, in turn, for the insulting embassy sent by the Dauphin. Proceeding with a range of **close** and **mid shots** recording the responses of all protagonists, by the end of the scene Henry has united his own court and impressed the ambassador Mountjoy with a strength of character displaying the potential force of his rule – and his resolve to take France. This is despite the fact that the scene is *also* shot to convey something of the way the play arouses doubts about the legality of the planned war.

Branagh uses the close and mid shot most carefully when revealing a Henry having doubts as well as certainties – his 'on the king' soliloquy at the end of the night-time sequence (in 4.1) being the best example. Such shots are employed nowhere more effectively to make emotional connections with the audience than when showing the male camaraderie Henry develops with his men as the prerequisite to military success; this is revealed in the camera's close record of their response to his highly rhetorical 'once more unto the breach' speech at Harfleur. But Henry starts building the 'male-bonding' process in earnest when responding to Westmoreland's anxious wish before Agincourt for but 'one ten thousand of those men in England/That do no work today!' 'What's he that wishes so?' calls out Branagh's Henry, and as he begins what will become the famous St Crispin Day speech, his men trail after him toward the cart where he will finish it, the up-tilted camera among them capturing his authoritative lead. An important moment occurs when, with Doyle's stirring music gathering underneath, Henry articulates for them all in a quiet voice full of emotion how they who are about to fight together will 'be remembered, / We few, we happy few, we band of brothers. / For he today that sheds his blood with me / Shall be my brother. ...' (4.3.59–62).

As Henry speaks the phrase 'we band of brothers', there is a **reaction-shot** intercut (one of many during this and the Harfleur speeches) of a small group of his men photographed from above, faces shining with devoted enthusiasm at their king's words. Not only does Branagh's Henry seem spontaneous, natural and convincing, in contrast to Olivier's more controlled and declamatory style, but he is also more emotionally convincing. Branagh's determination to move his audience is conveyed nowhere better than in the muddy battle scenes with the French, in great contrast to Olivier's relatively 'clean' style of portraying battle. His appropriation of Vietnam war movie codes is at the heart of his emotionalising technique, the sequence in which Henry's cousin York dies being remarkable for its similarity to one in *Platoon*. This is when Stone's slow-motion camera in **medium-shot** captures the death of the stranded Sergeant Elias whose upflung arms as Samuel Barber's 'Adagio for Strings' plays so much suggest a Christ-like martyrdom. In the midst of Branagh's slow-motion battle sequence, also accompanied by a repeated musical figure using strings, York is shown holding his sword aloft ready to strike, when he is cut down by the French soldiers surrounding him, blood spurting from his mouth, his death becoming a kind of ritualised sacrificial offering for what will be Henry's final victory.

Despite its also borrowing much from the grimly effective shooting techniques of Welles's battle sequence in *Chimes at Midnight*, the conclusion of Branagh's Agincourt battle scene is very much his own, an interesting combination of the sentimental and the serious. The sentimental strand begins when Fluellen discovers the French have killed all 'the poys [boys] and the luggage' (4.7.1) in the English camp. Branagh's script (and film) omits the fact that Henry orders his soldiers to cut the throats of all their prisoners as a strategic move in response to the military regrouping of the French (not obvious in Shakespeare's text but recoverable from Shakespeare's source, Holinshed). Instead, the action is carried forward by implying that Henry's statement 'I was not angry since I came to France / Until this instant' (4.7.47–8) is a response to the killing of the English boys.

When it becomes clear the English have triumphed, in what Branagh calls the 'greatest **tracking shot** in the world', he then has an exhausted Henry carry Falstaff's dead Boy (Christian Bale) the whole length of the corpse-littered battle field, finally depositing him upon a cart already bearing youthful corpses. The serious point Branagh undoubtedly wants to make by offering this end-of-battle scene is conveyed by his hope that in providing the sequence (together with Doyle's music producing a 'tremendous climax') 'There would be no question about the statement this movie was making about war' (Branagh, 1991, 235, 236). Olivier had gone to much trouble to construct in Ireland a set of tracks for the camera that would ultimately capture a very long travelling shot of the French on horseback speeding along for their attack on the English, carrying the viewer *into* battle.

Although exploiting the emotions of the audience by thrusting forward the image of children killed in battle to deliver an anti-war message, at least Branagh makes his serious point by using a long tracking shot to carry the viewer *out* of battle, but in a way that shows the human price we pay for entering into it.

Laurence Olivier's *Richard III* (UK, 1955)

Medium: VistaVision-Technicolor, 35 mm, *c*.150 minutes

Main actors: Laurence Olivier (Richard III); Ralph Richardson (Duke of Buckingham); John Gielgud (Duke of Clarence); Cedric Hardwicke (Edward IV); Alec Clunes (Lord Hastings); Laurence Naismith (Lord Stanley); Claire Bloom (Lady Anne); Andrew Cruickshank (Brackenbury); Norman Wooland (Catesby); Mary Kerridge (Queen Elizabeth); Pamela Brown (Jane Shore); Stanley Baker (Richmond)

Director: Laurence Olivier

Producers: Laurence Olivier, Alexander Korda

Script: Laurence Olivier, Alan Dent

Photography: Otto Heller

Design: Carmen Dillon, Roger Furse

Music: William Walton

Sound: Bert Rule

Laurence Olivier's third Shakespeare adaptation developed and took forward stylistic features of his earlier films *Henry V* and *Hamlet*. Indeed, an identifiably 'Olivieresque' Shakespearean cinematic style could be said to have emerged in these movies, combining four distinctive areas of approach. First, the structural design of each film carries what Anthony Davies has called a 'broad cyclical movement', the concluding frames of every film returning to and repeating those which opened it. Then there is the device introduced in *Henry V*, and developed significantly in *Hamlet*, where Olivier turns his camera into a kind of probing, actively 'showing' narrator. *Richard III* takes this narrative device one audacious step further when the eye of the camera (at least for the first half of the film) is put under the narrative authority and control of Richard himself. Thirdly, each movie evidences a balance consistently struck by Olivier between a theatricality of dramatic action and forms of cinematic expressiveness that are never less than ingeniously effective. A final yet significant feature inextricably bound up with Olivier's desire to showcase his own considerable acting talents is the fact that the principal characters he plays in each film are monarchs or princely leaders in conflict with the society around them. Henry V's goal is to prove himself to be heroically worthy of the crown to a sceptical English court and country; Hamlet has been cheated of the crown and aims to retrieve it by avenging Old Hamlet's killer; the amoral Richard of Gloucester sweeps all before him as he plots, manipulates and ruthlessly murders his way to the English crown.

Olivier noted special difficulties in bringing *Richard III* to the screen, as he told Roger Manvell after filming was completed in 1955:

> To start with it's a very long play. It's not until the little princes come on that the story forms that nice river sweep, going swiftly to its conclusion from about half way through the play. The first part up until that moment is an absolute delta of plot and presupposed foreknowledge of events. After all, *Richard III* forms the last part of a cycle of four plays, the other three being parts of *Henry VI* ... Yet it's always been a popular play – as Dr Johnson said, its popularity derives from the character of Richard.
>
> (Manvell, 1971, 48)

Olivier here identifies a key problem and a key solution in approaching his own adaptation: the 'absolute delta of plot' is as he says the most formidable obstacle facing the understanding of a movie audience, yet it is by focusing on 'the character of Richard', so evil and yet so compelling, that the audience can be helped to engage with the world of the film. To provide a **backstory** for the beginning of *Richard III* Olivier opens with the final scene of 3 *Henry VI*, which presents the coronation of Richard's eldest brother, Edward IV (5.7). Starting this way allows Olivier to introduce a range of visual elements to engage the audience's attention, chief of which is the actual image of the English crown. We have already read rolling titles informing us how the film's story begins as the 'White Rose of York was in its final flowering' that is, towards the end of that period of conflict known as the Wars of the Roses. As the ornate lettering cues us into the history, the swelling sonorities of Walton's regal score, so evocative of a grand historical English heritage, soothes our ears. That sense of stability is soon shaken after we read, 'Here begins one of the most famous and at the same time most infamous of the legends that are attached to: The Crown of England' – for as the frame proclaiming this **dissolves** to a close-up of a pendant golden crown, so does the stately music shift gear into high, rapidly bowed shrilly notes on the strings, newly linking the crown with a sense of terror and danger. This crown image that starts the film proper with Edward IV's coronation will also end it prior to Richmond's being crowned first Tudor king of England as Henry VII. Olivier's visual/acoustic image of an English crown connoting terror and danger is in fact a precise **metonymic** for the character and the theme which thread unerringly through the play – Gloucester, and his murderous contrivings to become and to remain king.

With Technicolor stock conveying for Edward's coronation the kind of eye-catching pageantry that made Olivier's *Henry V* so visually attractive, one would not know from viewing the sequence that this ceremony occurs only because the Lancastrian Henry VI had been murdered by Yorkist Richard in the Tower. This was shortly after Richard, Edward and the middle brother Clarence had together stabbed to death Henry's son Prince Edward (3 *Henry VI*, 5.6, 5.5), thus removing the immediate Lancastrian occupier and inheritor of the English throne. All is not therefore what it seems, and Olivier's shooting of the scene offers hints that the crown is not secure on Edward's head, that intrigue and intrafamilial strife in fact lurk under the surface of courtly gentility. An initial shot of the cardinal lowering the crown toward the new king's head is replaced by a shot over Richard's shoulder where the latter's placing of a crown on the long, luxuriantly thick curls of his own head significantly obscures the crowning of the king. At the third cry of 'Long live King Edward IV!' from the assembled court, Richard spins round to leer at the camera and (as we think) us – the cinema audience. But we are wrong. Although there will be many occasions to come when Richard does address us via the camera, Olivier this time tricks us: the following shot of Buckingham blinking attentively and a return to Richard's gaze reveals the **shot/reverse shot** sequence actually consisted of Richard and Buckingham exchanging significant conspiratorial glances. The sequence of glances continues, in what amounts to Olivier's introduction of all the main characters, when Buckingham glances toward brother Clarence, who in turn looks benignly on the scene while trumpet fanfares sound and Edward, after receiving blessings from the Cardinal, descends to be joined by Queen Elizabeth as they process through to the adjacent throne room of the Palace, where he addresses the court. On the way, he pauses to gently touch the arm of his mistress Jane Shore with the royal mace – to the Queen's obvious annoyance. Shore is a character only mentioned in Shakespeare's play, yet Olivier includes her as a frequently visible (although non-speaking) figure, almost certainly to provide sexual interest, but also perhaps to make up for the film's excision of Queen Margaret, the forthright and martial-minded widow of Henry VI.

The coronation scene over and the crowds dispersed, we are made to encounter 'crookback' Richard, the camera nosing its way into the throne room of the palace where he hovers, a dark, hook-nosed, crow-like figure awaiting us, we whom Olivier implicates in Richard's scheming by forcing us to be party to it. The famous – but ironical – opening lines of *Richard III*: 'Now is the winter of our discontent / Made glorious summer by this son of York' provide the first of many occasions when Olivier has Richard audaciously break through the imaginary 'fourth wall' of the cinema screen to address us via the camera, affronting the normal cinematic conventions. Olivier has explained how he self-consciously performed the first seventeen lines of his celebrated soliloquy 'as though to each one of us personally' – 'you can do that on film' (Olivier, 1987, 187), he observes, revealing his understanding of film technique. The direct address works here, as elsewhere in the film, because Olivier knows (from his work on *Henry V*) that he can only rant when further away from the camera, and he also keeps the camera moving, as if it (i.e. our **POV**) is a character attentively listening to him (which we are). What we therefore see in the opening sequences and at other places in the movie are Olivier's skills in deploying a clever combination of theatrical and cinematic techniques both to dramatise Richard's perverted designs and to put us in touch with 'the mind behind the mask'.

Richard's flirting with the cinema audience is shortly followed by his flirting seduction of Lady Anne. This scene of the play is difficult enough to carry off persuasively in the best of performances, Richard having assassinated both Anne's husband Prince Edward and his father Henry VI. Although Olivier reports that on stage his 'hideous wooing of Lady Anne' had worked brilliantly (modesty never being one of Olivier's faults), he perceptively realised that 'if it's too sudden on the screen the unaccustomed audience' would not be persuaded. He therefore decides to slow down the duration of the seduction by splitting the scene into two parts, rearranging the lines so that Richard then gets 'two glorious climaxes': 'I'll have her, but I will not keep her long', and 'Was ever woman in this humour woo'd? / Was ever woman in this humour won?' (Olivier, 1987, 184) At the end of each sequence, Olivier introduces the dramatically effective visual device of shadows, a **motif** which will recur to convey the evil lurking behind all of Richard's darkly calculated manoeuvres. The earliest deployment of this motif is at the conclusion of the first part of his seduction of Anne, when Richard performs more lines borrowed from 3 *Henry VI*: 'Clarence, beware; thou kept'st me from the light – / But I will sort a pitchy day for thee. / For I will buzz abroad such prophecies / That Edward shall be fearful of his life, / And then, to purge his fear, I'll be thy death' (5.6.85–9). These lines are spoken as if emerging from

Richard's bulky, bat-like shadow as it slopes off from Westminster Abbey, filling the frame on the word 'death'. The camera follows his shadow until we see it stooping to 'buzz' the ear of Edward's throne-seated shadow with the requisite lies, while monks are heard chanting, providing an ironically 'holy' counterpoint to Richard's 'pitchy' (dark) plotting. His evil messaging done, Richard kisses the royal hand, and as he moves away passes close to the camera, showing us in significant close-up the Gloucester heraldic badge pinned to his breast – a snarling boar. (A close-up in the closing frames of the film has the camera lingering on the motto of the Order of the Garter emblazoned on the upper part of Richard's boot – his dead body being slung across a horse – which reads: 'Honi soit qui mal y pense' – Shame to him who evil thinks.) The second key use of the shadow motif follows Richard's subduing of Anne, and is again triggered by a performance of his lines. This time, preening himself on his success, vanity prompts the comment: 'Shine out, fair sun, till I have bought a glass, / That I may see my shadow as I pass' (*Richard III*, 1.2.249–50). Richard now kicks open the door of Lady Anne's apartment, and his long vampire-like shadow is shown engulfing the white dress-clad form of Anne who, standing near her bed, turns toward him. The implication of impending sexual conquest is inescapable, and this is confirmed (though indirectly) by the next shot where, to the accompaniment of a chirpy flute tune we cut to a Richard merrily pulling on his gloves in a significant **close-up** that shows them to be decorated with his personal emblem – the snarling boar.

Walton's musical score frequently provides an appropriate heightening of the film's various dramatic moods. In emphasising Richard's terrifying control over events and our viewpoint, this heightening occurs powerfully in the sequence when Clarence relates his bad dreams to Brackenbury in the Tower, music and clever camera work subtly combining to create chilling effects. From gentle monks chanting and the closing up of their missal, we suddenly cut to the green-tinged stony gothic-arches of the Tower's subterranean vaults, a dissonant clash of brass, woodwind and percussion simultaneously sounding every bit as frightening as the horror genre scores that will come to characterise the music of Hammer films starting to appear in the mid-1950s. The dissonant fanfare succeeds to a sinister chugging and pounding rhythm in the low register of woodwind and strings as we are shown Clarence moaning in his 'ghastly dreams' of drowning, until the music spirals into a crash of cymbals at his waking in terror. He is seen recounting his dream to Brackenbury in a mixture of (mostly) **two-shots** filmed from within the cell, but after Clarence sinks to rest again, the camera cuts to a perspective of him from the high barred window. More surging dissonant brass and woodwind then quickly segue into a sinister flurry of strings while the camera pulls back to reveal the ominous shadow of Richard's hat and long hair framing our view of his doomed brother through the cell window, the music suddenly halting when Buckingham's cheery greeting, 'Good time of day unto your royal grace!' breaks the spell of our watching. Richard spins round alarmed and we cut to a **mid shot** of him responding with relief to the man he refers to elsewhere as his 'other self'. Until this moment there was no clue that the events we had been witnessing were being seen from Richard's narrative **POV**, this brilliantly contrived sequence exemplifying Olivier's cinematic skill in enforcing our complicity with Richard's outlook and manipulative methods.

There are further chilling moments created by Olivier that deploy frenzied Hammer-like scoring, and more examples too of his capacity to blend cinematic inventiveness and theatricality. The terrifying music accompanying the stuffing of Clarence's body into the malmsey butt (wine barrel) is not only of the Hammer variety but his murderers are played by two actors to appear repeatedly as villains in future Hammer horror films, Michael Gough and Michael Ripper, as will Patrick Troughton, playing Tyrell, murderer of the young princes. The **deep-focus** shooting Olivier used so extensively in *Hamlet* is deployed to good effect again in *Richard III*, the Vistavision camera giving solidity of image in **wide shots** and detailed expression in **close-ups**. When Richard and Buckingham are shown quietly plotting at the window of the throne room, the young Prince Edward standing in the background, the power of the former over the latter is amply visualised through their relative size differences in the film frame. In this scene too there is the visual device of the vertical window bar ironically prefiguring the estrangement to come between the currently amicable pair, a near-repeat of the image where they conspire at the foot of King Edward's deathbed. There, the vertical line of a narrow wall-column between them also suggests inevitable division. The part played by Charles Laughton in *The Hunchback of Notre Dame* (1939) seems to have provided Olivier with an irresistibly relevant image to apply to the crippled Richard when, following the latter's 'reluctant' agreement to accept the crown, he slithers down a bell rope to join the conspirators whom he compels to bow down before his twisted body, the bell ringing manically as a signal that the crown is now his.

Richard having attained his goal, there is little remaining to rival the compelling interest generated by his manipulative rise to power. The theatricality of action so expertly managed throughout the film (helped in great part by a studio set where Abbey, Palace and Tower locations are immediately contiguous) in some ways comes to the fore in the film's late scenes, where Richard's strangely attractive combination of the demonic and the witty are very evident. There is a kind of comic vitality in the throne room scene (end of 4.4.) where Richard is assailed by numerous messengers bringing him news of hostile forces up in arms from all corners of the kingdom; while his death on Bosworth Field has a certain grotesque and desperate comedy about it. In the play, Richmond kills Richard in single combat, but Olivier has Richard mobbed and assaulted by Richmond's men. After his throat has been cut, they draw back and we all watch him twitching violently about on the ground. His jerky movements are punctuated – somewhat comically – by the stabbing sound of trumpets stepping up in pitch, while he vainly jabs the air with his sword. This he eventually thrusts aloft by the blade as if – performer to the end – proclaiming his essential calling, that of the soldier and military tactician.

Richard Loncraine's *Richard III*
(UK, 1995)

Medium: Eastman colour, 35 mm, *c.*100 minutes

Main actors: Ian McKellen (Richard III); Jim Broadbent (Duke of Buckingham); Nigel Hawthorne (Duke of Clarence); John Wood (Edward IV); Annette Bening (Queen Elizabeth); Duchess of York (Maggie Smith); Robert Downey Jr. (Rivers); Jim Carter (Lord Hastings); Edward Hardwicke (Lord Stanley); Kristin Scott Thomas (Lady Anne); Donald Sumpter (Brackenbury); Tim McInnerny (Catesby); Adrian Dunbar (Tyrell); Bill Patterson (Ratcliffe); Dominic West (Richmond)

Director: Richard Loncraine

Producers: Lisa Katselas Paré, Stephen Bayly

Screenplay: Ian McKellen, Richard Loncraine

Photography: Peter Biziou

Design: Tony Burrough

Music: Trevor Jones

Sound: David Stephenson

The key strategy of the Loncraine/McKellen *Richard III* adaptation is to relocate what Ian McKellen calls this 'family drama of power-politics, more tragic than melodramatic' (McKellen, 1996, 24) to a 1930s Britain where Richard's rise to power is made to resemble the deadly contemporary dictatorships of Germany, Italy, Spain and the USSR. The rigid, aristocratic haughtiness of McKellen's army commander-in-chief Richard Gloucester specifically echoes that of baronet-politician Sir Oswald Mosley, who broke away from 1930s consensus politics to lead the blackshirt-garbed British Union of Fascists. The film was therefore set in the most recent period when a dictatorship like Richard III's might credibly have assumed power in the United Kingdom. This design originated in Richard Eyre's successful stage production of *Richard III*, which McKellen was enthusiastic to extend to a wider audience through popular film, an aim accomplished by a unique combination of two essential inputs. The first was the deep knowledge of Shakespeare that enabled McKellen to produce a draft screenplay cutting the text by over 70%, while retaining enough dramatic excitement to capture the filmic imagination of a moviemaker able to translate his screenplay into popular cinema. McKellen was fortunate to secure this second essential input in the form of prominent commercial and feature film-maker Richard Loncraine and his long-time cinematographic collaborator, Peter Biziou.

In much of what follows I will trace and comment on examples of what James Loehlin calls the movie's pattern of 'interwoven and overlapping visual codes derived from historical and film iconography' (Burt and Boose, 2003, 175) These visual codes are Loncraine's cinematic means for bringing the invented historical setting and design to dramatic life, such that this complex play of intertwined characters becomes accessible to a regular film audience (Loncraine's radical cinematic approach to this challenge is also discussed in the Introduction and in Part III). Firstly, I want to identify some of the ways in which this 1995 adaptation differs from Olivier's 1955 mediaeval-costumed film. McKellen has said that the 'crucial advantage of a modern setting is clarity of storytelling,' and for those who are unfamiliar with *Richard III* (let alone the *Henry VI* plays) a clear storyline is vital. The characters are therefore dressed in costumes visibly reflecting their status and profession in the social order, instead of forcing the audience to distinguish one mediaeval dressed figure from another. Of course, the audience will have no problem identifying Olivier in his 'star vehicle' approach of foregrounding the grotesque, insinuating, 'witch-like' characterisation (Olivier's description) of a Richard so very reminiscent of the cajoling 'Vice' figure of mediaeval religious drama. McKellen's Gloucester by contrast is played as a military tyrant whose grim obsession to rule gains coherence and a plausible chilling interest by making the dynastic political 'family' conflicts of the play reflect the realities of a weakly led and old-fashioned mid-1930s British state potentially ripe for totalitarian take-over.

The film's casting of American actors Annette Bening as Queen Elizabeth and Robert Downey Jr as her brother Lord Rivers gives the new 'interloping' Woodvilles a social identity so distinctively different from the traditional British aristocratic York family we are shown, that the audience will immediately discern the cultural contrast from their accents and performances. Of equal importance, with the film set in 1936 Britain, the historical resonances of Edward VIII's abdication that year to marry American divorcée Mrs Wallis Simpson, leaving the British throne in some disarray, are all too apt and suggestive (as is the fact of Edward's pro-German sympathies). A further and astute form of the film's economising narrative method (all of a piece with a general reliance on short, clear sequences) is the way some of the characters are omitted, while others are 'blended' together. Neither film includes the hate-filled figure of Queen Margaret, resentful widow of the

Lancastrian Henry VI. But while the female characters of Olivier's film are portrayed as either relatively quiescent – as in the case of the Duchess of York and Queen Elizabeth – or are only there to arouse sexual intrigue – as with the (silent) figure of Jane Shore – in Loncraine's film the deep animus of Margaret is felt through the forthright characters of Maggie Smith's Duchess of York (who is given some of Margaret's lines) and Annette Bening's Queen Elizabeth. And while Olivier included both of Elizabeth's sons Dorset and Grey to no great filmic effect, Loncraine omits these characters and instead makes the identity (and loss) of the male Woodville line felt more strongly by embodying it in the single figure of Elizabeth's brother Rivers, brilliantly played by Robert Downey Jr. A final 'user-friendly' method that Loncraine deploys throughout to communicate the story to his audience is by introducing elements from a whole variety of film genres. Downey himself is a star icon from light comedy (*Chaplin*, 1992) whose destiny is to be horrifically murdered in a manner derived from the slasher film. Action films, science fiction, the Western, musicals, the British Heritage film (if in parodic form here, it gives Shakespeare-naïve audiences a 'key' into some of the film's characters via familiar heritage film icons Maggie Smith *et al.*), and above all, the traditional American gangster film genre. I will conclude with a discussion of the way this genre is cleverly used to shape the film as a whole.

Loncraine's visual storytelling method is exemplified by the series of connected sequences in the first nine minutes or so before Richard begins his famous opening speech, though the initial three-minute sequence actually starts not with images but (partly echoing Olivier's opening) with a seven line written explanation orientating the viewer to 'the story so far':

> Civil war divides the nation. The King is under attack from the rebel York family, who are fighting to place their eldest son, Edward, on the throne. Edward's army advances, led by his youngest brother [5 second pause for dramatic effect until the final line is added]   Richard of Gloucester.

While this statement in blood-red appears – a signal of the carnage to come – in the background there is a clacking tickertape machine operating, heard more loudly when revealed in **close-up** detailing grim news for King Henry and his son Prince Edward at their battlefield HQ in a country mansion: 'Richard Gloucester at hand. He holds his course toward Tewkesbury.' Looking every inch the well-groomed British senior officer, Edward settles at his desk to a traditional

English supper with wine, his faithful black Labrador gnawing a bone before the open fire – a most homely scene (though the bone-chewing is an early register of the animalistic appetites to be released by Richard's evil later). The comfortable scene is shattered by the long snout of a tank's gun bursting through the fireplace wall, a gas-masked soldier emerging to shoot Edward stone-dead with a bullet between the eyes. His hoarse breathing scarily dominating the soundtrack, this masked figure seeks out King Henry and shoots him in the back of the head while he prays, the shot triggering a blood-red 'R' on to the screen. As Henry's executioner wrenches off his mask, the 'snout' of which has made him resemble (for those who know the play) the boar's head of Richard Gloucester's personal crest, further heard gunshots seem to blast red letters on to the screen, the sound of ricocheting bullets and title leaving us in no doubt who this bloody killer is: RICHARD III. Not only has 95% of this three minutes of **backstory**-infilling been achieved visually, but the effects used draw on a range of popular film genre codes, Richard's icy power being conveyed through the hoarse Darth Vader-like sounds heard from behind his gas mask – a horrifying aural variant on the shadowy visual echo of Darth Vader used to evoke regal power near the beginning of Branagh's *Henry V*.

The first sequence moves into the second with a **sound bridge** of ricocheting gunshots segueing into the smooth saxophone rhythms of a Thirties' swing dance band as we join a pensive and anxiously smoking Richard being swept along in his military staff car to the Yorkist victory party being held at the royal palace. The two minutes following use short scenes to introduce triumphant royal family members preparing for the party, the sequence ending with Clarence (a keen amateur photographer trying to capture on camera a world he cannot fathom) dashing up a staircase for the York family photo, his camera on timer-release. As the shutter's click freezes the colour film frame into photographic black and white, a **metacinematic** hint of how alert this movie is to the transformative shifts taking place in the 1930s media technologies, is neatly made. A cut takes us into the third sequence of three and a quarter minutes and the victory ball proper. Here, all are entertained by glamorous chanteuse Stacey Kent crooning lines from Marlowe's poem *The Passionate Shepherd to His Love* set to a catchy 1930s style tune, while she and the Glen Miller look-alike band leader make eyes at one another. (Shakespeare's initials decorate the music stands.) Dialogue is once again absent as more principal characters and relationships are revealed through 'showing' their interactions with one another. The king's ailing condition is confirmed by his cutting short a dance with the vivacious queen, who comes alive with the arrival of her brother Rivers. His offhand treatment of the royal platform and spontaneous embrace of Elizabeth on the dance floor produces visible disapproval of the American *arrivistes* among royals and courtiers, the beginnings of a potential social division that Richard Gloucester will ruthlessly exploit, widening it for his own ends.

A key alliance in his manoeuvrings is suggested when the camera, showing both he and Buckingham observing the Queen's daughter Elizabeth and Richmond getting up to dance, then finds them laughing and shaking hands heartily together, as if the crookback plotter and the oily yes-man had instinctively discovered common conspiratorial cause in what they have seen. Firmer evidence of Richard's plotting comes when the camera, following his gaze as he takes pause during uneasy efforts to be sociable, shows him watching a whispered exchange between Catesby and King Edward before it **pans** across to reveal his brother Clarence being arrested and led away by Brackenbury and two (tuxedoed) soldiers. 'Plots have I laid ... To set my brothers, Clarence and the King, / In deadly hate, the one against the other', Richard will be telling us soon. Evidently satisfied by his scheming efforts, he grimly stubs out his cigarette, coolly making his way to the bandstand to begin his 'Now is the winter of our discontent' speech. Squeals from the loudspeakers and his tentative tapping of the microphone draw our attention again to the new thirties sound technology, and as Richard does start to speak at the mike we are given a foretaste of how he will look when as British dictator he comes to address a mass rally of Blackshirt followers.

That moment is as yet some way off, but within a minute's screen time we see Richard shifting in style from the clever public rhetoric Buckingham finds so entertaining, to what we are to suppose is a repetition of these words sneeringly spoken in the privacy of the Palace's spacious male urinal – though within our hearing. This transition from calculated public oratory to deeply resentful complaint is cleverly managed on a cut at the end of, 'And now – instead of mounting barbèd steeds / To fright the souls of fearful adversaries –, / He' – words hissed out through gnashing teeth an ultra-**close-up** exposes to us in all their nicotine-stained griminess. Richard completes the ironic lines – '... capers nimbly in a lady's chamber / To the lascivious pleasing of a lute' while hobbling toward the urinal, the deep sigh he exhales while peeing not only seeming quite natural to the moment, but an action entirely suited to the words of bitter regret shortly to follow. These concern the physical limitations preventing him from performing 'sportive tricks' or courting 'an amorous looking glass' – his being 'deformed, unfinished, sent before my time / Into this breathing world, / Scarce half made up'. Although seeming to make light of his bodily deformity, Richard actually reveals a psyche deeply troubled by it, a vulnerability never apparent in the stage version, where it is only in the 'nightmare of despair' sequence he weakens, his conscience for multiple murders temporarily getting the better of him.

Yet for the most part, McKellen plays Richard as the ultimate narcissist whose feelings of rejection persuade him that the only way to gain power and control is to murder those who stand in his way. The strategy of utter self-reliance which in the play leads him to utter the extraordinarily bleak and Samuel Beckett-like declaration, 'Richard loves Richard; that is, I am I', emerges in the clever use of mirrors in the men's room scene. The moment he turns about after peeing, adjusting his clothing with military briskness, he advances toward and actually begins to 'court' the men's room mirror, gazing with close confidence into his own reflection, determining to 'smile, and murder while I smile', to wet his cheeks with 'artificial tears', and to frame his face 'to all occasions' (3 *Henry VI*, 3.2.182, 185). Even though while speaking these confidences to his entranced mirror image he catches sight of us / the camera watching him, he is by no means fazed, but turns round and boastfully confesses his resolve 'to prove a villain / And hate the pleasures of these days,' beckoning us to look and see his brother Clarence being taken away across the river to the Tower. Of far more forbidding aspect than the mediaeval Tower of London, the vast anonymous edifice of the Bankside Power Station (now the Tate Modern art gallery) fittingly resembles for this periodising film the kind of 1930s state prison of terrifying reputation that someone of Richard's fearsome and murderous methods would control (e.g. Stalin's notorious Lubianka prison in Moscow).

From the film's mid-point, when the Duchess of York snubs Richard following the deaths of Clarence and Edward, and Buckingham for the first time addresses him as 'my Lord Protector', the pace of the movie quickens. This is signalled by light martial music being played as Richard and Buckingham sweep into Richard's gigantic new headquarters as Lord Protector in a limousine very similar to the large black sedans favoured by mobster leaders of the 1930s. (Scenes in the Lord Protector's HQ were filmed in the grand marbled interior of London University's Senate House building, built in 1936 and occupied in the

Second World War by the Ministry of Information; George Orwell had this modernist building in mind when creating the headquarters of the 'Ministry of Truth' in his novel *1984*.) The assassinations that remove all obstacles to Richard's rule soon follow: Rivers; Hastings (after which the black fascist uniform of Richard's private army are introduced); the young princes. There is also what we assume must be the drug-induced death of Lady Anne, indicated in the horrific shot of a spider crawling across her immobile face, a visual **metonymic** cleverly recalling Elizabeth's hissed description of Richard as 'bottled spider'. Richard's last assassination – the garrotting of Buckingham – is one that removes his chief henchman at court, leaving him without senior support ('He has no friends', says Stanley) to battle it out with Richmond's army and Stanley's RAF near the Tower.

I started by mentioning McKellen's description of *Richard III* as a 'family drama of power-politics, more tragic than melodramatic,' his reflection on how later twentieth-century productions (including his own) had eschewed the 'one-man show' approach in favour of giving the supporting characters more prominence. The traditional melodramatic style from Colly Cibber to Olivier had functioned pretty largely as 'star vehicles' for the main player, while the 'tragic' style emphasises the intractable *circumstances* driving a central character to behave in ways that will eventually destroy them. In this film, the cursing outburst against Richard by the Duchess of York his mother (4.4.167ff, 186ff) exemplifies (in McKellen's words) 'the verbal and emotional abuse which from infancy has formed her youngest son's character and behaviour' (Mckellen, 1996, 22). For once, we here see Richard at a loss, his visible dismay in response to her attack shockingly exposing the vulnerability of a man supposedly impervious to normal human feelings. This susceptibility to the mother's influence and rejection is treated as part of the 'circumstances' which make Richard a tragic figure in the film. Nowhere apparent in Eyre's stage version, this dramatic inflection seems a key element in the psychological structure introduced by Loncraine so that Richard's rise and fall in the play will adapt closely to the story contour of the classic Hollywood gangster genre, a genre familiar to cinema audiences since the 1930s.

The final confrontation between Richard and Richmond on the smoking girders of the Tower elaborates and confirms the use of the gangster genre by Loncraine in a very specific way. Simultaneously echoing the genre styles of Western showdown, gangster movie cop and villain shoot-out, as well as the pursuit-and-kill climax of political thrillers, Loncraine also explicitly alludes to the final scene of the classic gangster movie *White Heat* (1949), where James Cagney as the deserted mother-obsessed mobster shoots into gas tanks and immolates himself by leaping into the flames while defiantly shouting 'Made it Ma, top of the world!' As with the many gangster movies in which a fleeing villain seeks escape by climbing a building only to topple to his death, McKellen's Richard climbs the burning Tower pursued by the ruggedly handsome and clean-cut Richmond until, with nowhere to go, he holds out a hand to his rival offering the mock invitation: 'Let's to it pell-mell, if not to heaven, then hand in hand to Hell.' Of course this is originally spoken in the play by Richard to his troops before battle, but his ironical delivery here before leaning back to plunge into a blazing inferno grinning insanely at the camera, is not the only element suggesting disturbed mental fixations are at work in this denouement. While the style of suicidal exit and the soundtrack of Al Jolson singing 'I'm sitting on top of the world' (from the first sound film ever made, *The Jazz Singer* (1929)) code Richard as an asocial maniacal criminal, there is also our final view of the supposedly 'heroic' Richmond to reckon with. For as he tumbles, Richmond fires two revolver shots into Richard, a superfluous gesture since the man is already plunging to his death. Yet this gesture is then compounded by the knowing smirk he offers the camera, leaving us with the chilling thought that perhaps life is as cheap to him as it was to Richard, the man who had also liked to share his viciously evil outlook with us. In these last highly filmic 30 seconds of the movie, as the fall of Richard III gives way to the rise of Henry VII, we seem to be left with the kind of question around which Jan Kott's cynical reading of the Shakespearean histories revolve: has one tyrant been defeated only to be succeeded by another?

3. Tragedies

INTRODUCTORY NOTE

Of all the dramatic genres for which Shakespeare wrote plays, it is his tragedies which have proved most attractive for directors to adapt to film. It is not difficult to see why this should be. There are inherent problems in successfully accommodating the stage conventions of comedy to those of the screen (see Introductory note to **Comedies**), while Shakespeare's history plays tend to have a limited interest for modern screen audiences. By contrast, Shakespeare's tragedies have maintained a consistent appeal for both film directors and their audiences, new adaptations of particular plays being made repeatedly over the years.

The tragedies to have been filmed most often are *Hamlet, Macbeth, Romeo and Juliet, King Lear* and *Othello*, their main attraction probably centring on the compelling creation of powerful conflicts between powerful characters whose strong passions we like to identify with, these conflicts being so intractable that only the death of the principals caught up in them seems to offer a resolution to the problems experienced. Ultimately, our experience of being carried along on the emotional 'roller-coaster ride' that identification with the clashing characters portrayed offers, is still likely to be linked to the 'purging' effect on our roused passions that Aristotle argued in his *Poetics* to be the real value of watching tragic dramas, over two millennia ago. Furthermore, since each of these plays offers a superbly structured story with plot and dramatic development providing the kinds of twists, turns, tensions and releases that appeal to the most demanding movie-goer, it is not surprising that so many film versions of them do appear.

The full range of cinematographic techniques for conveying these emotionally demanding plays on film tends to be used, though style and approach over the years have varied. One indispensable camera technique used for most of these films is the **close shot**, since it is obviously important to convey to the audience with some precision a character's emotional feelings or state of mind. There can be enormous emotional or intellectual pressures bearing in on the central characters of these dramas, access to their often conflicting thoughts and feelings being what we want most of all – as in a novel – so that we can become involved in and hopefully be entertained by making some sense of what is going on. From the 1940s of the twentieth century onward, Freudian theory, psychoanalysis and a massive interest in in-depth psychology made its impact felt in films perhaps more than in any other medium of artistic expression.

The brooding figures of Welles's *Macbeth* and Olivier's *Hamlet* in their 1948 films communicated themselves even more broodingly to audiences because of the gloomy, shadowy sets in which their dramas were paced out, access to Hamlet's mind being afforded particularly effectively by use of the **voice-over** technique. Polanski's later use of the same technique for his *Macbeth* – the most extensive of any Shakespeare adaptation – gives us even more privileged access to the innermost thoughts and desires of the Thane and his wife. The approaches of Branagh and Almereyda to their *Hamlet* films are quite different, the former broadening his out to present an epic, full-text version expressing all the play's themes and characters in the context of a precarious nineteenth-century political state. Almereyda's low-budget movie focuses on the way media technology in the ruthless, high-powered corporate setting of modern Manhattan shapes and cramps communication and the creative integrity of youthful aspiration. The two extremely popular versions of *Romeo and Juliet* by Zeffirelli and Luhrmann discussed here concern themselves more with techniques of presenting colourful, exciting imagery and using the power of music to sway emotions in the audience, than finding ways of exploring complex states of mind. Exploring complex states of mind is not a priority in popular cinema at the time of writing.

Franco Zeffirelli's *Romeo and Juliet* (UK/Italy, 1968)

Director: Franco Zeffirelli

Producers: Anthony Havelock-Allan, John Brabourne

Script: Franco Brusati, Masolino D'Amico, Franco Zeffirelli

Medium: Technicolor, 35 mm, widescreen, 132 minutes

Main actors: Leonard Whiting (Romeo); Olivia Hussey (Juliet); Milo O'Shea (Friar Laurence); John McEnery (Mercutio); Michael York (Tybalt); Pat Heywood (Nurse); Natasha Parry (Lady Capulet); Paul Hardwick (Capulet); Robert Stephens (Prince Escalus); Bruce Robinson (Benvolio); Antonio Pierfederici (Montague); Esmerelda Ruspoli (Lady Montague); Keith Skinner (Balthazar)

Photography: Pasquale De Santis

Costume design: Danilo Donati

Music: Nino Rota

As with so many other successful Shakespeare film adaptations, Franco Zeffirelli's *Romeo and Juliet* was preceded by a stage production, and in this case one that was not only hugely successful in 1960 at London's Old Vic theatre (world famous for its Shakespeare productions) but equally so in 1961 at the City Centre in New York. The essential reason for its enormous stage success was the same as the movie version's triumph later in 1968: they both connected with the emotions and understanding of contemporary youth. Since the teenage cinema audience would be all-important for moviemakers in the decades to come (including Shakespeare moviemakers of course), it is well worth considering first of all what ingredients Zeffirelli brought to his Old Vic production that made it so appealing to these new consumers of Shakespeare.

Old Vic general manager Michael Benthall had seen Zeffirelli's sunny production of the Italian opera *Cavalleria Rusticana* in the winter of 1959 at London's Royal Opera House. So impressed was he that he asked the opera director and designer to inject the same bright magic into a new *Romeo and Juliet*, to bring to the production (according to Zeffirelli's own report) 'the feel of Italy, not the Victorian interpretation that still dominated the English stage but something truly Mediterranean … sunlight on a fountain, wine and olives and garlic, new, different, real, young' (Zeffirelli, 1986, 157). Fresh from a 1960 summer during which he experienced the Olympic Games in a 'joyful, colourful, sunny Rome awash with bright, healthy young people from all over the world', he returned to England feeling that 'even at the very beginning of the 1960s ... young people were about to give everyone a very pleasant jolt, and it was this that I wanted to bring to the London stage' (160, 167). Years of training as assistant to neo-realist Italian filmmaker Luchino Visconti had given Zeffirelli the imaginative credentials to create such a theatrical jolt, his strategy including a determination to 'demolish' the 'Norma Shearer/Leslie Howard approach' of George Cukor, replacing it with 'a real story in a plausible mediaeval city at the opening of the Renaissance'. Instead of the usual set-piece balcony scene tastefully positioned amid 'Italianate verandas and artificial flowers', Zeffirelli had Juliet (a young Judi Dench) step out on to the more realistic battlement of 'a Capulet fortress built to keep foes out and treasures in' (163), forcing Romeo (John Stride) to climb a cypress to get to her, for in this erotic production it was powerful 'young love, impetuous, unstoppable', that had transformed them into 'amorous young animals who had been kept apart' (164). Such passion, played by youthful actors whom Zeffirelli insisted could not use wigs but had to grow their hair long (both boys and girls) for a natural Renaissance look, was a long way from the bleak 'kitchen sink' dramas then playing on London stages.

Despite a predictably savage response from the London drama critics who saw Shakespeare being destroyed by an irreverent Italian opera director ignorant of Shakespeare and verse speaking, the day was saved when leading critic and future dramaturge of the National Theatre Kenneth Tynan saw fit to praise Zeffirelli, calling his *Romeo and Juliet* 'a revelation, perhaps a revolution ... a masterly production ... a glorious evening' (164). Thereafter, the theatre was packed out night after night, often by young people who by the end of the play's extended run were also wearing the long hair soon to be made fashionable by The Beatles. Even the Shakespearean theatre's senior player John Gielgud, who had sat in the audience 'surrounded by laughing, crying kids', had to admit afterwards that 'I've never had the luck to have an audience like that.' (165) By the time it was evident Zeffirelli's first Shakespeare movie *The Taming of the Shrew* (1966) was going to be a worldwide hit, he and its stars Liz Taylor and Richard Burton all agreed that the only logical thing for him to do next was a film of his theatre hit *Romeo and Juliet*: 'that youthful production at the Old Vic had somehow to be translated on to film for the vast international audience we felt sure would flock to see it' (223). Luckily Paramount's head of productions in Europe Bud Ornstein had seen the original stage production, declaring that 'If this man can put one-tenth of the energy from that stage play on screen then we ought to do it' (224). Unfortunately Paramount in the US were less confident, willing only to back a movie that could recover the $800,000 offered (an amount described as 'derisory' (225) by Zeffirelli) from an **art house** audience and television sales. For them Shakespeare was still bad box office, despite the evidence of *Shrew*, the success of which was seen as entirely due to the bankable international movie stardom of Burton and Taylor, whereas (as with the 1960 theatrical perform-ances) the two leads for the *Romeo and Juliet* film would be unknowns: an essential and necessary risk for Zeffirelli, who refused to cast the older actors who traditionally played the roles.

The film began shooting in Italy during the hot 'summer of love' of 1967, exterior locations being found at Tuscania, Pienza and Gubbio, while interior sets were built at Cinecittà studios near Rome. Whether filming interiors or exteriors, Zeffirelli's twin skills of designing sets and settings for opera and of assisting Visconti in the design and mak-ing of his meticulously visualised neo-realist Italian films now came to the fore. With the same realistic, energetic and colourful style of approach used to film *The Taming of the Shrew*, he applied his experi-ence to produce the right 'look' of *Romeo and Juliet*. As a native Florentine passionate about his city's art, architecture and culture, the 'look' produced by Zeffirelli is primarily concerned with seducing the eye by rich colours and textures, gracefully reconstructed Renaissance interiors and costumes recalling old master paintings (the film won best costume design and cinematography Academy Awards), images being typically bathed in that special soft, golden light for which Italy is so famous. The impact of light is made apparent from the seemingly quiet opening frames of the film. Here we are shown a panoramic view of Verona shrouded in pale morning mist, soon to be dispersed by the hot sun, while the voice of Laurence Olivier speaks the grim tidings of the prologue over one of the simple but compelling tunes that Nino Rota provides for the movie. In fact, this opening (the aerial **pan** being a tribute to the beginning of Olivier's *Henry V* that inspired Zeffirelli toward theatre and film in 1945), offers in condensed cinematic form the contrasts of cold tragic death (the white veil of mist) and the pas-sions of love and hate (the circle of burning sun) of which the prologue speaks, appropriately distanced from the life of Verona below to suit its sombre register.

But such distancing does not last long, as the camera takes us down to ground level and into the colourful bustle of the Verona market, where we encounter in the violent clash of the Capulets and Montagues three key aspects of Zeffirelli's cinematic style: his use of **close-ups**, rapid cutting and **pan shots**, and a distinct preference for action over dialogue. Of course, when a fight is at hand, that is what the audience (especially a youthful one) wants to see, and the fast-cutting, **zooms** and blurred pan shots all effectively convey the excitement and chaos of the violent mayhem. Nevertheless, the sparcity and nature of the dialogue as spoken in the film could be seen as an issue, since Zeffirelli retains only 30% of Shakespeare's lines. But to Zeffirelli himself the beauty of the original poetic language of Shakespeare 'is not what makes it internationally unbetterable, with no peers'; he feels instead that 'to the author, youth was more important than enunciation' (162) in this play. Clearly it is the heartbreakingly sentimental *story* of *Romeo and Juliet* which appeals so much to this film-maker, and one commentator has gone so far as to say that the film is a 'version of the Romeo and Juliet narrative more like Shakespeare's sources'. To some extent this may be true, since Zeffirelli has said that in one of the source tales Juliet is dancing with two men at a masked ball, one having a cold clammy hand, and the other, Romeo, having a warm, gentle one. Zeffirelli comments: 'So by the touch of the two hands she knows their characters' (162). This not only points to Shakespeare's own emphasis on hands in the 'shared sonnet' voiced by Romeo and Juliet when they meet at the Capulet ball, but also explains the extent to which 'hands' are factored in as a key visual **motif** of meaning throughout this movie.

In fact, it is by deploying a whole range of *non-verbal* devices in the film that Zeffirelli succeeds so well in conveying his interpretation of the Romeo and Juliet story to us. I have already mentioned his preference for 'showing' the dramatic actions and reactions of characters over and above verbal 'telling,' as well as providing the eye-pleasing contrasts of vivid and subtle colours all bathed in the golden Italian light. Just as important for this director are the use of gesture, of looking, of touching, and of using music and the choreography of bodily movement – especially the dance at the Capulet ball and the open-air sword fights – to communicate the dramatic story. In addition to their touching of hands and lips, it is when they visit their clinging gazes upon one another at the Capulet ball that Romeo and Juliet fall in love: the Moresca dance and the cleverly inserted sentimental song 'What is a youth?' triggering the remaining emotional effects both on them and us, the susceptible screen audience. For the young of the film, words are an inadequate means for communicating the powerful impulses of lust, love and hate in the world they are forced to live by their elders, and instinctively distrust the language that governs it. Tybalt needs no words but only one *look* at the entranced Romeo to discover what his enemy is up to at the Capulet ball; Juliet asks 'What's in a name?'; Mercutio in the sweltering Verona square impatiently responds to Benvolio's repetition of the Prince's cautions with his dismissive 'blah, blah, blah;' a Romeo hot to couple with Juliet impatiently completes the sentences of hackneyed sayings Friar Laurence counsels him with prior to their marriage. No more outstanding example of Zeffirelli's drive to replace shot for text can perhaps be noticed than when he has the young men of the feud signify their masculinist sexuality by ceaselessly brandishing and thrusting forth their weapons; the references to the male member pervading the play text are repeatedly 'spoken' by the bodily gestures and rapier jabs of Mercutio and his like.

Despite the bright colours, busy action and rich visual detail that in many ways are appropriate for the more 'comedic' first half of the film, the darker and bleaker episodes of the movie, which occur after the deaths of Mercutio and Tybalt, are sometimes foreshadowed by visual moments that erupt in and interrupt this first half. For example, we see Mercutio bellowing about 'nothing' and 'the frozen bosom of the north' (1.4.96, 101) into the empty square bathed in an ominous blue light (a colour sometimes associated with death) at the end of his Queen Mab speech; there is the strange 'betwixt and between' moment when Juliet pauses in the shadowy Capulet courtyard by the statue after the ball, listening to different voices calling in the night for her and for Romeo; and we see Romeo being pursued along the narrow, claustrophobic streets of Verona. For the second half of the film, it is important to note how Zeffirelli fittingly changes the film's visual style, suspending the hectic activity and fast-cutting, and emptying the screen of its vivid colour to reflect the darkening shift of tone that Shakespeare's gives to this part of the play. What we see now is a range of more subdued images and sometimes longer takes: there are the white tones of Juliet's room; the gloominess of Friar Laurence's cell and his blowing out of the candle after giving Juliet the potion, an action even he catches himself noticing as dangerously symbolic; the darkness of the Capulet house; the sombreness of Juliet's 'funeral'; the dim interior of exiled Romeo's Mantuan room; the grimness of the Capulet tomb; and finally, when all of those we have been made to care about are dead, there is the desolate wind-blown square filled with mourners in black, the 'scourge laid upon their heads' being the price to be paid for the reconciliation between opposing households we observe taking place as the former enemies file into church side by side. However, important as all these cinematic meanings and effects are, none of them would matter unless the actors playing Romeo and Juliet were believable and attractive lovers, attractive and believable in the way that those previously playing the roles in Cukor's and Castellani's films were not. Fortunately, trained in the Italian school of Visconti's cinematic neo-realism where acting skills were frowned upon in favour of a beautiful 'look', Zeffirelli by having Olivia Hussey and Leonard Whiting as his two principals was immensely lucky. As the director himself so truly says, 'the cinema with its huge close-ups exaggerates everything', so that his Romeo and Juliet would need be 'extra beautiful and exceptionally talented' for the film to be successful. At fifteen the voluptuous Hussey had a 'magnificent bone structure', possessed 'wide expressive eyes,' and altogether presented a 'gawky colt of a girl waiting for life to begin' (226), while Zeffirelli felt that 17-year-old Whiting was 'the most exquisitely beautiful male adolescent' (228) he had ever met (and in fact the director makes sure we are able to gaze longer on the naked body of this male than that of Hussey, in the scene after Romeo and Juliet's night of love). When Richard Burton was shown early rushes of the film, he broached the perennial problem of inexperienced actors being cast for the parts of Romeo and Juliet: 'You've got problems with the verse.' However, as if realising as quickly as he had said it that for *this* film, being shown at this *time* – towards the end of the very first 'decade of youth' – perhaps the conventional objections of the seasoned Shakespearean on correct verse-speaking did not apply: 'But perhaps it doesn't matter – you're probably right. It certainly looks great' (228). It is true that neither teenage actor speaks Shakespeare's verse very skilfully. But then neither does the rest of the cast, except perhaps for John McEnery's Mercutio, whose Queen Mab speech is so expertly 'physicalised' into meaning for us: for the most part the actors were all encouraged to speak and act as naturalistically as possible. Nevertheless, without the emotional energy and physical spontaneity that Hussey and Whiting bring to their playing, the film could not have succeeded. As it is, that energy was powerfully present, especially in the case of initiative-taking Hussey, without whose beguiling glances and attractively spontaneous energy the film would lack sympathy and appeal for the viewing audience.

The year 1968 was before the days of the test screenings now used by film companies to gauge audience reaction to a movie, taking action where necessary to avoid a failure. In the case of *Romeo and Juliet*, when Zeffirelli ran out of funds halfway through filming, the response of one teenager who saw the rushes was decisive both in ensuring further funds would be released to complete the movie, and in illustrating that it was the response of *youth* which would matter most to the success of this film. Charlie Bluhdorn as head of Gulf and Western – the oil company that owned Paramount – was the only one able to authorise the money to finish the film. Yet he was utterly bewildered by the scenes he was shown – until his teenage son Paul interrupted proceedings in tears to say that he liked what he'd seen: 'He understands, well can ya beat that! An' I thought we were gonna haf to dub it' (229), said the baffled Bluhdorn.

Baz Luhrmann's *William Shakespeare's Romeo + Juliet* (USA, 1996)

Director: Baz Luhrmann

Producers: Gabriella Martinelli, Baz Luhrmann

Script: Craig Pearce and Baz Luhrmann

Medium: Color De Luxe, 35 mm, 115 minutes

Main actors: Leonardo DiCaprio (Romeo); Claire Danes (Juliet); Pete Postlethwaite (Friar Laurence); Harold Perrineau (Mercutio); John Leguizamo (Tybalt); Miriam Margolyes (Nurse); Diane Venora (Gloria Capulet); Paul Sorvino (Fulgencio Capulet); Vondie Curtis-Hall (Captain Prince); Dash Minok (Benvolio); Brian Dennery (Ted Montague); Christina Pickles (Caroline Montague); Jesse Bradford (Balthazar)

Photography: Donald McAlpine

Costume design: Kym Barrett

Production designer: Catherine Martin

Editor: Jill Bilcock

Music: Nellee Hooper; original score composed by Craig Armstrong, Marius de Vries, Nellee Hooper

As with Zeffirelli throughout his career, Luhrmann has worked in the theatre and opera house besides making popular films, and the benefit of these professional experiences can be seen in *William Shakespeare's Romeo + Juliet* (hereafter cited as *Romeo + Juliet*). A key 'theatrical' site in the movie is the ruined proscenium theatre arch at the beachside Sycamore Grove, one of the film's three key locations (the others being Verona Beach and the Capulet mansion), important because it was 'the originating image of Luhrmann's design, imagined and built as a model two full years before shooting began in Mexico City'. I will return to this aspect of Sycamore Grove, where 'real performance' in what is effectively a post-theatrical and a post-cinematic space may be seen to provide a kind of challenge to the image-saturated televisual and corporate power 'realities' that dominate the film. Yet almost the first area to explore is the movie's notoriously dense deployment of the kinds of images and sounds already discussed to a degree in Part III concerning the 'intertextuality' in film, that is, the way (especially post-) modern movies frequently refer to 'other works, genres and styles, whether as homage, parody, simple imitation, or even unconscious duplication' (Hayward, 1996, 259–72).

I say almost the first area, because prior to everything else is the fact that the whole substance and story of this film is 'contained' by its status as (a decidedly long, admittedly) 'item' on a TV news programme, delivered from the screen of a 1970s style television set that appears in the centre of the frame at the very opening of the movie. There is an audible clicking of the dial telling us that (click) 'Twentieth Century Fox presents' (click) 'A Bazmark Production', a final click bringing up an African-American newscaster who speaks the play's Prologue with the predictable blandness of modern TV reportage. The same TV screen appears again centre frame at the end of the film when the reporter returns to relate the play's gloomy epilogue in the selfsame bland tones. What this highly self-conscious 'containing' filmic device suggests is not only that what we see between Prologue and Epilogue is in a sense no more or less than another news 'story' rather than 'Shakespeare', but that communications through screen and image in modern culture are so pervasive that there is little difference between our experience of reality and its media representations. This suggestion becomes more assertive in the opening sequence when a slow **zoom** enlarges the TV image to reveal over the newsreader's shoulder a projected headline icon, 'Star-Cross'd Lovers.' Next to this is an image of Romeo and Juliet's broken wedding ring, and as the newsreader speaks the line 'two hours' traffic of our stage' (*Prologue*, 12) studio coverage 'goes live'. We are now catapulted *through* the TV screen into a film **montage** of **slam-zoom** images of urban violence too fast-changing to register clearly, while an ostentatious choral piece parodying Carl Orff's 'O Fortuna' assaults our ears. We are being shown what passes for **establishing shots** of the cityscape of Verona Beach, which the film's production website describes as 'a violent otherworld, neither future nor past, ruled by two families, the Montagues and the Capulets', but which the bold letters of a title card (twice) ironically proclaims is 'Fair Verona'. It would be nearer the truth to say that Verona Beach and Sycamore Grove bear a similar relationship to each other as do Los Angeles and Venice Beach. (Sycamore Grove is so named because Benvolio soon tells the concerned mother of Romeo how 'underneath the grove of sycamore/ ... So early walking did I see your son' (1.1.114, 116) – such trees were once associated with melancholy lovers who were 'sick-amour').

Aerial shots of Captain Prince's police helicopters striving to control outbreaks of urban violence below are now intercut with images of giant statues of Christ and of the Madonna, flanked and dwarfed – significantly so, we will come to realise – by the skyscraping towers of Montague and Capulet business corporations. The frame then cuts from video footage to a slow **zoom**-out of newsprint imaging Christ's monumental head surrounded by members of the feuding families, and we hear the Prologue being spoken again, this time voiced with nervous deliberation by Pete Postlethwaite, the British Shakespearean actor who will play Friar Laurence. Illustrating his speech are various shots intercutting images of the Montague and Capulet parents and newsmagazine photo versions of Jesus and Mary, with snatches of the Prologue shown in newsprint. In the white gothic lettering on black that becomes the film's trademark print style we finally read that 'a pair of star cross'd lovers take their life', the 't' of 'take' being in the form of a cross, the first of many to appear in this movie.

We are now introduced to the story's main protagonists in freeze-frame shots that use titling evocative of the opening of *The Good, the Bad and the Ugly* (a style repeated to introduce the Capulet and Montague 'boys' later) – except that we are only given a tiny glimpse of Romeo (unnamed) in the briefest of proleptic shots as he opens a church door to reveal the cross-blazoned aisle leading to Juliet's 'death bier' towards the end of the film. Juliet herself is neither shown nor named, but we do get further proleptic glimpses of future events in an amazing 7-second montage of 26 shots spliced together in such rapid succession that they can only be subliminally registered – just one of the devices used by Luhrmann to engage the young MTV audience. The last of these subliminal images is of a Montague gang member being gunned down, followed by a **match cut** to the falling body that forms a cruciform shape briefly in space before being replaced by a fiery red gothic cross with a tiny ampersand at its centre, this finally shrinking to the '+' of the white block lettering of the film's titling frames, 'William Shakespeare's Romeo + Juliet'. (The ampersand is clearly imaged in the packaging publicity for the DVD, though the screenplay book cover prints 'William Shakespeare's Romeo and Juliet', suggesting that the cross/ampersand conjunction was a late addition to the whole production).

Following the **wipe** that removes the titles, we are taken into a densely-packed six-minute sequence using a variety of cleverly inspired camera techniques that introduce us to members of the

Montague and Capulet youth gangs in violent but witty confrontation. It does this by imitating or parodying previous film styles, principally deploying the fast-cutting and speeded-up action movie approach of John Woo as the gangs shoot it out. Luhrmann also quotes from the tough-guy acting styles and gestures of Clint Eastwood in *A Fistful of Dollars* and Charles Bronson in *Once Upon a Time in the West*, while the twanging guitar and haunting whistles that punctuate the entry of the dapperly sinister Tybalt echo the trademark scores of Ennio Morricone in both Sergio Leone films. Despite its fast-cutting, slo-mos, **whip-pans, slam-zooms** and ultra close-ups, the excitement of this narrative sequence is almost wholly conveyed by very short **shot/reverse shots** no more than a few seconds long at most, filmed tight on the gang members' faces as they act and react hysterically to each other. Among the punning references to Shakespeare and visual jokes in the sequence ('hubble bubble toil and trouble', 'add more fuel to your fire'), the cross motif is highly visible: crucifixes that hang around the necks of a convent college girl, and opposing gang members, and which dangles from Benvolio's gun; a cross shaved on the head of Petruchio Capulet; the crosshairs of the telescopic sight on Tybalt's gun; the flaming cross formed on the gas station forecourt when gasoline is ignited by Tybalt's discarded cheroot. The Christian iconography is most noticeable when Tybalt declares, 'Turn thee Benvolio, look upon thy death', and opens his jacket not only to reveal two holstered pistols, but also on his bullet-proof vest an image of Christ displaying the Sacred Heart. This depiction at least could argue for a more complicating account of what otherwise becomes a repetitious crowding of the film with signs of the Christian 'brand' among other noticeable 'brand names', including those drawing on the play so that modern weapons could be included: Sword, Longsword, Dagger and so on. The effect of juxtaposing such holy signs with deadly weapons or the various scenes of violence – including the violence visited on his daughter in her cross-festooned bedroom by Fulgencio Capulet – is to suggest that the Christianity proclaimed in Verona Beach is always likely to be shaped by the needs of ruthlessly violent corporate rivalry, or the ritual blood sacrifices associated with the feud ('fuel') helping feed it.

In this film, there is a strong sense that one man at least – albeit a possibly drug-addicted priest – has the faith to believe that such a feud might be ended. This sense emerges in the cinematically inventive sequence of Friar Laurence's 'vision', where a succession of converging images that include a white dove of peace entering the Sacred Heart of Christ, inspires him to attempt a resolution of the feud through the marriage of Romeo and Juliet. His vision is supported by the relatively weak but sincere efforts of a Romeo whose impulse to create peace and harmony comes only after his confused 'doting' on Rosaline is replaced by his love for Juliet. There is some justification then for Luhrmann's view that Romeo is 'a young rebel in love with the idea of love itself', although his true rebellion is in abandoning the Montague boys' gang for a female – Juliet. This is a desertion registered most acutely in the hurt response of Mercutio, whose homoerotic feelings for Romeo are made clearer in this film than in any previous adaptation. Despite the astute casting of teen heart-throb de Caprio to code the film for success with its target audience, in many ways it is the anti-macho impact – 'wimpishness' even – conveyed by his performance, that tends to win out over his heterosexual appeal.

Luhrmann's use of water as the element emblematising the love-bond of Romeo and Juliet is probably a response to two of their statements in the play (unvoiced in the film): Romeo's response to Juliet's problem over his name being to tell her to 'call me but love, and I'll be new baptized' (2.2.50) (he 'new baptizes' both of them of course when they first plunge into the Capulet pool); while she declares later that 'My bounty is as boundless as the sea, / My love as deep' (2.2.133–4). Water is repeatedly associated with the lovers at different points in the film, linking them together in romantic and peaceful escape from their discontented lives. We first encounter Juliet dreamily submerged in a bath tub, unable to hear her mother and Nurse calling her. And after we see him plunging his head in a bowl of water to shake off the effects of Mercutio's drug at the Capulet party, Romeo and Juliet glimpse each other for the first time through an aquarium of blue and yellow tropical fish, colours which are associated with the Madonna, but which are increasingly identified with Romeo and Juliet as the film progresses. Such identification culminates in their final scene together at Juliet's 'death bier' when he swallows the yellow poison (sold to him by the apothecary/Globe Pool Hall owner who pulled it from its hiding-place inside a Madonna lamp), both of them being bathed in the glow of golden yellow candlelight and surrounded by a virtual 'sea' of illuminated blue crosses. A reprised freeze-frame shot of them kissing in the underwater retreat of the blue-lit Capulet pool is our parting view of Romeo and Juliet.

For some, this last drawn-out scene in which Romeo and Juliet are left to themselves and their 'tragic' destiny, may be the most moving and memorable of the film, as it is no doubt meant to be, the gently closing strains of Wagner's *Liebestod* providing a fittingly romantic and sad conclusion. Such a conclusion is made possible not only because Luhrmann alters the death scene in the same way that Thomas Otway had done for his Restoration version of the play in the late-seventeenth century, cutting and manipulating the dialogue so that Juliet wakes before Romeo dies, allowing for a reunion. Other changes are made too, shots included in the published screenplay involving Friar Laurence and Captain Prince's police rushing into the Madonna chapel being excised, permitting the lovers to be uninter-rupted in their last moments together. Yet it is also possible to see this ending as rather contrived and sentimental, and to point to other parts of the film as providing both more interesting and genuinely 'performative', as well as more tragic moments. In terms of theatrical-ity, there are of course the early Capulet mansion scenes where a nar-cissistic, pill-popping and neurotic Gloria prances down the staircase half-dressed as Cleopatra. In fact, Diane Venora's Lady Capulet pro-vides more interest as Tybalt's would-be lover, a situation registering the intensely dysfunctional nature of the play's families – although her 'speeded-up' antics do offer a prelude of sorts to Mercutio's more exhibitionist and campy descent in silver-sequinned mini-skirt and top later, miming to Kym Mazelle's 'Young Hearts Run Free'.

The sentimental 'set-piece' ending gives us the beautiful and almost identical 'Anglo' faces of Romeo and Juliet looking their last on each other before the TV anchor woman and the seventies TV set reduce what we have seen to insignificant 'news media history'. But it is worth recalling how Luhrmann's first design for the film had been the ruined proscenium theatre arch at the beachside Sycamore Grove. It is here that his cinematic achievement is greatest, assembling the most inter-esting visual commentary on what it means to film Shakespeare in a post-theatrical, post-cinematic and postmodern period, when mass culture is so dominated by screen-mediated versions of reality that it is hard for the performative of 'real life' to find a location for express-ing itself. Luhrmann claims that the film's 'created world' comprising twentieth century icons and images 'are there to clarify what's being said' in the Shakespeare text. Yet we are forced to conclude that it is really the icons and images of the film, and Luhrmann's cinematic flair in delivering them, which dominate, turning much of the Shakespearean dialogue, which for 'the most part, the actors speak with toneless naturalism' (Loehlin, in Burnett and Wray, 2000, 123), into the film's subtext. In wanting to 'make it easier for the audience to receive this heightened language', Luhrmann seems to fall into the trap of treating the Shakespearean text with kid gloves. Thankfully, it is the inspired cinematic language he uses to convey his concept of how to deliver *Romeo and Juliet* to a worldwide youth audience in 1996 that becomes 'heightened', leaving the Shakespearean text to survive as best it may in the American and Latino voices he so rightly wanted to bring forward in his production.

This cinematic language is nowhere better deployed than in the scenes at Sycamore Grove where Mercutio meets his death. There is always the danger in any production of *Romeo and Juliet* that this halfway point of the play can seem like its climax, since most of the engaging 'action' occurs in the early acts and in the aftermath of Mercutio's death when Romeo kills Tybalt. Yet the scenes around Mercutio's death are probably the most dramatically powerful and cinematically insightful of the whole movie. The culturally decayed stretch of beach and the amusement park at Sycamore Grove, inhabited by drunks, whores, hustlers, the poor and marginalised, is a horizontal open space where the feud-entrapped Montague and Capulet boys can express their real dissatisfactions without interference. It is a liminal space ideally suited for them to 'play out' their own frustrated destiny, literally so on the ruined **proscenium arch** stage whose only audience is themselves. Following the well-paced sequence of fast-cut **shot/reverse shots** tracking the 'fight' between vengeful Tybalt and peace-loving Romeo, Mercutio is stabbed by Tybalt using a shard of glass from a shattered window of the old theatre. Mortally wounded – though no one knows this – he climbs on to the stage, and announces with an Olivier-like theatrical gesture that he has 'a scratch' (3.1.89), a parodic flourish shown in **wide-shot** giving him the massive scope as solo stage performer that he so relishes. It is only then that he reveals his fatal wound, shouting 'a plague on both your houses' at Romeo and Tybalt, chief members of his audience, and it is a shout that Luhrmann has echo around the whole location, implicating us all. Meanwhile, **matte**d-in **shots** of storm clouds are seen through and behind the open stage, accompanied by the rumbling thunder of the gathering storm that actually hit on the day of shooting.

This is building to an effective virtual climax during the saddest moments of the film, Tybalt's anguished gazing on the death scene from the stage reinforcing the feeling of tragedy which the soaring voices of the **non-diegetic** choir now express with such power and

finality. After we see the faces of the comprehending and uncompre-
hending alike who happen to be around watching, we are left with a
wide shot of the now deserted stage and beach; waves beating on the
shore can be seen through the jagged opening of the proscenium arch;
night is shown falling through **time-lapse photography**. In a film so
often dominated by hi-tech flashiness, it is a sequence encouraging us
to reflect on how the tragedies of life might best be represented.

Laurence Olivier's *Hamlet* (UK, 1948)

Director: Laurence Olivier

Producers: Laurence Olivier, Reginald Beck

Script: Laurence Olivier, Alan Dent

Medium: Black and white, 35 mm, 152 minutes

Main actors: Laurence Olivier (Hamlet); Eileen Herlie (Gertrude); Basil Sydney (Claudius); Jean Simmons (Ophelia); Felix Aylmer (Polonius); Norman Wooland (Horatio); Terence Morgan (Laertes)

Photography: Desmond Dickenson

Music: William Walton

Although Olivier's *Hamlet* may now look rather dated, in conception and execution the film is even more of a dramatic success than *Henry V*. This is because Olivier is able to make a cinematic version of Shakespeare's most complex play accessible to all by drawing on contemporary Freudian theory, and especially cinematic codes and techniques already used successfully in German Expressionist film and in American *film noir*. A musical score again specially written by William Walton was also key to this screen dramatisation. But the main filmic qualities making this *Hamlet* such a cinematic *tour de force* are embodied in three powerful elements meshing with great dramatic effect: the 'oedipal' conception of Hamlet's character; the film's imaginative design and setting; and its innovative use of the camera. These interwoven elements come into play from the outset, and are observable working very effectively in the first ten minutes of the movie, where all its main themes are introduced.

Olivier's *Henry V* had begun with a bird's eye view of Elizabethan London, and *Hamlet* also starts with a **high-angle** camera, but this time moving in on the ramparts of Elsinore from above while Olivier's **voice-over** solemnly recites from Hamlet's 'vicious mole of nature' speech, also provided on screen for us to read. Filling our eyes and ears with the famous Prince's words instructs us in how we are to think of this Hamlet – as a damaged melancholic. Giving words from the play text also suggests to a general audience that this view of Hamlet is underpinned by 'Bardic authority'. In fact the speech is torn from its original context (in Q2, not in F) where Hamlet explains to Horatio the predilection of Danes to drunkenness (on the occasion of Claudius's rowdy 'wassail' to celebrate his marriage to Gertrude) as they wait for the ghost of Hamlet's father to appear on the ramparts (1.4.18.7–20). The view we are to accept is that it is 'the stamp of one defect … breaking down the forts and pales of reason' which results in 'a tragedy of a man who could not make up his mind' (Olivier's words, not Shakespeare's) – the tragedy of Hamlet. As Olivier voices his own psychological explanation for the 'destiny' of the Prince of Denmark, we are shown a sombre night-time tableau in which the dead Hamlet is held ceremoniously aloft by pall-bearers on a castle tower.

Just as Olivier created a fairly straightforward 'heroic' character for his Henry V by much textual excision, by the same method he fashions a Hamlet whose 'problems' are reckoned to be the outcome of an aberrant mind. The 'external' political dimensions of the play are cut out by removing Fortinbras and all mention of Norway, and also by removing Rosencrantz and Guildenstern, who work for Claudius as spies on Hamlet. This allows Olivier to deliver a *Hamlet* focusing on its more 'internal' psychological dimensions, with signals that the mysteries of the mind are to be key for the film's approach occurring in the first scene, set amid the swirling mists atop Elsinore castle. (This is one visual **metonymic** indicating both ghostliness *and* an unfocused mind, just as later a metonymic of mental instability is provided by an image of the swirling sea inside Hamlet's troubled brain before he recites the 'To be or not to be' speech again atop the battlements of Elsinore.) Grateful to be relieved of his watch by Barnardo on the castle ramparts, Francisco states that 'It is bitter cold', but then pauses before saying, with puzzlement on his face, ' – and I am sick at heart', as if afflicted by some strange (possibly mental) distemper. Then, as Barnardo is explaining what 'we two nights have seen' to Marcellus and Horatio, a pounding heartbeat is heard on the soundtrack, signalling anxiety. The camera moves in and out of focus to the pulsing beat as it closes in on the face of a Marcellus whose perceptions have been disturbed by the presence of Old Hamlet's ghost, and who now observes: 'Peace. Break thee off', before screaming, 'Look where it comes again'. Finally, that there is a distemper afflicting the inmates of Elsinore is strongly indicated by Marcellus speaking his line from 1.4.67 somewhat ahead of time – 'Something is rotten in the state of Denmark' – at which point he and Horatio together turn to gaze significantly at the camera as if toward another character (us), expecting a response. The camera now provides our **POV**, tracking to the right as if bidden to search out the cause of the 'rottenness', and now journeying through the castle, nosing its way down a stone staircase, past two empty thrones in a dark hall, pausing to view an archway while an oboe theme to become associated with Ophelia plays pleasantly on the sound track. A more jagged, disturbed theme from the strings now enters, the search proceeding rapidly into Gertrude's bedchamber, thematic heart of Olivier's film. As if satisfied it has found its goal, the camera zooms in, lingering on the 'enseamed bed' of Denmark, before the image **dissolves** to a **close-up** of Claudius drinking greedily from a goblet in the Great Hall, courtiers laughing around him as he drunkenly celebrates with Gertrude the acquisition of Old Hamlet's throne and wife, Hamlet's mother. The logic of the camera's search and discovery is clear: if something is rotten in the state of Denmark, this has been brought about by Gertrude's incestuous marriage with Claudius, and we are amply prepared to meet a young Hamlet tormented by an 'oedipal conflict'.

As the Great Hall scene develops, both this conflict and the isolation of a troubled Hamlet are conveyed visibly by Olivier's deployment of the camera. Olivier has stated that for the most part the film 'realised the drama through Hamlet's eyes', and 'when he's not present, through his imagination – his paranoia'. A great deal of the cinematic shape and logic of the film falls into place when we are told this, such as the camera's probing of Elsinore in search of 'rottenness': the 'character' that Marcellus and Horatio had turned to for an explanation was the paranoic mind's eye of Hamlet, given to us through the camera's eye. But for Olivier, the 'core of Hamlet is his loneliness and desolation after the death of his father, and his feeling of alienation from the new court' (Olivier, 1987, 178). This is conveyed very effectively by Olivier's use of **deep-focus** photography, evident in much of the film, and beginning with the Great Hall scene. Black and white film stock not only facilitated this technique, which, by keeping everything in the frame in focus, allows Olivier to show Hamlet as visually connected with those around him *at the same time* as he is at a physical, social and emotional distance from them. Black and white was also used because the 'tangerine and apricot faces' of Technicolor were not the faces Olivier wanted to haunt his 'melancholy Hamlet'. In this Great Hall scene, after a **shot/reverse shot** sequence featuring the faces of Claudius, Polonius and Laertes, there is a six-second deep-focus **long shot** from the perspective of Hamlet (whom we have yet to see). This is followed by a **medium shot** of Polonius rising, succeeded by another deep-focus long shot tableau of the whole court with the blond-haired Hamlet in the left foreground. (Olivier wanted his Hamlet to stand out from those around him, so giving him blond hair made him 'conspicuous in long and middle shots', but also helped to

Illustration 1   **Laurence Olivier's *Hamlet*, 1948.** This shot of Oliver as Hamlet and Jean Simmons as Ophelia exchanging looks at a distance is a fine example of the film's frequent use of deep-focus cinematography. This technique, by keeping both foreground and background in focus, has the effect of suggesting how characters may be both simultaneously connected to, *and* alienated from, one another.

'get well away from the glamorous brunette of a mediaeval king' – his look in *Henry V*.) This deep-focus shot enables Olivier to present simultaneously both Hamlet's perspective of what is going on around him, but also to establish his estrangement from an environment in which he is virtually a prisoner. The 'oedipal' element enters when, after Claudius remonstrates with Hamlet for the 'unmanly grief' he shows in mourning his father's death, Eileen Herlie as Gertrude bends close toward the seated Hamlet. To her plea that he 'Go not to Wittenberg', Hamlet replies, 'I shall in all my best obey you, madam', gazing deeply into his mother's lowered cleavage as he does so. Her response is to plant passionate, lingering kisses on his mouth before an irritated Claudius is forced to break up the lover-like exchange: 'Madam, come' (1.2.119–22). Such an exchange will be repeated between them at the end of the closet scene (3.4) on Gertrude's bed.

The court's departure from the Great Hall, leaving Hamlet alone, is shot from a **high angle**, emphasising his isolation and powerlessness, expressed vocally by the 'O that this too too solid flesh would melt' soliloquy. This is mainly spoken by Olivier in the 'interiorised' **voice-over** style as he paces around empty regal thrones and chairs, a visual **motif** repeated throughout the film to signal the absence of Old Hamlet. Instead of next having Horatio, Marcellus and Barnardo enter to report their sighting of the Ghost, Olivier introduces 'light' as a contrast with Hamlet's darkness by moving away from an enclosed space toward a series of arches opening out on to the light of day and the white-gowned figure of Ophelia. She is saying goodbye to her brother Laertes, who chides her for receiving the attentions of Hamlet, a chiding presently repeated by Polonius after we have been given a deep-focus shot of Hamlet from her **POV**, turning to gaze at her from far away at the other end of an arched corridor. The shot is then reversed and we see Ophelia in deep focus from over the shoulder of a seated Hamlet, a moment described by Olivier as when

> Hamlet sees Ophelia, in her innocent Victorian dress, an eternity away down the long corridor (150 feet away, actually), sitting in a solid wooden chair – in focus – with love clearly in her eyes. (Olivier, 1987, 179)

Deep-focus photography not only enables Olivier to suggest both connection and alienation between characters. By a refusal to focus exclusively on individuals, the technique also has the effect of depriving these human beings of significance.

As well as describing Olivier's *Hamlet* as a 'film about insanity,' script co-author Alan Dent also wrote a review of the film comparing its cinematic style to that of Robert Wiene's Expressionist master-piece *The Cabinet of Dr Caligari* (1920). Expressionist films like *Caligari* or *Nosferatu* (1922, Friedrich Murnau's version of Bram Stoker's *Dracula*) offer what Guntner calls a 'dramaturgy of light and shadows' to convey mood, emotion and an atmosphere expressive of anxiety, uncertainty and mental instability. Such **chiaroscuro** lighting and cavernous sets are also used by Olivier to communicate the dark, brooding and oppressively mysterious atmosphere of a claustrophobic Elsinore, all provided as a visual analogue of the insecure and angst-ridden interior worlds of the film's characters, in particular of course, the alienated inner world of Hamlet. Shadows especially tend to signal impending doom, and in conjunction with staircases, the doom of the person ascending or descending. Examples abound in *Hamlet*, such as when Hamlet is led up the tower stairs by the Ghost, or is followed by his own shadow going up to Gertrude's bedchamber. Estrangement is conveyed using stairs when Olivier objectifies an Ophelia abandoned, isolated and left helpless by Hamlet in the 'nunnery scene', the camera viewing her from a rising **crane shot** as it spirals up and up a winding staircase while Hamlet climbs to the battlements to make his 'To be or not to be' speech. (This is re-positioned from its textual location *before* the nunnery scene, which has the effect of suggesting that the agonised debate on suicide is caused by his troubled relationship with Ophelia, excluding the wider range of (political) pressures upon him.) As Guntner observes, in both the Expressionist film and **film noir**, stairways serve frequently 'as a bridge between appearance and reality, bourgeois normalcy and the unexplored depths of the human soul, the conscious and the subconscious' (Klein and Daphinoff, eds, 1997, 139).

The *film noir* tradition largely established by German émigré direc-tors like Fritz Lang, Otto Preminger and Billy Wilder in the 1940s are typically films in which an alienated hero struggles single-handedly to solve a crime (usually murder) in 'a strange, dark and threatening world in which the real and the unreal are very close to each other'. By 1948, Hollywood film audiences were so familiar with *noir* thrillers and detective movies infused with a bleak, claustrophobic fatalism, that Olivier's *Hamlet* would seem to be addressing familiar psycho-logical territory, albeit in the language of a Shakespeare tragedy.

Kenneth Branagh's *Hamlet* (UK, 1996)

Director: Kenneth Branagh

Producer: David Barron

Script: Kenneth Branagh

Medium: Colour, 70 mm, 242 minutes

Main actors: Kenneth Branagh (Hamlet); Julie Christie (Gertrude); Derek Jacobi (Claudius); Kate Winslet (Ophelia); Richard Briers (Polonius); Nicholas Farrell (Horatio); Michael Maloney (Laertes); Brian Blessed (Ghost)

Photography: Alex Thomson

Music: Patrick Doyle

If Olivier was obliged to cut the lines of *Hamlet* by half to make a film that cinema audiences accustomed to watching two-hour entertainment movies would find acceptable, Branagh was enabled to realise his vision of a 'full text' *Hamlet* extending to over double that length, making it the longest Shakespeare movie adaptation ever made. He had been trying to finance such a film for years, but (as ever) 'the perpetual reluctance of film companies to finance Shakespeare had frustrated each attempt'. Yet the man who had more or less single-handedly re-launched the Shakespeare-on-film genre with his *Henry V* (1989) and *Much Ado About Nothing* (1993) successes, now made the astute move of making *Mary Shelley's Frankenstein* (1994). The $22 m that this movie snatched in its 7-week cinematic release must have persuaded its financiers Castle Rock Entertainment to back Branagh's dream of making an epic-length film of Shakespeare's most famous play.

Basing his screenplay on a conflation of Folio and Q2 texts, Branagh wanted to present a *Hamlet* 'both personal, with enormous attention to the intimate relations between the characters, and at the same time epic, with a sense of the country at large and of a dynasty in decay' (Branagh, 1996, xiv–xv). Quibbles there may be about the degree to which the film achieves these aims. But by delivering the maximum amount of text possible, and then managing to find effective cinematic means to keep us watching the so-called eternity version of *Hamlet* for 242 minutes, Branagh has managed to convey all the themes of the play. The epic (political) dimensions of the story excised by the two major film versions of Olivier and Zeffirelli are restored here, being given visual emphasis in various ways. Hamlet's personal dilemmas and struggles are set in the context of military struggles between Denmark and Norway, the 'Fortinbras plot' being realised fully at the beginning, middle and end of the film, containing the epic dimensions of the story in a coherent dramatic framework. Branagh has in turn developed the political dimensions of the play more than any previous film version, reminding us in the process that a situation involving the struggle of a thwarted son to assert himself is not confined to the Danish royal family.

The film's nineteenth-century setting in a war-alert military state with most male characters in military uniform (Claudius and Polonius ostentatiously so) and martial training frequently seen in progress in the background emphasises that there are uncompromising imperialistic ambitions at stake here. This perspective is established more emphatically by using Blenheim Palace for the Elsinore exteriors, Blenheim being the home of the Dukes of Marlborough since 1704, and where Sir Winston Churchill was born and grew up. Claudius is described as speaking 'with a great Churchillian flourish' in the screenplay when, after dragging a reluctant Hamlet on to the dais he declares how the world should take note that his nephew is the 'most immediate to our throne' (1.2.108–9).

The aspects of political intrigue so integral to *Hamlet*'s dramatic edge are in this version brought out clearly by giving prominence to characters and parts of the play text usually cut. The first half of 2.1 where Polonius instructs his 'agent' Reynaldo in the techniques of spying on his son Laertes in France is invariably removed, its reinstatement here revealing how Polonius is as much a deviously hard-headed schemer as he is an old and bumbling senior state official (the way he is frequently played). Rosencrantz and Guildenstern – absent from the Olivier version – are shown here treacherously complicit with the usurping king against Hamlet, and their underhand willingness to comply with Claudius's deadly plan to have their old school friend assassinated in England clearly shows that 'they did make love to this employment', as Hamlet later reports to Horatio (5.2.58). Playing the full version of the scene in which Claudius skilfully manipulates Laertes into a plot to kill Hamlet in revenge for the death of his father Polonius (4.7), as Branagh himself says, helps to 'flesh out a richer portrait' of Claudius, instead of making Old Hamlet's murderer the 'conventional stage villain'.

Beyond the fuller account that all these textual restorations give to *Hamlet*'s scope as a political play, two other areas which benefit from the process concern the Ghost, and Hamlet's interactions with the visiting Players. The beginning of the film does all it can to suggest the uncanny atmosphere and anxiety implied by the play's opening words, Barnardo's inquiry, 'Who's there?' Without cast list or indeed any credits whatever, the first image seen in epic 70 mm film gauge is what Branagh (in the screenplay) calls 'the screen-filling legend carved deep in the stone, HAMLET', the word turning out to be carved on the stone plinth of the tomb upon which a statue of the (murdered) Old Hamlet stands. The director achieves several weighty effects simultaneously with this unmediated portentous articulation: a signal, of course, that we are about to see the 'legendary' Shakespeare play which has attained this status partly because of its worldwide fame and reputation as an impenetrable work of art. But it is portentous also in *exhibiting* a name that in one gesture symbolically displays the whole text on the screen at the same time as its location on a tombstone suggests that what follows may be associated with destiny and death. A few frames later, having shown us the icy grandeur of Elsinore's exterior and Barnardo's terror, the camera pulls back to focus on the hand of the statue shockingly wrenching the sword from its scabbard: we are being prepared for the chilling event of a Ghost's appearance. For the first time in any *Hamlet* film adaptation of this scene, the camera assumes the **POV** of the (advancing) Ghost, swooping us along and 'down on the retreating figures racing across the snow', who, just in time 'fling themselves behind a pillar'. Branagh here seems to have taken a lesson from the kind of horror film in which the audience is implicated in the visceral atmospherics of terror by being compelled to pursue victims from 'POV the monster'.

'Point of view' is without question an important area of concern for the way that Branagh shoots this movie. The delivery of a full text and no less than 45 (silent) visual interpolations to 'illustrate' various elements of the story mean that Hamlet's point of view in the drama is no longer distinctly privileged over the viewpoints of other key characters (as it is in Olivier's version, for instance). Such postmodern 'decentring' here can only be accentuated by Branagh's use of international stars to play some of the minor roles: for example, Gerard Depardieu as Reynaldo, Billy Crystal as First Gravedigger and Robin Williams as Osric. I shall return shortly to this key area of viewpoint, in relation to spying, and **identification**. The film gives a brilliantly played version of the scene where Hamlet, having in fantasy killed Claudius while he is at prayer in a confession box (a murder we see in a subliminal flash), actually refuses the opportunity (3.3.96–8). Hamlet is unwilling to kill Claudius at prayer because by doing so he will 'send to heaven' the selfsame 'villain' who had denied such a passage to Old Hamlet by murdering him 'with all his crimes broad blown' (3.4.77–8, 81). This spiritually motivated refusal, together with the uncut, highly dramatic delivery of the Ghost's speeches in this *Hamlet* conveys very potently how real the fears of a Catholic purgatory were in the still newly Protestant England of 1600–01, and how dangerous the tangling with other-worldly visitations were felt to be. (Towards the end of his second soliloquy, Hamlet worries that the spirit he has seen may 'be the devil, and the devil hath power / T'assume a pleasing shape', an idea concerning ghostly visitations still common in Shakespeare's era.) A surprisingly potent *religious* context is thus provided in this version for Hamlet's continuing uncertainties about life, death and the afterlife in the play, a context entirely missing in Zeffirelli's 'action' *Hamlet*, where the Ghost is virtually left out. The establishing of this context in turn makes us realise how important for the play Hamlet's words to Horatio are after he has been discoursing with the Ghost, in his statement that: 'There are more things in heaven and earth, Horatio, / Than are dreamt of in our philosophy' (1.5.168–9). The deficient 'philosophy' he refers to here is the Lutheran-based creed they have imbibed at their *alma mater*, Wittenburg (where the anti-Catholic Martin Luther had actually taught).

It has been said that *Hamlet* is 'a meditation on the multiple uses of theatrical conventions', that the theatre is the 'mode, the subject, the driving force and the central metaphor of the play'. If this is so, then Branagh, who has an equal facility for playing Shakespeare in the theatre and on film, here points up analogies between stage and screen, and in drawing our attention to the conventions of both filmic and theatrical representation, makes **metatheatrical** and **metacinematic** statements. Two illustrations must suffice. In the play-within-the-play, the stage and audience spaces are distinguished by using a flat horizontal stage for 'theatrical' space, and an almost vertically raked stack of bleachers for the auditorium in front. On the one hand, Branagh as Hamlet moves between stage and audience, blurring both the line between the two spheres, yet by doing so he also signals his role as player and director *within* the play, providing additional metacinematic comment on his role as film-maker. A further, more variable code is introduced in this scene by making the gazes of different characters determine where the actual performance or stage 'space' *is*, for the spectacle keeps shifting, depending on *who* is being watched by *whom*. For example, Horatio's spying gaze through his opera glasses is

Illustration 2   **Kenneth Branagh's *Hamlet*, 1996**. © Castle Rock Entertainment. Licensed by Warner Bros. Entertainment Inc. All Rights Reserved. Branagh as Hamlet confronting his own image while deliberating on the prospect of murder – or his own death (3.1.58–90 – the famous third soliloquy). The sequence provides a disturbing and doubly reflexive metonymic of menace for the viewer, who identifies with Hamlet's dilemmas even as the Prince (unknowingly) faces his mortal enemy Claudius, the regicide spying on his troublesome nephew from behind a two-way mirrored door.

focused on how Claudius, Gertrude and Ophelia are 'acting' when Hamlet taunts them during the progress of the play; while a shocked and fascinated court audience turns in alarm toward the king and queen to gauge their response when Hamlet publically blurts out his various scandalising comments (3.2.85–138, 209–48).

A second, brilliant conjunction of devices for exposing and exploring how theatrical and filmic convention may convey meaning is when Branagh performs Hamlet's third soliloquy while advancing menacingly upon his own image in a mirrored door. This occurs after the cleverly shot sequence in which Branagh's camera circles round and round the figures of Claudius, Rosencrantz, Guildenstern, Gertrude, Ophelia and Polonius as they debate the causes of Hamlet's 'crafty madness'. The instability of the situation is here reproduced by the camera's refusal to settle for any single **POV** adjudged reliable, the viewpoints of all being tainted in one way or another by ignorance or deception. Polonius and Claudius hide behind the two-way mirrored door, for the purpose of spying on the actions of Hamlet, to whom Polonius has 'loosed' his daughter Ophelia, and they jump in terror when he suddenly whips out a dagger at the lines 'When he himself might his quietus make / With a bare bodkin' (3.1.77–8). As the camera continues to close toward the mirror with Hamlet, we come to see his self-threatening reflection almost from his POV, thus forcing us to reflect, along with him perhaps, 'who's there?' The effects of using the mirror in this way are multiple. We unfold ourselves along with Hamlet and become him as, with dagger drawn, he confronts both himself and his enemies Claudius and Polonius behind the mirror. But not only do we have here a visual expression of the processes of **identification** at work in the soliloquy: the reflective mechanism deployed shows how Shakespeare's own definition of the function of drama – 'to hold, as 'twere, the mirror up to nature' (3.2.20) – can work for film as well as for theatre.

Running at four hours as it does, Branagh's *Hamlet* may not always manage to sustain the tautness of dramatic effect that more economically cinematic translations of Shakespeare's play might accomplish, such as Zeffirelli's film. And errors there may have been in casting, such as Jack Lemmon's Marcellus, whose articulation is embarrassingly wooden. Or in design, where the ground splintering under the feet of Hamlet as he pursues his father's ghost is a brilliant attempt to reproduce the terror of the underworld that Elizabethan audiences would have felt, but which is realised here in ways that verge on the clunky and clumsy. But this is a *Hamlet* whose blemishes are minor. It features much fine acting, making the full text utterly accessible and providing a dramatic delivery in settings that uniquely reveal on film a coherent wide-arcing plot at the same time as multiple thematic resonances are repeatedly exposed. The movie also breaks new ground, not only by melding and toying with theatrical and cinematic conventions already noted, but also by creating a new cinematic device. These are the silent flashbacks and inset sequences introduced by Branagh to visualise elements in the **backstory** of the play, or to offer visual extrapolations implied by various reported situations in it (e.g. the preparations for war, or the 'invented' love sequence between Ophelia and Hamlet shown as Polonius reads Hamlet's letter to Claudius and Gertrude). These are often far more than unsophisticated visual illustrations of the text, which they may seem to be at first glance. At their best, they not only offer an imaginative method of enabling the director to blend together elements of film and theatre, they can also be seen as the cinematic equivalent of Shakespeare's own dramatic insets, films-within-the-film in dumb show which inform and entertain at the same time as a homage of the silent screen to the silent stage is presented.

Michael Almereyda's *Hamlet* (USA, 2000)

Director: Michael Almereyda
Producer: Amy Hobby and Andrew Fierberg
Script: Michael Almereyda
Medium: Colour, 35 mm (enlarged from 16 mm), 106 minutes
Main actors: Ethan Hawke (Hamlet); Diane Venora (Gertrude); Kyle MacLachlan (Claudius); Julia Stiles (Ophelia); Bill Murray (Polonius); Karl Geary (Horatio); Liev Schreiber (Laertes); Sam Shepard (Ghost)
Photography: John de Borman
Original Music: Carter Burwell

Forced by tight funding to shoot his *Hamlet* 'fast and cheap' on 16 mm stock, Michael Almereyda was nevertheless sufficiently assured by the example of what Welles called his 'rough charcoal sketch' – *Macbeth* (1948) – to believe that 'you don't need lavish production values to make a Shakespeare movie that's accessible and alive. Shakespeare's language, after all, is lavish enough' (Almereyda, vii). In other words, if a director can offer imaginative visual translations of Shakespeare's verbal text to communicate its meaning well enough, there may be less of a need for this text to be spoken in full: a little of Shakespeare's rich poetic language may go a long way on screen. A viewing of Almereyda's film confirms this, for despite utilising only about 40% of the play's lines and running at a mere 106 minutes – well over two hours shorter than Branagh's 'unexpurgated, all-star treatment' (as Almereyda calls it) – it is a pleasant surprise to discover that this very American adaptation captures much of the dramatic essence of Shakespeare's *Hamlet*. Shifting the royal court of Elsinore into an 'omnipresent Denmark Corp' that rules supreme in 2000 Manhattan's glossy but cutthroat business world, Almereyda's Shakespeare update with its soundtrack mix of modern music and hip-youth lead actors would seem to be following in the footsteps of Luhrmann's *Romeo + Juliet*. But the film offered here is targeted at an **arthouse** rather than MTV audience, and uses film technique, codes and language with a subtlety and power seriously different from the brilliant but ultimately flashy and sentimental effects achieved by Luhrmann.

Crucial to this cinematic re-visioning of *Hamlet* was Almereyda's determination to maintain

> a parallel visual language that might hold a candle to Shakespeare's poetry. There was no wish to illustrate the text, but to focus it, building a visual structure to accommodate Shakespeare's imagery and ideas.
>
> (Almereyda, x)

The skilful weaving of cinematic language and editing to realise this aesthetic mode produces many brilliant shots and sequences, some examples of which are discussed below. But perhaps the principal device used to invest the movie with the essential dramatic energies and meanings of Shakespeare's play is that of presenting two radically contrasting visual worlds and viewpoints. One world, represented and shot in colour from some notionally 'objective' **POV** using the 'master' Super 16 mm camera, provides the dominant visual and narrative structure of the film, displaying the glitzy but controlling modern terrains of Claudius's Manhattan business empire. The other world is Hamlet's, a radically intimate perspective frequently presented through the lens of his work as amateur film-maker (Ophelia is a young photographer). Hamlet's POV and world is often shown to us in the grainy black and white images of his own pixelvision camera's video diary, or in *The Mousetrap: A tragedy by Hamlet, Prince of Denmark*, since here the 'play within the play' becomes a 'video within the film', Hamlet's successful device for inciting Claudius to 'unkennel' his 'occulted guilt' (3.2.74, 73). We are admitted to Hamlet's painful consciousness so effectively compared with the world of scheming corporate power led by Claudius, that the understated, fragmented approach used creates a strongly sympathetic alternative reality for the viewer. For this postmodern Hamlet with a conscience, Manhattan is a prison-house of ruthless commercialism – and it's personal.

One reason Almereyda's *Hamlet* turns into what he calls 'the most condensed straight film adaptation in English' is that a lot of the footage shot to reproduce scenes from the play was discarded, many of the 'best and worst ideas' being 'sacrificed for the sake of clarity and momentum' (Almereyda, xii). An excellent example of how such cutting becomes necessary to satisfy the expectations of the screen audience comes at the beginning of the film, where the original opening playing a version of 1.1 in the lobby of the Hotel Elsinore was found at a test screening by Miramax to have yielded the second worst scores in the company's history. As Almereyda says, not only was the Elizabethan language exchanged by Bernardo, Horatio and Marcella (a female version of Marcellus, re-cast as Horatio's girlfriend) too confusingly dense and fast for the audience to follow, but 'it was troublingly clear that Hamlet's first appearance in the film came too late and felt flat' (Almereyda, 135). Realising that 'a more urgent start' was required, a new introduction now not only brought in Ethan Hawke's Hamlet more quickly, but it demonstrated how a little of Shakespeare's rich poetic language can indeed go a long way on screen, dramatically speaking. The first 13 minutes embodying five sequences take us up to the moment that the Ghost (Sam Shepard), refusing Horatio's appeal to speak to him, **dissolves** into this film's version of purgatory, a Pepsi drinks machine, offering a sequence of events whose meaning and drama are conveyed with superb filmic economy.

The very first two-minute sequence inserted prior to the white-on-red title of HAMLET appearing on screen offers a brilliant collage of images and words setting the Manhattan scene and an introduction to the figure and character of Hamlet himself. From the rear-window of Claudius's stretch-limo advancing toward Times Square at night we see the bright colours of neon-lit buildings looming high and flashing by while onscreen appears a series of pithy statements giving 'the story so far':

- New York City, 2000
- The King and CEO of Denmark Corporation is dead
- The King's widow has hastily remarried his younger brother
- The King's son, Hamlet, returns from school, suspecting foul play ...

When the limo stops, Hamlet in Nepalese Bhote woolly hat slouches across the street toward Hotel Elsinore with shoulder bag full of camera gear, moving out of frame right to leave Almereyda's lens lingering long and close on the Hamlet Corporation logo fixed high up on a giant plasma screen bearing the equally large legend, 'Panasonic'. The message that visual representation and communication are to be compelling themes here is confirmed when, backed 'by a cross-mix of Morcheeba and orchestral music by Niels Gade', we are shown the face of 'poet/film-maker/perpetual grad student' Hamlet in close-up grainy black and white pixelvision pictures, confiding to his own camera some of his character's most heart-felt lines from the play. These short, fragmented takes of Hamlet on himself are cut together to give dramatic emphasis to his performer/film editor's cynically tortured outlook on a world pervaded by man's inhumanity to man:

> I have of late – but wherefore I know not – lost all my mirth
> What a piece of work is a man! How noble in reason, how infinite in faculties, in form and moving how express and admirable, in action how like an angel, in apprehension how like a god –

A ringing phone forces Hamlet to interrupt his 'take', the video diary resuming with images cut in to include TV shots of a Stealth bomber creating explosive devastation, while his flat-solemn **voice-over** offers a verbal statement on man in severe ironic contradiction:

> – the beauty of the world, the paragon of animals

As the sound track brings in Morcheeba again, he mutters his bleak, questioning conclusion:

> And yet to me, what is this quintessence of dust?

We now pull back to see Hamlet in the 16 mm 'real time' of the colour film/master narrative as at editing desk he cuts together further shots of his own attempt 'to be' Hamlet. These are the first of many **metacinematic** statements of the film; the camera 'invading' his clamshell editing screen that first turns to snow before dissolving to the white-on-red HAMLET title beginning the film proper: what kind of status and value will the succeeding edited-together visual representations have for us?

This two-minute sequence of visual fragments that now 'kickstarts the movie' not only gives 'the Prince a series of intimate close-ups and a private (pixelated) language', as Almereyda says. This engaging opening **montage** also offers both a concentrated slice of the film's overall approach to representing and involving us in the mind of its main character, as well as demonstrating the typical way its cool style of 'focusing' the Shakespeare text will deliver that very 'visual structure' the director wanted in order 'to accommodate Shakespeare's imagery and ideas'. The glossily explicit colour master-narrative of the enclosing 'frame' film starts and continues to convey the Manhattan spaces and surfaces among which it is shot as hard and impersonal, creating the feeling of an excluding and insensitive prison – a 'hot' medium in the jargon of Sixties' mass media guru Marshall McLuhan. By contrast, Hamlet's grainy, cynical and agonised black and white movie of himself and the cruel world around him is conveyed inclusively and sensitively, supplying a 'cool' and involving account of 'the Hamlet dilemma', if ever there was one.

When we follow Hamlet into the Hotel Elsinore press conference where Claudius is announcing his take-over of Denmark Corp and his marriage to Gertrude – who like a 'first lady' stands supportively at his side – it is once again apparent that this film is to be all about competing visual representations of the world in which Hamlet finds himself. Pixel camera and clamshell monitor in his hands, he moves about conspicuously filming the event hordes of press photographers are also recording. Out on the sidewalk, Almereyda uses Wellesian **low angle** shooting to convey a powerful family in crisis as the mystified Gertrude and a dapper, irritated Claudius (his ever-present bodyguard in tow) quiz Hamlet on his melancholy condition while they walk along. Hamlet's halting on the sidewalk to tell the queen that he has 'that within which passes show; / These but the trappings and the suits of woe' is a rare moment when Hamlet's power 'to be' is asserted over the 'seeming' of Gertrude and Claudius. Shortly after, the tense power relation of mother, son and uncle is conveyed in one of the most effective filmic images of the movie. This is when Gertrude, now sitting in the limousine, winds her window halfway down, and takes off her sunglasses to plead with Hamlet not return to Wittenburg. While she speaks, we also see Hamlet and his deadly enemy Claudius reflected in the car window, standing side by side against the Manhatten skyscrapers so emblematic of the power of this usurper.

Hawke's film-making Hamlet uses his pixelcamera and editing machine to reflect on and to become the character/persona of the Shakespeare text, going so far as to shoot himself about to shoot himself (gun to head) before the master-camera gets to secure the 'objectifying' setting for his 'To be or not to be' soliloquy. This is performed by Hawke in **voice-over** as he paces irritably up and down the 'Action' aisles of a Blockbuster video store, ironically showing us the thwarted man of action surrounded by numerous video-films counterfeiting 'Action'. Reflections and refractions suggesting the devious, sinister, evasive and oblique nature of much of the reality of the Manhattan Hamlet world are also communicated on and through glass and other surfaces in the movie, occurring almost as pervasively as the facilitating yet entrapping items of electronic communication gadgetry that find their way into nearly every scene. Ophelia is frequently seen and sees herself reflected in water: that of Claudius's penthouse pool, and especially in the Guggenheim Museum water feature where she will drown. We see Rosencrantz asking Hamlet

Illustration 3 **Michael Almereyda's 'Manhatten'** *Hamlet,* **2000.** Ethan
Hawke as Hamlet roams the 'Action' aisles of a Blockbuster video store while
performing the 'to be or not to be' soliloquy (3.1.58–90). Visual ironies abound
as Hamlet, surrounded by numerous videos counterfeiting and arresting
'action' on tape, reflects on how his own 'native hue of resolution/Is sicklied
o'er with the pale cast of thought', causing the currents of his own impulses to
revenge to 'lose the name of action'.

where Polonius's dead body is, their images reflected in the round
glass door of a Laundromat washing machine as the prince gazes at his
bloodstained clothes going round and round. We see Hamlet complet-
ing his 'How all occasions do inform against me' soliloquy while gazing at himself in a toilet mirror on the plane in which Rosencrantz and
Guildenstern are taking him to England. One of the film's most resonant reflections occurs just before Kyle MacLachlan's sleek but rat-
tled Claudius confides his plot to kill Hamlet to Laertes. Here we see
the king gazing into the wardrobe mirror shattered and splintered by
the bullet from Hamlet's gun that had killed Polonius. 'Where th'of-
fence is, let the great axe fall', he mutters, unaware that the mirror he
abstractedly looks into as a reminder of Hamlet as killer, offers to *us* a
fractured image **metonymically** conveying *him* as a murderer whose
diabolical scheming sets him apart as the guilty instigator of a commercial dynasty suffering collapse.

As I said at the beginning, this is a film which gains much of its power from using two counterpointed visual discourses. The fine actors playing the parts of the 'older generation' characters, MacLachlan's Claudius, Diane Venora's Gertrude, Bill Murray's Polonius and above all Sam Shepard's chillingly naturalistic Ghost, all are given space and time to speak their lines often in continuous takes, conveyed by the colour master-camera. But it is the contrasting, more visually and verbally cross-cut and uneven discourse conveying the emotional plight of young Hamlet and his friends – especially Julia Stiles's so-young and victimised Ophelia and Karl Geary's laid-back but movingly loyal Horatio – that is brought forward to impress and convince us. Furthermore, the film undoubtedly gains much of its power from the surly anguish with which Hawke invests his Hamlet, a power drawing on American cinema history to make itself felt. This is revealed when, without the impassioned acting of the Player King for him to respond to, TV images of James Dean 'suffering beautifully in *East of Eden*' (as Almereyda states in the screenplay) are used to incite Hamlet to his 'O what a rogue and peasant slave am I' soliloquy. In coming to reconstruct *Hamlet* for an **arthouse** film audience, Almereyda says he kept remembering the 'adolescence-primed impact and meaning' that this play had always held for him, and the 'rampant parallels between the melancholy Dane' and his 'many doomed and damaged heroes', among them James Dean and Holden Caulfield ('antihero' of *The Catcher in the Rye*).

Ethan Hawke's complementary reading of the play is made plain when he states that the reason Hamlet had for him always come off 'so annoying, infantile, and self-indulgent is that the guy playing him is 10 to 20 years too old for the part':

> He is a bright young man struggling deeply with his identity, his moral code, his relationship to his parents and with his entire surrounding community. Hamlet was always much more like Kurt Cobain or Holden Caulfield than Sir Laurence Olivier. (Almereyda, xiv)

These readings of Hamlet by the film's director and leading actor partly explain why this skilfully cut-down but cleverly shot film delivers such a rich visual and aural translation of Shakespeare's language for a modern film audience. Never before had there been a *Hamlet* film in which the Prince was played by an actor in his twenties: even Branagh was 35 when he shot his *Hamlet*. At 27, Hawke was not only the right age for the Hamlet of the play, but by consistently presenting the Prince as a smoulderingly melancholic James Dean figure done down by a power-obsessed corporate culture, a fine American Shakespeare film has been made. It is a movie that speaks 'with most miraculous organ' to the youthful audience who are the prime target for Shakespeare film-makers of the new millennium.

Orson Welles's *Macbeth* (USA, 1948)

Director: Orson Welles
Producers: Charles K. Feldman, Orson Welles
Script: Orson Welles
Medium: Black and white, 35 mm, 107 minutes
Main actors: Orson Welles (Macbeth); Jeanette Nolan (Lady Macbeth); Edgar Barrier (Banquo); Dan O'Herlihy (Macduff); Peggy Webber (Lady Macduff); Erskine Sanford (Duncan); Roddy McDowall (Malcolm); Alan Napier (a holy father); John Dierkes (Ross); Keene Curtis (Lennox)
Photography: John L. Russell
Music: Jacques Ibert

Coming from the maker of *Citizen Kane* (USA, 1941), the virtuoso experiment in cinematic style and technique which many still regard as one of the greatest twentieth-century movies, one might expect Orson Welles's film adaptation of *Macbeth* to display similar filmic sophistication. It does do that in many ways, despite such restrictions as Welles having to work with the facilities of low-budget Hollywood 'B' movie studio Republic Pictures, and a tight 23-day shooting schedule. The film bears some comparison with Olivier's *Hamlet* of the same year (1948), since both black and white movies use Expressionist techniques of **chiaroscuro** lighting to create claustrophobic sets conveying the sense of psychological oppressiveness and anxiety which inhabit both plays. Despite the technical brilliance of Olivier's movie, Welles's approach to Shakespearean adaptation here involves a more self-consciously cinematic re-working. The endeavours of Welles in his various drama projects were always best focused when making films as works of art, a process in which he drew as inventively as possible on the grammar of film – sometimes even extending its language somewhat – in order to achieve the dramatic effects he wanted.

The dramatic effects established from the outset in *Macbeth* are ones that focus on its potential as a mysterious drama of supernatural malevolence; these are apparent from the first sixty seconds of the film prior to opening titles and credits. Against a background of ever-moving clouds and mist, the figures of the three witches in silhouette are seen bending over a steaming, bubbling cauldron cackling their incantatory chorus from 4.1: 'Double, double, toil and trouble, / Fire burn, and cauldron bubble'. As Welles has them continuing to mutter more lines of magical formulae from the play, we see close-ups of the fiercely bubbling and fiery 'hell broth' being concocted, until out of it they draw a figure hand-fashioned from the clayey mixture, holding it aloft and uttering the name 'Macbeth!' – the film title which now appears on screen. The arched brows of this clay doll's visage give it a remarkable resemblance to Welles as Macbeth. At the outset the assumption is therefore established that by magically fashioning his likeness, the witches are able to exert an evil power over the thane similar to the way voodoo witch doctors of Haiti are able to do over their victims. Welles had produced an all-black 'voodoo' production of *Macbeth* ten years before in Harlem, New York, so evidently draws on his earlier production, but also uses other 'pagan' elements too. However, the key point to note in this opening is the pictorial method by which Welles conveys chilling meanings and effects prefiguring his approach to the whole screen adaptation. For instance, everything glimpsed among the swirling clouds, mists and hideous broth of the cauldron, except for the doll's visage, is indistinct and murkily anonymous. This indistinctness not only applies to the figures and faces of the witches, only ever visible in **backlit**-created silhouettes, but also applies to camera shots that continually **dissolve** one into another, reproducing cinematically the very fluidity of magical transformation performed by the witches.

Welles omits completely 1.2, where Duncan greets the bleeding Captain and hears his report of the battle. This could be because he wants to foreground not a specifically historical, social, political or military situation for the play, but provide rather a blurred, de-contextualised state of affairs in which the evil manipulations of the witches over Macbeth are the most powerful forces present. This creates a space of dream-like psychological terror for the dramatic events to unfold in, rather than a space of realistic, everyday surfaces. The impenetrable and swirling mist thus becomes a kind of external simulacrum of Macbeth's disturbed and metamorphosing thoughts as the witches' spells activate his susceptible ambitions: the mixture of 'fair and foul' elements in what we see is a kind of preparation for the mental torments that are to afflict Macbeth. The obscure and terrific effects established by the witches in the mist develop when we see Macbeth and Banquo riding through it toward them. For after we hear on the soundtrack the second witch's incantation from 4.1, 'By the pricking of my thumbs, / Something wicked this way comes', comes Macbeth's innocent comment to Banquo of how 'so fair and foul a day' he has not seen, ominously announcing the fortune that is shortly to be visited on him. 'Hailing' him as Thane of Cawdor, the witches in their cat-like screeches reveal that Macbeth 'shall be king hereafter', the Cawdor regalia being hung around the voodoo doll's neck and a miniature crown set on its head. These are the very head and crown that will be lopped off at the end of the film, a clever device to avoid having to depict Macbeth's decapitation, yet which will signal the end of his bloody reign. The Gothic atmosphere is now intensified as, brandishing a large Celtic cross, 'a holy father' arrives and the witches, hissing, are forced to back off like vampires subdued by a crucifix. The genre conventions and style of 1930s black and white horror films like *Dracula* and *Frankenstein* appear not to have been very far away from Welles's mind in his design of the *mis-en-scène* for this film. The 'holy father' character wholly invented by Welles is introduced to provide the film with a 'good versus evil' structure, a design evident from the original spoken prologue by Welles, dropped for the DVD/video releases. This statement had described the setting as an 'ancient Scotland, savage', where 'the cross itself is newly arrived' and where,

> Plotting against Christian law and order are the agents of chaos, priests of hell and magic; sorcerers and witches. Their tools are ambitious men.
> Men like Macbeth.

When Macbeth and his entourage ride off following the announce-ment of the witches' prophecy, we are left with a stunning image of the three witches atop their rock chorusing 'Hail!' while each grips (in a play tinctured throughout with the equivocations of evil) a forked stave in the shape of the letter Y. This cleverly suggests the sinister question Why? as a counterpoint to the 'newly arrived' but evidently feeble powers of the Christian Cross (what Anthony Davies calls a 'semiotic dichotomy'). That the Christian light is very limited in its powers to thwart evil is revealed in the remaining scenes of the film, where the forces of a primitive malevolence are shown to hold sway. As the holy father writes out the letter dictated by Macbeth to Lady Macbeth, we see that the metallic blisters on Macbeth's tunic echo the muddy, bubbling appearance of the witches' hell-broth, identifying him with their evil powers and purposes. This **metonymic**ally menac-ing connection is followed by another effective linking transition when, towards the end of dictating his letter, Macbeth's voice is displaced by that of Jeanette Nolan as Lady Macbeth, this 'verbal dis-solve' coinciding with a visual **dissolve** to his 'dearest partner of great-ness' reading it as she lies on the bed in their castle. Their collusion

visually and aurally established, her candle is ominously blown out by
the wind, leaving her in a fittingly 'thick night' to conjure up the evil
spirits she requires to help 'stop up th'access and passage to remorse',
an emotion inimical to her planned murder of Duncan, which will
facilitate the fulfilment of the witches' prophecy of Macbeth becoming
king. She begins this speech of darkness while sensuously stroking an
animal fur on the bed, suggesting bestial impulses that are echoed
soon after when Cawdor is led to the scaffold accompanied by the ritualistic pounding of primitive drums. Eroticism and violence are evidently in play when we see Macbeth and Lady Macbeth embrace
while the axe slices through Cawdor's head. And even though this execution is meant as a Christian rite, together with the collective ceremony overseen by the holy father as a prophylactic against Satan,
when the 'amen' is said, all present blow out their lighted candles,
strangely indicative of a pagan *denial* of the 'Christian light,' rather
than its affirmation.

   Camera movement is relatively rare in *Macbeth*, but the camera is
nevertheless used skilfully to convey meanings produced by
Shakespeare's text, primarily those associated with Macbeth's disturbed subjective state, or projecting the troubled relationship he
bears to other characters. There are two instances where **subjective
camera shots** are used to convey Macbeth's troubled interior state.
The first occurs in the long 'noirish' prelude to Duncan's murder, after
Macbeth emerges from the shadows where he wishes Banquo 'good
repose'. After we hear him speak (in **voice-over**) of 'withered murder'
moving 'like a ghost' from his second soliloquy (2.1.52, 56), the camera
dissolves from his image using blurred focus into a **close-up** of the
head of the Macbeth voodoo doll being 'penetrated' by a dagger blade
superimposed over it. This image then blurs back into that of Macbeth
advancing slowly toward the dagger-as-camera, failing in his attempt
to grab it: 'Is this a dagger which I see before me, / The handle toward
my hand?' (2.1.33–4). After more camera-blur dissolves into and out
of images that include for him the feared entrance to Duncan's room,
he sees that this and the 'dagger of the mind' are indeed 'false' cre-
ations 'proceeding from the heat-oppressèd brain' (2.1.38–9). The second example occurs at the banquet, when an anxious, sweating
Macbeth, now king, raises a toast to the absent Banquo. But his face
becomes fearful, and as he lowers his goblet in a trance, from his **POV**
the camera shows the diners imitating him, his stricken gaze transfixed
in terror by something at the end of the table. The shadow created by
the lowering of his arm now functions as a kind of **wipe** moving his

focus from the actuality of the banquet and its attendees, to the 'shadow realm' of his guilty mind, which has created Banquo's ghost before him. Gripped by this apparition, he asks, staring, 'Behold, look, lo – how say you?' (3.4.68), the camera following the movement of an elongated shadow of his pointing finger along the rough-hewn walls of the chamber toward the figure of Banquo's ghost, sitting alone at the end of the table, and seen, as it must be, from Macbeth's POV, for it is invisible to the POV of anyone else, as other camera shots reveal. It is a brilliant visual transition, soon matched by another in which Macbeth advances angrily toward his hallucination muttering 'Well, what care I?', the camera then cutting to the POV of Banquo's ghost focused on the man who ordered his murder. It is a remarkable shot, for in this **subjective camera** work the camera is viewing Macbeth's reaction to the consequences of his own actions, viewed from the POV of those grim consequences.

Welles's economic use of **montage** to create narrative energy and pace in the early part of the movie switches at certain points into a more theatrical mode, sometimes employing long unbroken takes, as with the ten-minute sequence featuring Macbeth and Lady Macbeth before and after the ('offstage') murder of Duncan. In this notable sequence (unaccountably cut by Republic in the film's original release), we see examples of camera use that are classically Wellesian, and the visual outcome of which captures some of the 'equivocating' elements so essential to the meanings of this play. It has been said of Welles's films that from being shown the spatial disposition and angles between characters, it should be possible without the aid of one word of dialogue to understand the relationships between them. Throughout this sequence, the power-relationship between Macbeth and Lady Macbeth tends to be defined by the vertical position of one to the other – the character looming above suggesting dominance over the lower one. This meaning-effect can also be enhanced by the position of the camera: a powerful figure looking down at the camera, and a weaker one looking up at it. For much of the early part of the sequence, before Macbeth goes to murder Duncan, we see the uneasy Macbeth – this is not long after the 'dagger of the mind' episode – being berated and sexually taunted for his equivocation by a Lady Macbeth standing above him. Though with reluctance, Macbeth now mounts the stairs to undertake the murder, thereby showing activity and some dominance. After killing Duncan, Macbeth descends the staircase, pausing on it above Lady Macbeth to say 'I have done the deed' (2.2.14), and so maintaining a dominant power relation. But once he walks on down past her, he stays below, until, refusing to put the bloody daggers back next to Duncan's drugged grooms, he is chastised by Lady Macbeth, this time for being 'Infirm of purpose!' (2.2.50) On her return from replacing the daggers, she pauses to stand above him on the staircase, maintaining her dominance while he stands lost in a daze, only disappearing from view for a time while he complies with Lady Macbeth's injunction to get on his nightgown. The cutaway that ends this single ten-minute 'theatrical' take shows Macduff running along the castle rampart from Duncan's apartment, and in the following five minutes there could not be more of a contrast in pace and style of shooting. No less than 45 camera shots of varying closeness and angle are swiftly cut together in these minutes to convey the confusion and agitation while numerous characters speak, move and interact in their various responses to the murder's discovery.

At the end of the movie, isolated by his tyrannical and murderous efforts to maintain power, Macbeth is slaughtered by the avenging Macduff, quick-cutting multiple **zoom** out **shots** of cheering troops holding blazing torches and crosses aloft seeming to confirm Macduff's proclamation that now 'The time is free' (5.11.21). Yet the final frames of the movie belong to the witches, bringing us back full circle to the film's unease-making use of visual and aural **dissolves**. For from brass fanfares and the reverse-zoom shots of torch-bearing troops conveying victorious dynamism, the camera **dissolves** to a crown-like image of Macbeth's castle continuing the slow-reverse zoom, a movement soon revealing the three witches and their 'questioning' Y staves in the bottom of the frame. The music has metamorphosed from a mood of boisterous triumphalism to that of quiet and sinister mystery, several more visual dissolves taking us through the mists of the film's opening to a close-up of the 'weird sisters', one of whom is given the film's last word: 'Peace: the charm's wound up' (1.3.35). Through its fluidity of images and sounds, this film without doubt not only suggests the torturing unease and ambiguity of the evil world Macbeth is drawn into and creates; through the fluxions of film technique that he commands so well, Welles also manages to convey the mutabilities of the mind, the desires and the emotions, phenomena which figure so pervasively in Shakespeare's tragic drama.

Roman Polanski's *Macbeth* (UK, 1971)

Director: Roman Polanski
Producer: Andrew Braunsburg
Script: Roman Polanski, Kenneth Tynan
Medium: Colour, Todd A-O 35 mm, 134 minutes
Main actors: Jon Finch (Macbeth); Francesca Annis (Lady Macbeth); Martin Shaw (Banquo); Terence Bayler (Macduff); Diane Fletcher (Lady Macduff); Nicholas Selby (Duncan); Stephen Chase (Malcolm); John Stride (Ross); Paul Shelley (Donalbain)
Photography: Gilbert Taylor
Music: The Third Ear Band

The opening of Polanski's *Macbeth* resembles that of Welles's film in two respects: it begins with the witches, and there is mist. But there the similarity ends. Much of the power of Welles's black and white movie comes from his use of expressionist and film noir conventions on a studio set of high artifice to convey a drama of mysteriously supernatural evil overcoming Christian good. Evil pervades Polanski's film too, but this is shown as emerging more realistically from the 'natural' psychological motivations of the characters, rather than through the 'supernatural' magic of the witches, not semi-ethereal beings here but 'practising' flesh and blood witches, living in a female community of their own. They, Macbeth, Banquo and the others are filmed realistically amid the bleak, rain-swept hilly landscape of North Wales, a natural exterior location assisting the projection of an eleventh-century Scottish society of quasi-tribal clans led by a king who rules by the warrior codes of courage and loyalty. It is a setting in which Polanski's understanding of *Macbeth* as a play exploring 'the violence at the heart of usurpation' (Kliman, 1992, 119) can be developed and exposed with some power. An apt location of this sort was important for providing the film with the appropriate tone of social rivalry Polanski wanted to establish in realistic characters inhabiting a raw, godless world of self-serving evil and violence. Yet this setting is only one of the many elements that make the film among the most enduring – because so artistically effective – Shakespeare adaptations ever made. Casting choices, ***mis-en-scène, montage***, use of colour, visual and sound **motifs**, careful textual editing, and chillingly effective 'period' music by The Third Ear Band – all these factors are creatively exploited to make a coherent and engaging dramatic mix by Polanski, and I will explore some of these in what follows.

It is useful at the outset to notice a good example of how Polanski manipulates both cinematic space and Shakespeare's text to make psychology predominate in character motivation. After Macbeth and Banquo have heard the witches' prophecies early on in the film, an intensely curious Macbeth dismounts from his horse to follow the weird sisters, who have retreated out of sight to the door of their underground lair, slamming it shut on him. Unable to see this, Banquo asks 'Whither are they vanished?' Macbeth replies with the lines the play gives him, but his report is a lie: 'Into the air / And what seemed corporal / Melted as breath into the wind' (1.3.78–80). Quickly seduced by the promise of a high destiny ('All Hail Macbeth, that shall be king hereafter'), Macbeth craftily keeps the location of the witches' lair to himself: later he will return to consult them and their oracular powers in pursuit of his own power-obsessed interests.

With a reputation for an interest and involvement in the macabre at the time of making *Macbeth* – especially through his 1968 Hitchcockian gothic melodrama *Rosemary's Baby* and the shockingly bloody murder of his wife Sharon Tate by the Manson gang in 1969 – Polanski said in an interview at the time that he was 'more interested in the behaviour of people under stress'. Certainly, from the moment that Macbeth hears the witches' prophesy that he will 'be king hereafter', he is a character under stress, a mind divided. This is in the play, revealed by his early conflicting reflections on the prophecy: 'My thought, whose murder yet is but fantastical, / Shakes so my single state of man that function / Is smothered in surmise, / And nothing is but what is not' (1.3.138–41). This reflection is spoken in **voice-over** interior monologue, a device that enables Polanski to emphasise the 'split state of man' motivating the mind of Macbeth, and which is sustained to such an extent that it is used more in this study of psychological obsession and its outcomes than in any previous Shakespeare adaptation. In a wider sense, Polanski also juxtaposes the everyday with the disturbed for much of the time, pursuing his typical filmic goal of presenting 'a realistic situation where things don't quite fit in' – the domesticity of Macbeth's castle co-existing alongside the bloody horror of Duncan's murder, for instance.

Apart from producing the first *Macbeth* to graphically depict several of the acts of violence always previously played 'offstage' in both theatrical and cinematic productions – mainly the murders of Duncan and Banquo, and the decapitating of Macbeth – Polanski also

broke new 'realistic' ground by casting young actors to play Lady
Macbeth and Macbeth. But instead of repeating what he saw as a
clichéd depiction of them as 'a couple of crowing gangsters', he
wanted to make the Macbeths at the outset a youthfully attractive
loving couple, sexually active and emotionally involved. 'She has to be
a woman for him, and not another witch', he has commented, and their
affectionate relationship is noticeable in the many **two-shot** close-ups
of young actors Jon Finch and Francesca Annis in the first third of the
film. Making the Macbeths young, good-looking and innocent on the
outside, but hatching evil plans within, also helps to convey the play's
pervasive ambiguity theme exemplified by the witches' expression,
'fair is foul'. At the same time, together with a tendency for the impact
of the Shakespearean verse to be reduced by the actors' speaking it
prosaically and the frequent use of 'internalised' voice-over, their
attractiveness could be thought to reduce their stature as tragic figures. This is especially so for Lady Macbeth, who does not speak the
lines concerning her plucking the nipple from her babe and dashing
out its brains, nor is she described as a 'fiend-like queen' by Malcolm
at the end. Instead, what we see in their 'squabbling couple' exchanges
at the first banquet is a Lady Macbeth shedding genuine tears of
frustration at Macbeth's initial refusal to kill Duncan, revealing her
naïve grasp of their plotting, seen as a kind of exciting game. She may
glide beautifully along the corridors of the castle like Kurosawa's equivalent of Lady Macbeth, Asaji, but she does not possess her menace.
Fainting at the sight of the severed heads of the guards whom Macbeth
kills, slowly sinking into madness after Banquo's murder while Macbeth
neglects her for the witches, murdering with increased obsessiveness to
secure the throne, she comes across as pathetic, rather than tragic.

It is true that Lady Macbeth's reproaches about his lost 'beast' at
the first banquet turn into a cajoling and coaxing full of sexual appeal
that in many ways restores Macbeth's sense of masculine purpose.
Yet there is something even more 'masculinist' motivating this crucial
sequence of the film, for prior to her winning him over comes a
moment of taunting perhaps more decisive in restoring Macbeth's
motivation to kill Duncan. This is when Malcolm gestures for Macbeth
to fill up his goblet with wine for him, then offering in effect a jeer
instead of a cheer with his 'Hail, Thane of Cawdor' – the toast functioning as a taunting reminder of the witches' crucial supplement to
this: 'All Hail Macbeth, that shall be king hereafter.'

But even if this is a sexy, naïve Lady Macbeth who lacks tragic
stature, the 'beast' which she accuses Macbeth of having abandoned is

nevertheless in evidence throughout the film, not only through numerous references to animals and animality, but by the use of cleverly deployed visual and aural **motifs**. We know this is a play where, from the moment that King Duncan asks 'What bloody man is that?' (1.2.1) to the chopping off of Macbeth's head by Macduff in their hand-to-hand combat, hardly a scene goes by without blood being spilt or an act of violence being committed. Polanski's film signals even earlier than this that blood and violence will be major themes. The opening frame shows a red dawn sky bathing the sandy ridges of a seashore in the same hue, and this is only the first of many blood-red dawns and sunsets that will create memorable visual motifs to energise the movie's dark yet vividly unrelenting interpretation. The first view of Macbeth's castle is against a blood-red evening sky. It is dawn when Duncan's murder is discovered, the faces of all in Macbeth's castle yard being tinted with red. The evening that his plot to kill Banquo is carried out Macbeth's gaze is on a deep red sunset. The speech where he admits that he is 'in blood so far ...' is made against a blood-red dawn. And he stands again in the glow of a red sunset on his castle ramparts when spotting the approach of Malcolm's rebel thanes with the English army, noting with grim appropriateness in his isolation how he begins 'to be aweary of the sun'.

The soundtrack over the opening frames delivers eerie sounds, sourced from a **diegetic** and **non-diegetic** mix, before **time-lapse photography** speeds our view of the same scene forward into the flat light of day. These sounds continue, until, with the cry of a gull and what sounds like the distant bellow of an elephant! – a cough is heard, and a witch's crooked stick punctures the frame from screen right, a mild enough action in itself, but which functions as and feels like a violation, the first of many much more cruel and brutal violations later. The murderous nature of what some of these will be are signalled by objects ritually buried in the sand by the three witches: a hangman's noose (the hanging of Duncan's enemies, including the execution of Cawdor); a dagger placed in the hand of a severed forearm (Macbeth's stabbing of Duncan, and the final severing of his own head). The emptying of a vial of blood over the burial place by the eyeless witch while all chant the ambiguous magical formula 'foul is fair and fair is foul' (their own appearance could be said to be a mixture of 'foul and fair'), marks the first spilling of blood in the film, but not the last. Indeed, as the witches walk off into the fog now filling the screen while the titles come up, the sounds of the battle mentioned by them is heard: horses galloping and neighing, metal on metal clashing, the murderous and desperate cries of those who kill or who are being killed. These sounds are not just more effective for being only heard, but bring the impact of the one act of violence that we do see committed – a half-dead soldier 'finished off' by a spiked iron ball repeatedly and bloodily thudded into his back (Banquo will later be axed to death in a similar way) – sickeningly home.

By bathing everyone and everything in the *mis-en-scène* in the colour of blood Polanski vividly reminds us of the hideous human cost that societies pay for maintaining ruthless tyrannies. But he also deepens the violence theme here by stressing in various ways the animality underlying the struggle for existence in this semi-tribal mediaeval society. Our first encounter with Lady Macbeth is in the bustle of a castle courtyard full of animals, and as she reads his 'partner of greatness' speech, two enormous dogs lick her hands. In preparation for the banquet in Duncan's honour, we see a squealing pig being caught for the feast, a grim reminder of which comes when Macbeth later plunges his dagger into Duncan's throat, producing what sounds like the grunt of a stuck pig. Bears figure large both in the play and in this film. (We should remember that in the public entertainment stakes, Shakespeare's Globe vied with the adjacent Bear Garden for business.) Prior to the banquet that celebrates his own accession to the crown, Macbeth gazes amusedly at a caged bear, declaring that 'Here's our chief guest' – an ironic comment in many ways, given that an animal struggle for existence will henceforth prevail under his kingship. This fact reveals its greatest personal relevance and force for Macbeth by the time all have deserted him, when he declares, glancing at the iron ring in the wall to which the bear had originally been tethered: 'I cannot fly,/But bear-like I must fight' (5.7.1–2).

A fascinating if grim pattern established through character plotting in this *Macbeth* by Polanski concerns the figure of Ross, made emblematic here of the screenplay authors' cynicism regarding the way power structures can attract self-seeking political opportunists. Ross, aptly described by Rothwell as a 'smirking sociopath', is a character offering a variation on the theme of 'foul and fair'. He is fair-haired, draws little attention to himself, but is in fact an amoral opportunist who without scruple attaches himself by turns to whoever has power and wealth and will serve his own interests. He appears first as the deliverer of treacherous Cawdor to Duncan, bringing the chain of office to Macbeth as the new thane, and obsequiously helping him on to his horse. He stares suspiciously when Macbeth declares that he has killed Duncan's grooms, and is one of the small circle of thanes who lift Macbeth on his coronation shield, remaining mute along with his neighbour Banquo when the 'Hail Macbeth! King of Scotland' is called, yet looking with a strange kind of glee at Macbeth's old friend, who remains emotionless. Gone over completely to Macbeth's side, he becomes the baffling third murderer, only failing to kill Fleance because Banquo downs his horse with an arrow. When the other two murderers are led into the castle dungeons, it is Ross who oversees their deaths, snatching the forked stick that serves as a crutch for the younger one (and as a 'hommage' to Welles's witches) to push him cruelly down a well himself. Ross invites Macbeth to the place where Banquo's ghost sits at the second banquet, and who organises the massacre of Macduff's family, while giving bland assurances to Lady Macduff and blessing in his arms the Macduff son who is shortly to be slaughtered by his accomplices. When he is casually passed over for advancement by Macbeth, he deserts to Malcolm's side, and with concerned looks breaks the news of the massacre and rape that he has stage-managed to Macduff. However, not only does Ross not suffer for his crimes in the end, but he joins Malcolm's new regime, wiping the blood from the crown he takes from Macbeth's severed head, and placing it as he offers the cry of 'Hail Malcolm King of Scotland!' on to the head of his new master.

The circle drawn in the sand in the film's opening frames by the sightless witch is but the first example of a key visual motif deployed by Polanski throughout. It recurs in the hangman's noose buried by the witches, and with the noose-like well-bucket hook seen swinging ominously back and forth in the long-held shot in Macbeth's castle yard after Duncan's murder. We see it in the golden crown which falls spinning to the ground from Duncan's head as Macbeth butchers the king, and in the golden goblet that not only also falls spinning to the ground when Macbeth hallucinates Banquo's ghost, but from which Macbeth drinks the witches' potion, after which he sees the various visions by gazing into their circular cauldron. We see the circle motif in the giant shield upon which Macbeth is raised at his coronation, and we see it in the iron collars around the necks of Cawdor and the bear, as well as in the chains of office slung around the necks of all those caught in Macbeth's lethal web. When Macduff destroys this web by slicing off Macbeth's head, the most macabre use of the circle motif is created not only by seeing the head whirled about on a pole to the delight of Malcolm's soldiers, but also by **subjective camera shots** giving us glimpses of their jeering faces from its wildly spinning **POV**.

The use of sound to stimulate the fearful capacities of what Shakespeare famously calls the 'mind's eye' is also exploited in the kind of music we hear at many points in the film. The Third Ear Band's often harshly sour music on period instruments is very effective in suggesting a feeling of sinister threat, most pointedly with the drearily unpleasant droning bagpipe tune played whenever we are shown the witches' lair. A remarkable use of this music accompanies Duncan's approach to Macbeth's castle: it begins light and pleasant, but gradually falters and slows as Duncan and his entourage's procession snakes its way along the serpentine road, descending lower and lower in pitch, until, in deep, drab discords, it finishes with a dull, twisting twang – the finality of death lies here, it seems to say. Music is important at the end of the film too, with the addition of a scene not in the play, but which makes for a feeling of awful enclosure and inescapable repetition. Macbeth has been killed, and Malcolm crowned. But the camera then cuts to the exact same spot that Macbeth and Banquo had at the beginning encountered the witches, and the familiar sour bagpipe motif linked to this place enters once again, as we see the figure of Malcolm's younger brother Donalbain riding across the heath in driving rain just as his predecessors had. Lured to dismount by the sound of the witches' chanting, he disappears out of sight into their underground lair, closing credits coming up as a primitive five-note phrase is plucked repeatedly over thin, harsh, wind instrumental sounds. The camera pulls back to objectify the moment, making the emphatic point: as one usurper of the crown drawn into his wild obsession by 'fair and foul' prophecy is vanquished, so is another victim seen being drawn into the same process. The pessimistic implication in this final 'circle' is that the lure to possess absolute power will go on in an endless cycle of temptation, desire, deceit and death.

Part V

Shakespeare on Television

1

Film and TV: The Key Differences

Whether we watch dramas on film or television the visual images we see are mediated by screens, so why not use the term 'Shakespeare on screen' to embrace both situations? It is convenient to do so in a broad sense, but the ways that the two forms of visual media record and communicate their dramatic content to an audience differ greatly. The communication technology used is distinct in each case and the conditions of production, performance and reception for film and TV operate differently too. Having explored the practices of communicating Shakespeare on stage and film in Part I, I will begin this concluding part with a discussion of how TV producers and directors of this less obvious yet significant form of conveying Shakespeare to yet another kind of audience have approached the task.

Shakespeare on two kinds of screen

The distinguishing feature of the cinematic film format is that it is *photographic*, supplying a fast-moving sequence of large images of high definition and fine texture, chemically 'fixed' on celluloid. These are highly articulated motion pictures projected on to a screen that the filmmaker uses to provide detailed visual information for a large audience sitting in the dark semi-public space of a movie theatre. By contrast, television images are *electronic*, not photographic, being produced by scanning electronic beams in continual motion illuminated on to the screen from within a TV set. The TV receivers convey these moving images to viewers who are, typically, watching in a private domestic space. From the 1990s, digital technology and larger, wide format screens provided pictures of very high definition, with excellent stability and colour. Yet even the largest TV screen systems are still many times smaller than the screens of local commercial cinemas. This means that despite the convenience of our being able to view a DVD or video version of made-for-cinema films on a domestic screen delivering high definition photographic images very effectively, the relatively small size of the TV screen will always reduce the amount of information containable in its image, and certainly offer far less to the viewer than is visible on the large theatrical screen.

As was pointed out in Part I, the small-screen viewer nowadays benefits increasingly from the fact that many directors and producers of movies, anticipating a significant small-screen market for their films in post-theatrical release, will shoot their movies with the needs of the domestic viewer in mind. This can be seen at work in Radford's *The Merchant of Venice* (2004), where most of the sequences are in **mid** or **close shot**, aiming to capture the significant glances of an actor's eyes. But compared with their effect when seen on the big screen, even facial close-ups such as these lose much of their expressive force when viewed on the small screen. At the other end of the scale, a **wide**-angle landscape **shot** impressively received on the big screen will have a negligible impact when seen on TV (Corner, 1999, 25–6). Furthermore, even if directors of Shakespeare film adaptations with an eye to the follow-up DVD market *do* shoot their films with the needs of a small-screen viewer in mind, the decisions they take about (for instance) the organisation of a set, or the **depth of focus** of shots, or the duration of shot sequences, may frequently have to be influenced by the 'first-release' needs of *cinema* rather than TV audiences. Ultimately, the needs of the movie audience are defined by a desire-led expectation of gazing on compellingly detailed pin-sharp big-screen images in what is a uniquely magical context: the darkened cinema space. Here, the moviegoer gains voyeuristic pleasure from gazing on an image 'marked by present absence', a situation afforded by the 'sense of cinema's consent to the act of being watched' (Ellis, 1992, 138).

Film hot, TV cool

The situation experienced by someone watching TV is different, since broadcast TV constructs an image for a viewing regime marked by (as John Ellis notes) 'co-presence of image and viewer'. As long ago as 1964, Marshall McLuhan noticed some key divergences between film and TV as communicating media when he characterised the movie as 'a hot, high-definition medium', while the TV image was of 'low intensity or definition', with the result that 'unlike film, it does not afford detailed information about objects' (McLuhan, 1964, 318, 313). This contrast of image definition we have already taken note of, but McLuhan also asserted that with a 'hot' medium of high definition like film, 'participation is low', whereas a 'cool medium' like TV 'leaves much more for the listener or user to do than a hot medium' (319). He does not elaborate on what he means by the viewer's 'participation', or explain what kind of activity he refers to when viewers 'do' more or less in each watching situation. By his saying 'participation is low' for movie watchers, I do not take him to mean that the intensity of involvement with what is happening on screen is low, but assume he is referring to the *kind* of involvement we are experiencing with the screen. This is the voyeuristic type of involvement already noted, where we as movie watchers gaze at and invest the projected images moving on the screen in front of us with a 'fictional reality' (the film **diegesis**).

In the crisp but subtly articulated world of the big film image we are presented with a fluidly dynamic modelling of characters interacting in a whole variety of pictorially realistic settings, where what is *said* by those characters is often of secondary importance to the way that they and their world are visually conveyed. By contrast, it is what the characters have to *say* in the world of the small TV screen that usually takes precedence over the setting in which they are *seen*, for TV cannot provide an array of finely detailed images articulated within an extensive **depth of field**. What it *can* provide very effectively however is a sense of 'liveness' and immediacy, creating a situation in which the figures or characters on screen seem to be *speaking* to us personally in our living rooms. John Ellis has explored the distinctions between film and TV media in some depth:

> The image is the central reference in cinema. But for TV, sound has a more centrally defining role ... This is a tendency towards a different sound/ image balance than in cinema, rather than a marked and consistent difference. Broadcast TV has areas which tend towards the cinematic, especially the areas of serious drama or of various kinds of TV film. But many of TV's characteristic broadcast forms rely upon sound as the major carrier of information and the major means of ensuring continuity of attention. ... Sound tends to anchor meaning on TV, where the image tends to anchor it with cinema. (Ellis, 1992, 129)

Therefore, persuading a TV audience to *listen* will be crucial where the aim is to capture and hold the attention of viewers of a Shakespeare play, especially because the *verbal text* is such a vital dimension of his work. In this sense, the task of engaging the TV viewer's attention is not perhaps so very different from stage actors involving their audience: in both cases director and actors need the audience to *listen* as the precondition for communication to take place. Of course, a major difficulty in the TV communication compared to that of the stage – and this is not so very different from the situation with film – is that TV actors cannot *directly* interact with or respond to their audience, but must perform with and for each other – and for the director controlling the camera. So how *have* presenters of TV screen Shakespeare handled this challenge?

2

The BBC-TV Series: Shooting the Complete Canon

I want now to explore the BBC Shakespeare adaptations that were taped and broadcast between 1978 and 1985 on BBC-TV, and in the PBS *Great Performances* slot in the USA between 1979 and 1985. Uniquely, the series comprises the complete canon of Shakespeare's 37 plays and its commercial availability on DVD makes at least one small-screen version of each Shakespeare play accessible to any viewer. The adaptations were produced by three different producers over a six-and-a-half year period, with sixteen different directors bringing a range of often quite different perspectives, interests and skills to bear on these productions. Such diversity of interpretative style and dramatic approach draws on a significant range of methods for shooting Shakespeare on TV. For this reason, a brief critical exploration of the series enables us not only to assess BBC dramatic procedures and styles, but also offers a way into evaluating the approaches of other TV Shakespeare adaptations which have been broadcast, a number of which are also commercially available on DVD.

As Susan Willis has noted (following André Bazin), the core of the stylistic debate about presenting Shakespeare on TV revolves around whether drama should aspire to film or to the theatre, to a strong notion of *representation* aiming for realism of place, or to providing a *suggestivity* of place or space, a strategy often employed in open staging productions (Willis, 1991, 87). In terms of TV camera deployment, the choice is between using the cinematic technique of **montage** (cutting back and forth between different shots or short sequences) and the more theatrical practice of ***mis-en-scène***, composing and

manipulating what is to be seen into the totality of a single shot and its
depth of field. BBC directors responded differently from play to play
to the challenge of delivering full text productions using the resources
and techniques of the TV camera and studio. However, their
responses resulted in strategies which can be categorised under the
three broad headings of approach suggested by Michèle Willems: the
naturalistic, the *pictorial* and the *stylised* (Willems, 1999, 74).

The realistic/naturalistic approach

It was inevitable that many of the BBC directors would opt for a
'realistic' solution to the design of a production, given the series requirement to create settings that would convey the period implied by the
world of each play's story. At the beginning of the series especially, much
effort was put into constructing an 'authentic' representation of the
world of each play, resulting in a 'preoccupation that badges, banners,
and weapons should look genuine,' publicity proudly proclaiming (for
example) the 'authentic recreation of Caesar's Rome' for *Julius Caesar*,
and the filming of *As You Like It* in a 'real forest' (Willems, 1999, 75). The
rationale for this approach stemmed from the idea that the viewing
habits and perceptions of TV viewers unfamiliar with Shakespeare's
plays whom the BBC wanted to attract and educate were shaped by
news programmes and documentaries. Hence the view of Alvin Rakoff,
director of the first play to be broadcast, *Romeo and Juliet*, was that in
'order to grab the audience's attention you've got to do it as realistically
as possible' (Willis, 91). More often than not, doing it 'realistically' means
creating a large representational set designed to model historically accurate constructions for both interior and exterior settings of a play.

Where such representationalism supports the dramatic forwarding
of text and plot, this can be involving for the TV audience, especially
when interior settings suggest an atmosphere relevant to the text
being dramatised. Interior settings support the text well in Desmond
Davis's award-winning *Measure for Measure*. The settings move from
the Duke's elegant and formal audience hall where the gripping inter-
views between Angelo and Isabella are captured by imaginative two-
camera shots, to the rowdy clamour of the brothel styled like the
saloon of a western, while the prison set suggests the 'torch-lit, scream-
filled grotesquerie of a horror film' that the director wished to emu-
late. However, although Davis's staging of the last scene on a platform
is an apt elevation for the Duke's revelations and pronouncements
while also providing an allusion to the Globe, this exterior scene

'nonetheless suffers the same limits of stylised realism as the first season's other studio exteriors' (Willis, 199). Exteriors suffer most when the realistic approach is followed, for however elaborate or detailed a design is, the TV camera exposes any scenic artifice as a 'clunky' distraction from the all-important dialogue. This is the case even for an adaptation broadcast four years into the series, David Jones's *The Merry Wives of Windsor*. It may have won a design award for its painstaking reconstruction of Tudor Windsor, but not even outstanding actors like Ben Kingsley, Alan Bennett or Prunella Scales can rescue it from the deadliness of an exterior looking so studio-bound that the importance given to it 'is probably just as detrimental to the comic effect as the absence of a live public' (Willems, 1999, 77). Swapping the studio for the real outdoors may seem a solution, but Basil Coleman's *As You Like It* shot on location in a 'real forest' shows that it is not, the forest setting merely distracting us from the performance. As Susan Willis comments, 'it is not ultimately a play about trees' (Willis, 211). By contrast, when the (only) other play to be taped on location was shot, the less well-known *Henry VIII*, Kevin Billington was enabled to use the solid, stone walls and ceilinged rooms of Hever, Penshurst and Leeds castles to advantage, bringing the political intrigues and atmosphere of the Tudor court to life, and in the process producing an unexpected early success for the series.

Alvin Rakoff's *Romeo and Juliet* exemplifies the limitations of realistic and naturalistic approaches. With famous Shakespearean Sir John Gielgud as Chorus, a role he had already played in Castellani's 1954 film of the play, the opening seems promising. But Rakoff's attempt to mimic the market place setting of Castellani and Zeffirelli films feels deadly, the constructed piazza where Capulet and Montague youths brawl looking so obviously like a TV set rather than any kind of real place that the action and performance fail to convince, the same problem occurring with the arbour's painted drop, the balcony, the Capulet's ballroom and the tomb. Realism of representation is also tested out and found wanting in the casting of 14-year-old Rebecca Saire as Juliet, especially noticeable when her small girlish voice and undemonstrative acting encounter the fruity baritone of Patrick Ryecart's manly Romeo: when man and girl interact, little happens to interest us.

The pictorial approach

When BBC internal politics forced series architect Cedric Messina to stand down after two years, Jonathan Miller entered as series producer, who saw the series 'house style' as an opportunity to bring a Renaissance manner and look to the productions. He also brought in three new directors, Elijah Moshinsky, Jack Gold and Jane Howell, which ensured that nearly half of the remaining adaptations would be delivered with what Susan Willis calls a 'conscious aestheticism' of attitude, though each director would also develop their own lines of approach. Both Miller and Moshinsky use the TV screen in their productions like a canvas, creating *mis-en-scènes* that reproduce the style of specific artists and their paintings from the Renaissance and later: Dutch interiors out of Vermeer in particular, but also Veronese, Watteau and others.

For *The Taming of the Shrew*, Miller uses Dutch and Italian paintings to design the Paduan street and Baptista's interiors, all aspects of Vermeer's 'The Music Lesson' being exactly reproduced for the scene where Petruccio (John Cleese) woos Katherine. Although he does saturate most of his adaptations with ideas and images drawn from Renaissance paintings, for the Cyprus interior scenes of *Othello*, Miller provides a set 'carefully based on period architecture, a palace in Urbino, and the dark street in Cyprus based on a real street'. Surfaces and spaces are fashioned to help convey the play he thinks of as a 'closet tragedy', even rooms of 'airy spacious confinement' finally coming to feel like 'an awful prison' (Willis, 216, 123).

Miller's *Shrew* convinced Moshinsky of the value of following Vermeer's use of period space, as can be seen in the Roussillon and Widow's house sets in his *All's Well That Ends Well*. Another example of his artistic quoting occurs in *A Midsummer Night's Dream*, where the image of Titania reclining in her forest bower beautifully resembles Rembrandt's *Danae's Bower*, a delight for the eye, whether one knows the allusion or not. Moshinsky uses art-related effects so much he confesses that his *Love's Labour's Lost* is not merely set in the eighteenth century, it is 'set in Watteau' (Willis, 160). His goal of ravishing the viewer's eye is not only achieved by using the techniques of old master paintings that include **chiaroscuro** lighting effects derived from Georges de la Tour. He also draws on a skilful deployment of camera and **blocking** to frame numerous kinds of shot – **establishing, close, high angle, crane, subjective**. In addition he uses **voice-overs**, music, the **sound bridge** (a fine example of which opens *Cymbeline*), precision **montage** for effective continuity editing – and much more. His preoccupation with using highly studied and creatively lit camera shots for aesthetic effect, together with cutting techniques prioritising story continuity over capturing **two-shot** dialogue exchanges, can make Moshinsky seem like a frustrated big-screen film director, rather than an adapter for the small screen.

The stylised approach

Michèle Willems poses the key question regarding the use of a pictorial approach for engaging viewers in TV Shakespeare: 'Is there not a danger in this profusion of visual signs that the picture will interfere with the reception of the words?' (Willems, 1999, 79). In fact, the BBC directors who deploy a stylised approach do so because they want viewers to connect with and to understand the performance of a text *without* such distraction. It is perhaps no surprise to find that six of the ten tragedies are delivered as stylised productions, since the large amount of dialogue revealing the agitated inner lives of the main characters is of such primary importance in these plays: the frequency with which Rodney Bennett has Derek Jacobi confide Hamlet's innermost thoughts to the viewer in to-camera **close-ups** for his *Hamlet* production gives one obvious example. Although a number of directors use the stylised approach, I want to concentrate here on the work of Jack Gold and Jane Howell, since both use the approach exclusively and also offer valuable comments on its value and efficacy.

What soon becomes apparent from viewing the plays directed by Gold and Howell is their use of techniques creating theatre-like playing conditions in the TV studio. Given the intimate kind of contact that can be set up between actor and viewer with this small-screen domestic medium, it is no surprise to hear Jane Howell saying that 'what TV can give you is the excitement of an actor's performance' (Willems ed., 1987, 80). Since performing the text is at the heart of an actor's performance, and given the series requirement to present minimally cut plays means that the audience are required to listen to a *lot* of performed text, how can viewers be encouraged to listen in the way Shakespeare's audience would also have had to? Of course, as Jack Gold observes, Shakespearean dialogue 'is not our own. You have to concentrate'. And he asserts that the only way to encourage this kind of viewer-concentration is 'to get rid of everything on the screen that does not actually make clear what is being said' (Willems ed., 1987, 47).

Gold's stylised productions of *Macbeth* and *The Merchant of Venice* demonstrate how this approach works in practice. The theatrical playing conventions he deploys use minimal props and abstract set designs to *suggest* rather than to *realise* the kind of space conjured up by Shakespeare's dialogue. In the Scottish play, Gold therefore has Macbeth and Banquo hear the news of Macbeth's elevation to Thane of Cawdor on what he calls a 'not-quite-real-heath'. With an acute observation on how using several cameras to cut between shots makes 'most TV productions ... very static', he argues for retaining dramatic complexity and flow by employing long takes with a single camera, his approach differing from Miller, who he thinks 'does not compose enough' or 'use the camera's mobility and actors' mobility enough' (Willems ed., 1987, 47). A good example of this technique is seen during the first banquet, from when the camera **pans** along the banqueting table to a passageway where Macbeth mutters his soliloquy starting 'If it were done when 'tis done, then 'twere well / It were done quickly' (1.7). Lady Macbeth soon arrives to upbraid him for his cowardice, hatching her murder plan, convincing him that they will succeed, Gold ending the scene by having the camera follow their return hand-in-hand to the banquet, and **slow-zoom**ing in for an ironic close shot of Duncan's smiling face as they part hands. He explains the reason for this six-minute take: 'I thought it would lose the tension, the mood, if I did it on more than one camera. So I made *them* more mobile and the *camera* mobile. It took a lot of rehearsing' (Willems ed., 1987, 44).

Gold's style of working is very similar to that of Jane Howell, an experienced theatrical director whose first adaptation *The Winter's Tale* contains a 48-minute sequence played and taped without break, the country scene in Bohemia (4.4). Her approach to the direction and design of any play initially requires 'a spark', an idea – 'I don't like concepts', she says. The idea she had for this production concerns 'the sense of rebirth ... the returning of spring [being] obviously fundamental to the play'. The shifts in season are registered visually by changes in the colour and texture of the set, sparingly composed of two large wedges (between which the actors enter and leave) and a tree in the left foreground. Both tree and wedges change colour with the seasons, from Sicilia's wintery white to the stony grey of Bohemia's coasts, then to the gold of Bohemia's fields, with spring green appearing for the concluding scenes in Sicilia. Such a setting of seasonal rebirth also supports her idea of this play as one where 'everyone can have a second chance' (Willems ed., 1987, 84). Howell's commitment to melding the theatrical with the televisual is even more apparent in her four productions of the minor tetralogy, the three parts of *Henry VI* and *Richard III*, all broadcast in sequence over succeeding Sunday evenings in 1983. The unit set for these adaptations is simple but effective, comprising a wooden adventure-playground structure like a stockade with an upper level, swing doors at either side being used by the actors for their entries and exits. This provides a structure and a space fortuitously equivalent to the platform stage of Shakespeare's theatre, and very adaptable to the playing of outdoor or indoor scenes. Most importantly it is a design allowing Howell to offer an underlying visual reminder of an interpretation of these four Wars of the Roses histories in which the action starts with a kind of boyish playground brawling game, but then shifts into political manoeuvring and violence, powermongering struggles and battles that result in the piles of corpses darkly punctuating the end of each adaptation. 'It struck me', says Howell, 'that the behaviour of the lords of England was a lot like children – prep school children' (Willis, 167). This view of the nobles' behaviour is shown in 1.3 of *1 Henry VI* where Gloucester and Winchester confront each other on hobbyhorses as their men scrap, while soon after 1.4 begins, three French boys squabble over a toy longbow. (The use of young Lucius as a 'witness' to the nightmarish violence in her *Titus Andronicus* – borrowed by Taymor for her film *Titus* – is a related idea.)

Howell's decision to dramatise all four plays as a continuous story informs a key aspect of her 'theatrical' approach: her directorial relationship with, and use of the actors. With what is in effect a large-scale repertory company of about fifty actors, her casting of some of them in two or even three different roles throughout the sequence is done purposely to attract the audience's attention: after seeing their faces in various guises throughout the three plays (she says) '*Richard III* should be like a nightmare' (Willis, 170). Despite the seriousness of the material, Howell manages to get her large, talented and versatile company to bring out the inherent theatricalism of these histories such that the performance is **metatheatrically** celebrated *as performance*. For instance, near the beginning of *1* and *2 Henry VI*, the play titles are announced on banners over the door, in *3 Henry VI* the title is proclaimed on a shroud covering the pile of corpses, while Ron Cook as Richard chalks up the title on a board at the beginning of *Richard III*. Furthermore, with the numerous opportunities for ensemble playing in front of the camera that these plays afford, Howell not only demonstrates a sure grasp of how to place her actors in the playing space to gain maximum effect, but when they do perform, addressing and confiding in the camera far more in these productions than happens in other series adaptations, she conjures performances that make what are often thought of as difficult and dense plays, very clear for the TV viewer to follow. To say so is not mere assertion, for after the tetralogy was broadcast, Howell reports receiving 140 letters, 'all from families, not from critics or theatre-going people, families who said: 'we happened to watch the first one, we became interested, what are we going to do now they've stopped?' (Willems ed., 1987, 89).

3

TV Shakespeare: The Stage–Screen Hybrid

The BBC-TV Shakespeare adaptations mostly cast actors with experience of performing the plays on stage, yet none emerged directly from actual stage productions. There have been other 'made for TV' adaptations of note I shall discuss briefly later on – specifically Michael Elliott's 1983 *King Lear*, Andrew Davies's 2001 *Othello* and Tim Supple's 2003 *Twelfth Night* – but the productions I want to focus on next all emerged from celebrated stage performances reworked for the small screen. Many would agree that the primary motivation for creating such TV versions has been to make a permanent record of productions that enjoyed popular and critical success on the stage, and to provide confirmation of the undoubted truth expressed in Kenneth Rothwell's statement that 'acting remains the one crucial variable determining success on stage or [small] screen' (2000, 110). The chance for many more people via the TV screen to enjoy what a comparatively small number of people have enjoyed in the theatre is also a major reason for creating such productions (which in the US are often to be seen on the PBS Masterpiece Theatre series). I observed in Part III how, although Tony Richardson's film of his London Round House *Hamlet* with Nicol Williamson was shot on celluloid, the intimate camerawork of the production makes it very suitable for domestic consumption on the small screen, and no doubt many more people have viewed it on DVD or video format than ever saw the limited big-screen cinematic release.

Trevor Nunn: 'Shooting the text'

The same comment no doubt applies to the small-screen adaptations of Shakespeare stage productions directed by Trevor Nunn, his first being a reworking of *Antony and Cleopatra* staged as part of the 'Roman season' of plays put on with the RSC at Stratford in 1972. The **1974 ATV** network broadcast won a BAFTA TV award in London as best single play for 1975, and part of the reason for this is interestingly conveyed by Patrick Stewart (the production's Enobarbus), who commends Nunn's approach to Michèle Willems in an interview conducted on the occasion of his playing Claudius in the BBC *Hamlet*:

> I still think the style he adopted for that *Antony and Cleopatra* was so successful that many of the BBC directors should have observed it themselves. Rather than trying to build architecture for the play, sets and so on, he used light and smoke and gauzes only.

Miller tried for a minimalist set of 'drapes and boards' with his *Antony and Cleopatra* but the contrasting atmospheric settings created for Rome and Egypt and the inspired acting of a cast thoroughly attuned to their parts in Nunn's earlier production elevates the latter far above the BBC version. The contrast between Cleopatra's exotically sensuous Egyptian court and the martial exactitudes of a Rome that Antony has all but forsaken are conveyed from the outset with Egyptian scenes and costumes played in a soft, warm, golden glow further softened by a screen image often blurred at the edges; while the Roman scenes are monochromatic, the white and black costumes of Octavius's men providing a harder uncompromising edge. Neither are we left in any doubt of the power that the cunning allure of Janet Suzman's 'tawny fronted' Cleopatra has over Richard Johnson's shrewd but vulnerable Antony, revealed as this is by Nunn's camera consistently focusing (as Stewart notes) on 'the actors' faces and the text' (Willems ed., 1987, 94).

Nunn characterises the difference between film and TV Shakespeare production as between 'shooting the action' and 'shooting the text' (Willems, 2000, 40). Among the stage-to-TV-screen productions he has masterminded, there is none that exemplifies his approach to 'shooting the text' better than the ***Macbeth*** he transposed from an award-winning RSC production at Stratford's The Other Place in 1976 to the **Thames TV** dramatisation, broadcast in **1979**. The 'live' stage origins of this fine production are not only signalled by its title, 'A Performance of *Macbeth* by William Shakespeare', but the whole enterprise is designed to recreate for home-viewers the kind of chilling performance effects experienced by small audiences crammed into the intimate studio confines of The Other Place. The play is acted out within a ritualistic magic circle where a saintly looking white-bearded Duncan dressed more like a high churchman than a king, falls prey to a Macbeth (Ian McKellen) murderously infected with the malevolent designs of the sensuous Lady Macbeth (Judi Dench) who infatuates him. McKellen reports how in the theatre the effects were 'properly alarming', as shown by the fact that a 'priest queued for a returned ticket again and again, so that he could sit at our feet, discreetly holding out his crucifix to protect us from the evil summoned up in the stifling air'. With the whole production conveyed through **mid shots** or **close-ups** in a frequently smoky atmosphere minimally lit for maximum spookiness, the effect of actors playing close to the camera is so captivating that McKellen is surely right to assert that the small screen is able to communicate 'an intimate horror that is still thrilling' (McKellen, 1996, 9). This kind of impact is felt particularly with McKellen's Macbeth, which Patrick Stewart regards as 'so marvellous on the screen because he thinks so brilliantly, so brightly and quickly, and the camera observes the thought, and it's the thought that's full of impact' (Willems ed., 1987, 95). McKellen achieves this kind of performing brilliance throughout, but an especially unnerving moment occurs in the soliloquy beginning, 'Is this a dagger which I see before me.' Muttering as if under compulsion how 'withered murder .../ With Tarquin's ravishing strides, towards his design / Moves like a ghost' (2.1.52, 55–6) – when he moves toward the camera and a shadow passes across his face, for a moment we really feel as if this entranced being closing in on us, **is** 'like a ghost'.

Ten years later in **1990**, Nunn transferred his successful RSC production of **Othello** (again at The Other Place) to TV, and since this play is, like *Macbeth*, a drama of claustrophobic themes ideally suited for a studio space, the translation to the domestic screen was again fluently achieved, although Ian McKellen, who won honours for his Iago performance, did not feel this *Othello* surpassed Nunn's *Macbeth*. A further 10 years on, and **2001** saw Nunn creating a transposition to TV of his award-winning RNT production of **The Merchant of Venice**, the stage-like sets and costumes this time periodised for a late-1920s Europe that worked most effectively for this so-called 'comedy'. The setting was chosen, says Nunn, because 'it was that very period when anti-Semitic thought and anti-Semitic behaviour was becoming current and even – it's ghastly to think it – voguish and the subject of wit and amusement'. Such an approach allows Nunn to dramatise unflinchingly the sufferings visited upon and invited by Shylock (Henry Goodman), his daughter Jessica (Gabrielle Jordan) and Antonio (David Bamber). Shot and cut very like a film, Nunn's camera observes the actors' performance in a variety of **two**, three and ensemble **shots**, with the **shot/reverse shot** being put to efficient use for a drama of often hostile exchanges climaxing in a courtroom confrontation. Carrying some genuinely funny sequences at times, the adaptation nevertheless tends always to bring us back to a sombreness seeming to deny the possibility of social reconciliation. Nevertheless, it concludes with two elements of hopefulness in Belmont: learning of Shylock's humiliation, Jessica separates herself from the others in tears to sing a Hebrew song she and her father had earlier sung together, an assertion of her Jewish identity that is positive and which gains a kind of faint support from Portia's closing announcement that 'It is almost morning.' Without doubt it is Henry Goodman's deeply impressive (and award-winning) performance as the proud and sensitive Shylock which gives the adaptation its dramatic weight, his urgent portrayal of a committed orthodox Jew with strong Yiddish accent, yarmulke and tallit bringing an intense authenticity of feeling and drama to the part.

Three TV adaptations of the 1980s and 1990s

Six months after Jonathan Miller's BBC *Lear* was broadcast, Granada TV produced its own *King Lear* **(1983)** starring 75-year-old Laurence Olivier and a host of famous actors in the other parts, including Dorothy Tutin, Colin Blakely, Diana Rigg, Leo McKern and John Hurt. The $2 million production certainly showcased the acting talents of its star-studded cast, but as a dramatisation of an important Shakespeare play it is conventional in design, shooting and interpretation, failing to draw us into the horrors and anxieties of the play in any deeply imaginative way. However, the presumed aim of providing the elder statesman of British Shakespearean theatre and film with a vehicle for a fine farewell performance is certainly met by the production, a nice moment occurring early on in the Stonehenge setting when Olivier's Lear imperiously surveys with evident satisfaction each member of the court bowing low before him. This is an image which cannot fail to suggest how the long reign of the elderly fictional king has its counterpart in Olivier's sovereign position as the world's leading Shakespearean actor. The performance design tends to feed the image of an ailing king wronged by his ungrateful daughters and owed a justified sympathy, this valuation assisted (for instance) by the omission of Edgar's 'But who comes here?' (4.6.80) and related asides, persuading us to view Lear as a kind of 'unaccommodated man of nature' in what becomes almost a new scene of the old man joyfully fending for himself in the wild – not at all what the allusion to 'nature' means at this stage of the play.

The stage-to-TV-screen BBC2/WGBH Boston adaptation **(2004)** of **Richard Eyre's** award-winning 1998 RNT production of *King Lear* by contrast is not only a revelation of the great acting talents of Ian Holm, but a wrenchingly insightful exposure of the play's profound and diverse human themes. Observing that 'Every family is a state in miniature', Eyre achieves this exposure by presenting the play as a drama of failing family relationships. In Lear's family such critical dysfunction is occasioned by the tyrannical behaviour of a father seemingly driven by uncontrollable parental rages for most of his life. Notwithstanding his compact physical stature (indeed perhaps because of it), Holm drives the production along with acting of great emotional density, captured in **close** and **medium** camera shots. In contrast to Elliott's production, this adaptation does not endorse Lear's claim that he is 'a man / More sinned against than sinning' (3.2.57–8), for the close-observing camera also captures on many occasions (before malice enters their hearts) the shocked distress of Goneril and Regan as daughters who have long suffered the pressures of an overbearing father. Expressions of desperate hurt and unhappiness caused by Lear's vicious cursing tongue are especially noticeable on the face of Goneril. The clever use of lighting on a relatively bare set supports strong performances from a strong cast, with camera work revealing many moments of insight and feeling in the second half of the play. The camera **close-ups** allow us to witness an almost unbearably moving reconciliation scene between Cordelia and her father, one that would be more difficult for a theatre audience to register. Despite 'shooting a text' that is heavily cut in places, Eyre's riveting TV adaptation of *King Lear* is a revelation.

It was in the year **1988** that **Kenneth Branagh's** Renaissance Theatre Company first properly gained notice, the *Twelfth Night* he directed at London's Riverside Studios becoming a great theatrical hit following a Royal Gala Preview attended by the RTC's new patron, Prince Charles. Soon after, the production was adapted for the small screen and broadcast by Thames Television just before Christmas. Branagh designed the production to be set in winter, 'with snow covering a mysterious Victorian garden [to] bring out the brooding melancholy of the play'. The spare unit set, although unadventurous, offers a sound frame for delivering the bitter-sweet aspects of the play while also supporting both the boisterous scenes with Sir Toby we all enjoy, and the pivotal scene of Malvolio's gulling. The strong cast includes Anton Lesser as Feste and the versatile Richard Briers as Malvolio, his outstanding performance probably justifying the claim that 'a great comic actor can be a great tragic actor' (Branagh, 1989, 198). Unfortunately, however good the comic performances are, the problem of getting such Shakespeare comedies to work effectively on TV will remain so long as 'one important participant is missing: the reacting audience' (Wells, 1982, 272).

Post-2000: some innovative TV adaptations

A new century produced some interesting excursions in TV Shakespeare adaptation, and I shall conclude by considering four of these. The stage-to-TV-screen adaptation of **Gregory Doran's** acclaimed 1999 **RSC *Macbeth*** production originally staged at the Swan Theatre, Stratford, was shot at London's Roundhouse and broadcast by Channel Four in **2001**. Where Tony Richardson's 1969 *Hamlet* at this same location was filmed in **close** and **medium** shot throughout, Doran uses every available space in the cavernous Roundhouse to deliver his *Macbeth*, the dripping subterranean passages, enormous open arena and circling upper gallery each being lit to convey a variety of tense, forbidding and sometimes alarming effects. Many of the heightened effects are achieved by scenes being shot in confined passages or on stairways. For example, the frantic exchange which takes place on a narrow staircase between Macbeth (Antony Sher) and Lady Macbeth (Harriet Walter) after Duncan's murder provides an appropriately liminal location for the playing out of their morally agitated state. Agitation and instability are also frequently conveyed by the use of **hand-held** camera shooting, and although conventionally steady camera work of **close, medium** and sometimes **long shots** are also used, there are also surprises, as with the startling close-up but inverted head and shoulders shot we are given of a naked Lady Macbeth in her bathtub while her 'Come, you spirits' soliloquy is heard in **voice-over**. This is a punchy postmodern presentation which does not flinch from making contemporary political allusion either, the extraordinary Porter's speech which emphasises 'equivocation' so much including an uncannily accurate imperson-ation of the then British prime minister, Tony Blair.

'Based on the play by William Shakespeare', the made-for-**TV** *Othello* **written by Andrew Davies** and first broadcast near Christmas **2001**, this LWT and WGBH/Boston co-production (in association with the CBC) alludes much more specifically to British political and social life. It does this by showing a Blair-like prime minister and his 'spin doctor' promoting a senior black London policeman (John Othello) to the top job of Commissioner of the London Metropolitan Police for heroically quelling a race riot, and by-passing Ben Jago, not only Assistant Commissioner previously senior to Othello, but also his mentor and supposed friend. Enraged by being passed over, the smil-ing but deeply racist Jago persuades an all-trusting Othello that his new wife Dessie is having sex with her police bodyguard John Cass, with the result that an insanely jealous Othello smothers Dessie and then kills himself, Jago being left to inherit the Commissionership he regards as rightly his. The 'dark ending' Davies says he was looking for and found in this final twist is not the only surprising thing about his *Othello*, for Shakespeare's play text is nowhere heard in it. As a mas-terly adapter of classic novels like *Pride and Prejudice* and *Dr Zhivago* to TV mini-series, the response of Davies has been to say that when he sets out 'to make a modern powerful drama' like 'Othello at the Met', his priority is to use 'what I can of Shakespeare', the source for adapt-ing what he calls a 'great story' to a medium where language becomes 'proportionately unimportant', compared with what we see on the screen. This point seems borne out by the fact that this *Othello* won many TV drama prizes around the world on release, including two BAFTA TV awards for Best Photography and Lighting, and Best Editing. With Christopher Eccleston (Jago) and Eamonn Walker (Othello) giving outstanding performances, this is a powerful drama that effectively adapts the main *Othello* themes and characters to a relevant and important socio-political context and does so more con-vincingly than the American boarding school setting of Tim Blake Nelson's movie "O" (USA, 2001). Given its ambiguous relationship to Shakespeare's text, the status of this *Othello* must necessarily remain uncertain, perhaps controversially so, for it is not an adaptation in the sense I have used that word in this book. Yet even though it cannot be said to embody the dramatic depth of its source with the stylistic bril-liance or fluency of plotting that Kurosawa's *Kumonosu Jô* does in relation to *Macbeth*, such serious but 'accessible' forms of approach to dramatising Shakespeare's plays for TV must surely remain an important option for the future.

A TV version of *Othello* deprived of any of Shakespeare's text may be predictably controversial. It may be equally unsurprising to find a stage-to-TV-screen production by the legendary Shakespearean director **Peter Brook** called *The Tragedy of Hamlet* (**BBC4, 2001**) coming under fire for 'having the balls cut off' and 'anaesthetised' – especially when the comments come from the director of politically radical Shakespeare, Michael Bogdanov. For what has made the dramas of Brook so legendary in many ways is an existential-humanist approach that works to absorb the 'politically local' into a kind of cosmic exploration of the human condition. Applying this approach to *Hamlet* (which runs 128 minutes without an interval) Brook excises the political subplot about Norway and a good many other scenes and characters, the characters, scenes and speeches which remain being chopped and shifted about in order (as he puts it) to 'cut out all that's superfluous' so as 'to get to the essential'. The 'essential' for Brook seems to mean focusing closely on the emotional, psychological and spiritual development of a Hamlet (Adrian Lester) told by his father's Ghost (Jeffery Kissoon) to avenge his murder by Claudius (also played by Kissoon), but who must 'taint not' his mind in the process. Brook compares this task with that facing the hero of the *Mahabharata* Indian epic he dramatised and toured worldwide years before. Unlike that epic production, or Branagh's epic film version of the play, the stage *Hamlet* Brook toured round the world and finally taped for TV at his Théâtre des Buffes du Nord in Paris is more of a studio piece with many **close-ups** showcasing the subtle but emotionally powerful performing talents of the young black British actor Lester. The adaptation is performed by a small 'multicultural' cast of actors (some of whom play doubled parts) on a square of brilliant orange carpet sparsely dressed with a few cushions, candleholders, ottomans and small rugs, the whole performance being creatively punctuated by Eastern inflected music by Toshi Tsuchitori. This music not only supports a dramatic style of production designed to be coherently received by audiences of any cultural background, but in its semi-ritualistic effects suggests the *kind* of coherence Brook aims to deliver here. For this is a 'pared-back' dramatic approach inspired by Fate-driven Greek tragedy, rather than Renaissance-style tragic drama, an approach clearly illustrated by the Fatalistic pronouncement Brook has given Claudius to speak just before Hamlet stabs him to death: 'This must be so.'

Tim Supple's made-for-TV production of *Twelfth Night* broadcast by British Channel 4 in **2003** also uses a 'multicultural' cast, settings and music, though the style of its opening might prove confusing to anyone unfamiliar with the play. Beginning with a violent episode forcing the twins Viola and Sebastian to become Indian 'asylum seekers' in the land of Illyria, the action rapidly cuts between the development of this episode and Orsino's restless enjoyment of some ravishing music, before settling into the situation whereby the now isolated Viola (as Cesario) takes on the daunting task of being Orsino's young 'male' servant. With serviceable and mostly unobtrusive settings to support it, the production then advances coherently enough, with Parminder Nagra as Viola/Cesario offering by far the most penetrating and subtle performance. Exchanges in Hindi between her and Sebastian in the final recognition scene and between Antonio and Sebastian earlier lend depth to the interpretation, as do the effects of well-placed tabla music throughout. The idea of having a CCTV camera in the garden to enable Sir Toby, Sir Andrew and Fabian to watch Malvolio and his antics in the gulling scene is an inspired and efficient dramatic device. What does not work so well is the *tone* of a production whose cast of characters Supple claims are 'in a state of delightful delirium'. Rather, because much of what we see gets performed and presented too realistically, the drama loses its core of comedy through the characters (except Feste) taking themselves too seriously. This over-seriousness is felt after Cesario's 'wooing' of Olivia, when the latter's sudden infatuation is conveyed through a series of 'flashback' shots rapidly exploded on to the screen. From Maria's collapse into drunken distress following the interview Feste (disguised as Sir Topaz) has with Malvolio, there is a general tendency to perform what are meant to be farcical clashes and encounters of mistaken identity with an inappropriate seriousness. Notwithstanding the drama's reputation as a 'problem' play, to perform *Twelfth Night* as earnestly as this is to do it too much violence: a lighter touch in dramatic design might have brought us a better balance of both the darkness and delight animating Shakespeare's text.

As I hope the survey here has demonstrated, although the made-for-TV adaptation approach can be provoking and interesting, in many ways it is the TV Shakespeares initially nurtured into dramatic life and success in a theatrical context that have fared most impressively on the small screen – and long may this process continue.

Appendix 1: Box Office Data for Selected Shakespeare Film Adaptations on Theatrical Release in US Movie Theatres from 1989

Russell Jackson has said that the US domestic movie market is 'a crude but reliable index of the financial fortunes of English-language films' (in Jackson ed., 2000, 4), and although financial success does not of course necessarily equate with critical worth, an exploration of the data in the table allows us to make some inferences about the marketing and performance of some of the Shakespeare adaptations discussed in this book. A glance at opening dates tells us there are two main points of seasonal release, each linked either to the holiday periods of summer – Branagh's *Much Ado* (3), Hoffman's *A Midsummer Night's Dream* (7) and Almereyda's *Hamlet* (9) – or Christmas for all the rest. There is an obvious logic to releasing comedies in the summer, though bringing out Almereyda's *Hamlet* then may seem a puzzle until we realise that this is a film primarily targeting a summer youth audience. What, then, of Luhrmann's *Romeo + Juliet* (5)? – a teen-focused film product if ever there was one. Both this and Hoffman's *Dream* 'opened wide', meaning that they were Hollywood movies opening at a large number of movie theatres across the US (over 1000 venues in each case), and making around a quarter of their total earnings during their first week of release, when the massive publicity for new films such as these attract large audiences. The earning strategy of distributors marketing such Hollywood movies seems to be to draw in large numbers of moviegoers over a relatively short period (three months in both cases here), before interest in the movie wanes. Careful research told Fox that *Romeo and Juliet* would be a hit with teenagers, and it was. *Dream* did reasonably well, but even with big names like Kevin Kline and Michelle Pfeiffer starring, the returns for such a big-budget movie must have disappointed Sony.

The more common marketing strategy adopted by distributors uneasy about the hard-to-anticipate audience take-up for a Shakespeare film is to 'open narrow', in the hope that a movie's popularity will grow over a longer period, and then to build up the distribution to more and more cinemas so that good returns can be achieved over a longer period. This approach worked particularly well for small budget movies like Branagh's *Henry V* (1) and Almereyda's *Hamlet* (9). But where larger budget movies have failed to find big audiences despite playing star names – Branagh in Parker's *Othello* (4), Anthony Hopkins in Taymor's *Titus* (8), Al Pacino in Radford's *The Merchant of Venice* (10) – the theatrical returns are decidedly low. In such a situation, the hope must be that longer term DVD sales will help to recoup the original investment.

Table A1.1 Box office data for selected Shakespeare film adaptations on theatrical release in U. S. movie theatres from 1989

Title	Dates		$ Gross		Screens				Distributor
	Opening	Closing	Total	Opening	Opening	Widest	First Week%	Per screen	
Henry V	08–11–1989 (1)	16–08–1990	10,161,099	340,071	3	134	3.35	75,829	**Goldwyn**
Hamlet	19–12–1990 (2)	13–06–1991	20,710,451	3,406,300	4	624	16.45	33,190	**Warner Bros**
Much Ado Abt Nthng	07–05–1993 (3)	09–12–1993	22,538,421	1,024,306	3	280	4.54	80,494	**Goldwyn**
Othello	13–12–1995 (4)	15–02–1996	2,509,062	461,138	2	219	18.38	11,457	**Sony**
Romeo + Juliet	01–11–1996 (5)	20–02–1997	46,351,345	11,133,231	1276	1963	24.02	23,613	**Fox**
Hamlet	25–12–1996 (6)	17–04–1997	4,425,305	455,728	3	93	10.30	47,584	**Sony**
MND	14–05–1999 (7)	26–08–1999	16,066,563	4,285,620	1080	1099	26.67	14,619	**Fox Searchlight**
Titus	25–12–1999 (8)	18–05–2000	1,900,106	145,481	2	35	7.66	54,289	**Fox Searchlight**
Hamlet	12–05–2000 (9)	17–08–2000	1,568,749	155,384	4	64	9.90	24,512	**Miramax**
Merchant of Venice	02–01–2005 (10)	22–05–2005	3,752,725	69,868	4	107	18.61	35,072	**Goldwyn**

Explanation of headings: Opening and Closing dates – duration of theatrical release (i.e. release in cinemas/movie theatres); **$ Gross** – Total earnings over duration of theatrical release; earnings over the opening weekend of movie release; **Screens – Opening**: number of screens showing movie over opening weekend; **Widest**: peak no. of screens showing movie in release period; **First week** % – Earnings for opening week of release as percentage of total earnings; **Per screen** – average earnings per screen over duration of theatrical release.

Appendix 2: Kenneth Branagh's *Much Ado About Nothing* (1993) – Structure of Emotional Registers and Rhythms

There is a consensus that Branagh's *Much Ado About Nothing* is the most successful Shakespearean comedy to be adapted to film, and some of the reasons for this – setting, casting, and so on – are discussed in Part IV. However, a broader reason for its success lies in the way the screenplay creates a highly structured switchback ride of emotional intensities and suspense to engage and to sustain the viewer's involvement. As Branagh says in his screenplay introduction, a 'strong sense of the interpretative line' needs to be established when adapting Shakespeare's comedies for the screen. This is because the comedies lack the stronger narrative spines embedded in the histories and tragedies. The chart given here breaks down the film's screenplay and action into 26 sequences, tracing and describing the switchback rise and fall of the screenplay's 'interpretive line'. As one might expect for a comedy by Shakespeare, despite this author's predilection for creating a mixture of emotional registers in all of his plays, the general tendency is for him to create a preponderance of crests over troughs, the texture of the whole film edifice here being kick-started and carried along by Branagh's deployment of the song 'Sigh no more' at the beginning, middle and the end.

Table A2.1   Kenneth Branagh's *Much Ado About Nothing* (1993): Structure of emotional registers and rhythms

Sequence	Screen time (min)	Emotional register	Description	Screenplay (pages)	Norton Shakespeare reference
1	9	↑	Opening/setup: Sun & Song – arrival of Don Pedro *et al.* – exuberance-showering – Don P's men and Leonato's household meet face to face	5–13	1.1.1–1.1.76

(Continued)

Table A2.1   Continued

Sequence	Screen time (min)	Emotional register	Description	Screenplay (pages)	Norton Shakespeare reference
2	6	↑	'Skirmishing' of Benedick & Beatrice (B& B) – Claudio declares love for Hero – Don P. agrees to intercede on his behalf	13–21	1.1.77– 1.1.276
3	3	↓	Borachio informs Don John of overheard plan	21–23	1.3 (1.2 omitted)
4	4	↔	Beatrice's man problems (character exposition)	23–26	2.1.1–69
5	2	↑	Mask dance – banter between B & B, masked – Benedick 'insulted'	26–29	2.1.70–131
6	5	↓	Don J. begins deception on Claudio; serious falling out of B & B	29–35	2.1.139–262
7	4	↑	Claudio wins Hero; Beatrice refuses marriage proposal of Don P. – he hatches plot to bring B & B together as couple	35–39	2.1.263–336
8	10 s	↓	Don John has overheard – grim faced after removing red bird mask – shown as intrusive malevolent force	Not in screenplay	Not in play text
9	3	↔	Benedick's woman problems (character exposition); Balthasar sings 'Sigh no more'	39–41	2.3.8–77
10	7	↑	Gulling of Benedick in garden; lovesick he greets a furious Beatrice	42–48	2.3.84–228
11	3	↑	Gulling of Beatrice in garden; romantic dissolve shots of B & B in (individual) bliss against sunset	48–51	3.1.37–117
12	5	↑	Dogberry, Verges & the Watch on duty	51–3	3.3.1–83
13	2	↓	Don John agrees Borachio's plan to slander Hero	53–4	2.2.1–18

(Continued)

Table A2.1 Continued

Sequence	Screen time (min)	Emotional register	Description	Screenplay (pages)	Norton Shakespeare reference
14	2	↑	Fun at Benedick's expense	54–5	3.2.12–62
15	2	↓	Don J. 'shows' Claudio & Don P. supposed betrayal of Hero at her window	55–6	3.2.66–97
16	4	↔	Borachio's drunken boast to Conrad of slanderous deception overheard by Watch – arrest – Dogberry & Verges report to Leonato	56–9	3.3.84–153 and 3.5.1–57
17	7	↑ ↔	Wedding – aborted – Friar's plan to pretend Hero has died agreed	59–64	4.1.4–254
18	4	↑	B & B come together – Benedick commits to challenging Claudio	64–9	4.1.255–329
19	20 s	↓	Don J. laughing devilishly in cellar tunnel	67	Not in play text
20	4	↔	More 'comedy' with Dogberry & Co.	67–9	4.2.1–70
21	4	↔	Leonato & Antonio charge Don P. & Claudio with Hero's 'death'; Benedick challenges Claudio	69–73	5.1.1–188
22	7	↔↓	Borachio's (and Don J's) guilt exposed to Don P. & Leonato – Claudio's punishment begins – agrees to wed Hero's 'lookalike cousin'	73–5	5.1.201–312
23	4	↓	Torchlit procession to Hero's 'tomb' – Claudio penitent – lament sung	76	5.3.2–21
24	4	↑	B & B fully reconciled	76–8	5.2.22–87
25	7	↑	Weddings of Claudio & Hero, B & B	78–82	5.4.1–107
26	5	↑	Merriment, singing and dancing – final reprise of 'Sigh no more'	82–3	5.4.112–122

Emotional Registers Incited: ↑ Light/benign/positive; ↓ Dark/malign/negative; ↔ Neutral/variable (character exposition; plot forwarding).

References

Almereyda, Michael, 2000, *William Shakespeare's Hamlet: A Screenplay Adaptation* (London: Faber & Faber).

Ball, Robert Hamilton, 1968, *Shakespeare on Silent Film: A Strange Eventful History* (London: George Allen & Unwin).

Barber, C. L., 1972, *Shakespeare's Festive Comedy* (Princeton: Princeton University Press).

Bordwell, David and Thompson, Kristin, 2001, *Film Art: An Introduction* (New York: McGraw-Hill).

Branagh, Kenneth, 1989, *Henry V: A Screen Adaptation* (London: Chatto & Windus).

——, 1991, *Beginning* (New York: St Martin's Press).

——, 1993, *Much Ado About Nothing: Screenplay, Introduction, and Notes on the Making of the Movie* (New York & London: W.W. Norton).

——, 1996, *Hamlet: Screenplay and Introduction* (New York & London: W.W.Norton).

Brook, Peter, 1987, *The Shifting Point: Forty Years of Theatrical Exploration 1946–1987* (London: Methuen).

Buchanan, Judith, 2000, 'Virgin and Ape, Venetian and Infidel: Labellings of Otherness in Oliver Parker's *Othello*', in Mark Thornton Burnett and Ramona Wray (eds), *Shakespeare, Film, Fin de Siècle* (London: Macmillan), 179–202.

Buhler, Stephen M., 2002, *Shakespeare in the Cinema: Ocular Proof* (Albany: State University of New York Press).

Burch, Noel, 1979, *To the Distant Observer: Form and Meaning in the Japanese Cinema* (London: Scolar Press).

Burnett, Mark Thornton, 2000, 'Impressions of Fantasy: Adrian Noble's *A Midsummer Night's Dream*', in Mark Thornton Burnett and Ramona Wray (eds), *Shakespeare, Film, Fin de Siècle* (London: Macmillan), 89–101.

Cartmell, Deborah, 2000, *Interpreting Shakespeare on Screen* (London: Macmillan).

Corner, John, 1999, *Critical Ideas in Television Studies* (Oxford: Clarendon Press).

Crowl, Samuel, 2003, *Shakespeare at the Cineplex: The Kenneth Branagh Era* (Athens, Ohio: Ohio University Press).

Davies, Anthony, 1988, *Filming Shakespeare's Plays: The Adaptations of Laurence Olivier, Orson Welles, Peter Brook and Akira Kurosawa* (Cambridge: Cambridge University Press).

——, 1996, 'The Film Versions of *Romeo and Juliet*', *Shakespeare Survey*, 49, 153–62.

Dent, Alan (ed.), 1948, *Hamlet: The Film and the Play* (London: World Film Publications).

Donaldson, Peter S., 1990, *Shakespearean Films/Shakespearean Directors* (Boston: Unwin Hyman).

Ellis, John, 1992, *Visible Fictions: Cinema: Television: Video* (London & Boston: Routledge Kegan Paul).

Greenblatt, Stephen (ed.), 1997, *The Norton Shakespheare: Based on the Oxford Edition* (New York & London: W. W. Norton & Co.).

Guntner, Lawrence, 1995, 'Recycled Film Codes and "The Great Tradition of Shakespeare on Film" ', in P. Drexler and L. Guntner (eds), *Negotiations with Hal: Multi-Media Perceptions of (Shakespeare's) Henry the Fifth* (Braunschweig: Technische Universität Braunschweig), 51–61.

——, 1997, 'A Microcosm of Art: Olivier's Expressionist *Hamlet* (1948)', in Holger Klein and Dimiter Daphinoff (eds), *Hamlet on Screen* (Lampeter, UK: The Edwin Mellen Press).

Hayward, Susan, 1996, *Key Concepts in Cinema Studies* (London: Routledge).

Hoffman, Michael, 1999, *William Shakespeare's A Midsummer Night's Dream, Adapted for the Screen* (New York: HarperCollins).

Holland, Peter, 1999, 'Two-Dimensional Shakespeare: "King Lear" on Film', in A. Davies and S. Wells (eds), *Shakespeare and the Moving Image* (Cambridge: Cambridge University Press), 50–68.

——, 1997, *English Shakespeares: Shakespeare on the English Stage in the 1990s* (Cambridge: Cambridge University Press).

——, 1996, 'Hand in Hand to Hell', *Times Literary Supplement*, May 10.

Jackson, Russell, 2000, 'Introduction: Shakespeare, Films and the Marketplace', in Russell Jackson (ed.), *The Cambridge Companion to Shakespeare on Film* (Cambridge: Cambridge University Press), 1–14.

Jorgens, Jack J., 1983, 'Kurosawa's *Throne of Blood*: Washizu and Miki Meet the Forest Spirit', *Literature/Film Quarterly*, 11(3), 167–73.

——, 1991, *Shakespeare on Film* (Maryland & London: University Press of America).

Kael, Pauline, 1992, *Movie Love: Complete Reviews 1988–91* (London: Marion Boyars).

Kliman, Bernice, 1992, *Macbeth* (Manchester & New York: Manchester University Press).

Kott, Jan, 1974, *Shakespeare Our Contemporary*, trans. Boleslaw Taborski (New York & London: W.W. Norton).

Kozintsev, Grigori, 1967, *Shakespeare: Time and Conscience*, trans. Joyce Vining (London: Dennis Dobson).

——, 1972, ' "Hamlet" and "King Lear": Stage and Film', in *Shakespeare 1971: Proceedings of the World Shakespeare Congress Vancouver, August 1971* (Toronto & Buffalo: University of Toronto Press).

Lanier, Douglas, 2003, 'Nostalgia and Theatricality: The Fate of the Shakespearean Stage in the *Midsummer Night's Dreams*, of Hoffman, Noble, and Edzard,' in Richard Burt and Lynda E. Boose (eds.), *Shakespeare, The Movie II: Popularising the Plays on Film, TV, Video, and DVD* (New York & London: Routledge), 154–72.

Loehlin, James N., 2000, ' "These Violent Delights Have Violent Ends": Baz Luhrmann's Millennial Shakespeare,' in Mark Thornton Burnett and Ramona Wray (eds), *Shakespeare, Film, Fin de Siècle* (London: Macmillan), 121–36.

——, 2003, ' "Top of the World, Ma": *Richard III* and Cinematic Convention', in R. Burt and Lynda E. Boose (eds), *Shakespeare, The Movie II: Popularizing the Plays on Film, TV, Video, and DVD* (London & New York: Routledge), 173–85.

McKellen, Ian, 1996, *William Shakespeare's Richard III: A Screenplay Written by Ian McKellen & Richard Loncraine, Annotated & Introduced by Ian McKellen* (Woodstock, New York: The Overlook Press).

——, 1998, 'Shakespeare Is Up to Date: An Interview with Sir Ian McKellen', by Gary Crowdus, *Cineaste*, 24(1), 46–7.

McKernan, Luke and Terris, Olwen (eds), 1994, *Walking Shadows: Shakespeare in the National Film and Television Archive* (London: British Film Institute, 1994).

MacLiammóir, Micheál, 1994, *Put Money in Thy Purse: The Filming of Orson Welles's Othello* (London: Virgin Books).

McLuhan, Marshall, 1964, *Understanding Media: The Extensions of Man* (London: Routledge & Kegan Paul).

Manvell, Roger, 1971, *Shakespeare and the Film* (New York & Washington: Praeger Publishers).

——, 1979, *Theatre and Film: A Comparative Study of the Two Forms of Dramatic Art, and of the Problems of Adaptation of Stage Plays into Films* (New Jersey & London: Associated University Presses).

Metz, Christian, 1974, *Film Language: A Semiotics of the Cinema*, trans. Michael Taylor (New York: Oxford University Press).

Olivier, Laurence, 1984, Orig. 1945, *Henry V, Produced and Directed by Laurence Olivier* (London: Lorrimer).

——, 1987, *On Acting* (London: Sceptre).

Ritchie, Donald, 1975, *The Films of Akira Kurosawa* (Berkeley: University of California).

Rothwell, Kenneth S., 2000, *A History of Shakespeare on Screen: A Century of Film and Television* (Cambridge: Cambridge University Press).

Wells, Stanley, 1982, 'Television Shakespeare', *Shakespeare Quarterly*, 33(3), 261–77.

Willems, Michèle (ed.), 1987, *Shakespeare à la television* (Rouen: Publications de l'Universite de Rouen).

——, 1999, 'Verbal-Visual, Verbal-Pictorial or Textual-Televisual? Reflections on the BBC Shakespeare Series', in Anthony Davies and Stanley Wells (eds), *Shakespeare and the Moving Image* (Cambridge: Cambridge University Press), 69–85.

——, 2000, 'Video and Its Paradoxes,' in Russell Jackson (ed.), *The Cambridge Companion to Shakespeare on Flim* (Cambridge: Cambridge University Press), 35–46.

Willis, Susan, 1991, *The BBC Shakespeare Plays: Making the Televised Canon* (Chapel Hill & London: University of North Carolina Press).

Zeffirelli, Franco, 1986, *Zeffirelli: The Autobiography of Franco Zeffirelli* (New York: Weidenfeld & Nicholson).

Suggested Further Reading

Shakespeare on film

Anderegg, Michael, **Orson Welles**: *Shakespeare and Popular Culture* (New York: Columbia University Press, 1999).

Boose, Lynda E. and Richard Burt (eds), *Shakespeare, The Movie: Popularizing the Plays on Film, TV, and Video* (London & New York: Routledge, 1997).

Buhler, Stephen M., *Shakespeare in the Cinema: Ocular Proof* (Albany: State University of New York Press, 2002).

Burnett, Mark Thornton and Ramona Wray (eds), *Shakespeare, Film, Fin de Siècle* (London: Macmillan, 2000).

Burt, Richard (ed.), *Shakespeare after Mass Media* (New York & Basingstoke: Palgrave, 2002).

Burt, Richard and Lynda E. Boose (eds), *Shakespeare, The Movie II: Popularizing the Plays on Film, TV, Video, and DVD* (New York & London: Routledge, 2003).

Crowl, Samuel, *Shakespeare at the Cineplex: The Kenneth Branagh Era* (Athens, Ohio: Ohio University Press, 2003).

Davies, Anthony and Stanley Wells, *Shakespeare and the Moving Image: The Plays on Film and Television* (Cambridge: Cambridge University Press, 1994, repr. 1999).

Hatchuel, Sarah, *Shakespeare, from Stage to Screen* (Cambridge: Cambridge University Press, 2004).

Jackson, Russell (ed.), *The Cambridge Companion to Shakespeare on Film* (Cambridge: Cambridge University Press, 2000).

Jorgens, Jack J., *Shakespeare on Film* (Maryland & London: University Press of America, 1991).

Lehmann, Courtney and Lisa S. Starks (eds), *Spectacular Shakespeare: Critical Theory and Popular Cinema* (London: Associated University Presses, 2002).

Manvell, Roger, *Shakespeare and the Film* (New York & Washington: Praeger Publishers, 1971).

Naremore, James, 'The Walking Shadow: Welles's Expressionist *Macbeth*', *Literature/Film Quarterly*, 1, 360–66 (1973).

Rothwell, Kenneth S., *A History of Shakespeare on Screen: A Century of Film and Television* (Cambridge: Cambridge University Press, 2000).

Starks, Lisa S. and Courtney Lehmann (eds), *The Reel Shakespeare: Alternative Cinema and Theory* (London: Associated University Presses, 2002).

Welsh, James M., Richard Vela and John C. Tibbetts, *Shakespeare into Film* (New York: Checkmark Books, 2002).

Film

Bordwell, David, *The Way Hollywood Tells It: Story and Style in Modern Movies* (Berkeley, Los Angeles & London: University of California Press, 2006).

Bordwell, David and Kristin Thompson, *Film Art: An Introduction*, Sixth Edition (New York: McGraw-Hill, 2001).

Hollows, Joanne, Peter Hutchings and Mark Jancovich (eds), *The Film Studies Reader* (London: Arnold, 2000).

Monaco, James, *How to Read a Film: The World of Movies, Media, and Multimedia: Language, History, Theory*, Third Edition (Oxford & New York: Oxford University Press, 2000).

Reference

Rothwell, Kenneth S. and Annabelle Henkin Melzer, *Shakespeare on Screen: An International Filmography and Videography* (New York & London: Neal-Schuman Publishers Inc., 1990).

List of films discussed

Title	Director	Country	Date
As You Like It	Paul Czinner	USA	1936
As You Like It	Christine Edzard	UK	1992
The Children's Midsummer Night's Dream	Christine Edzard	UK	2001
Chimes at Midnight (Falstaff)	Orson Welles	Spain/Switzerland	1966
Hamlet, The Drama of Vengeance	Svend Gade	Germany	1920
Hamlet	Laurence Olivier	UK	1948
Hamlet	Grigori Kozintsev	Russia	1964
Hamlet	Tony Richardson	UK	1969
Hamlet	Franco Zeffirelli	USA	1990
Hamlet	Kenneth Branagh	UK	1996

(Continued)

Title	Director	Country	Date
Hamlet	Michael Almereyda	USA	2000
Henry V	Laurence Olivier	UK	1944
Henry V	Kenneth Branagh	UK	1989
Julius Caesar	Joseph Mankiewicz	USA	1953
King John	William Dickson	UK	1899
King Lear	Grigori Kozintsev	Russia	1970
King Lear	Peter Brook	UK/Denmark	1970
King Lear	Edwin Sherin	USA	1974
Kumonosu-Jô	Akira Kurosawa	Japan	1957
Love's Labour's Lost	Kenneth Branagh	UK	2000
Macbeth	–	USA	1908
Macbeth	Orson Welles	USA	1948
Macbeth	Roman Polanski	UK	1971
A Midsummer Night's Dream	Charles Kent	USA	1909
A Midsummer Night's Dream	Max Reinhardt & William Dieterle	USA	1935
A Midsummer Night's Dream	Peter Hall	UK	1968
A Midsummer Night's Dream	Adrian Noble	UK	1996
A Midsummer Night's Dream	Michael Hoffman	USA	1999
Much Ado About Nothing	Kenneth Branagh	UK	1993
The Merchant of Venice	Michael Radford	UK/Luxembourg Italy/USA	2004
Othello	Orson Welles	Morocco/Italy	1952
Othello	Sergei Yutkevich	Russia	1955
Othello	Stuart Burge	UK	1965
Othello	Oliver Parker	UK	1995
Richard III	James Keane	USA	1912
Richard III	Laurence Olivier	UK	1955
Richard III	Richard Loncraine	UK	1995
Romeo & Juliet	George Cukor	USA	1936
Romeo & Juliet	Renato Castellani	UK/Italy	1954
Romeo & Juliet	Franco Zeffirelli	Italy/UK	1968
Romeo & Juliet	Baz Luhrmann	USA	1996
The Taming of the Shrew	Franco Zeffirelli	USA/Italy	1966
The Tempest	Percy Stow	UK	1908
Titus	Julie Taymor	USA/Italy	1999
Twelfth Night	Trevor Nunn	UK	1996

Some useful websites

www.imdb.com	**International Movie Database**. Comprehensive historical source of information about all films generally released, including cast and crew, reviews, awards and nominations, company credits, release dates, business data, etc.
www.bardcentral.com	**Poor Yorick Shakespeare Catalogue**. Excellent source for obtaining Shakespeare on film/TV DVDs and videos, many of them not easily obtainable from the usual commercial outlets; also film and book reviews by professionals in the field.
www.boxofficeguru.com	**Box office data** on motion pictures released between 1989 and the present. Note that 'domestic box office' relates to earnings at American movie theatres (in US dollars); 'foreign' relates to earnings in non-US countries.
www.ddhe.co.uk	**DD Home Entertainment**: all of the BBC-TV Shakespeare adaptations on DVD may be obtained from this site.
www.bufvc.ac.uk/ Shakespeare	**International database of Shakespeare on film, television and radio**: ongoing project by the British Universities Film & Video Council aiming to compile information on every traceable film, television programme and radio broadcast, not only including selective video stage recordings and sound recordings, but extending to 'the full range of audiovisual Shakespeare, including plot borrowings, significant quotations, and appearances by WS himself'.
www.maurice hindle.com	*Author website*: for further discussion, forum, and upcoming projects around Shakespeare on film. Plus information on other of my publications, work in progress and downloads.

Glossary of Terms

ADR (automated dialogue replacement) – When actors re-record their dialogue in synchronisation (sync) with their lip movement in post-production. Becomes necessary (for example) when the speech recorded on set has been distorted by background interference.

Apparent motion – A quirk of human seeing whereby our eyes can be deceived into seeing movement if a visual display is changed rapidly enough. Besides applying to moving pictures, the illusory phenomenon occurs in flashing neon signs created by static lights flashing off and on at a specific rate.

Arthouse – Movies the aesthetic style and/or intellectual content of which appeal to a limited audience whose tastes are geared to these elements; as opposed to the (usually) less demanding 'Hollywood' films relying on more 'formulaic' construction and casting.

Back-lighting/back-lit – Where a person or object is thrown into shadow by being lit from behind, often producing a ghostly effect.

Backstory – Narrative elements added to give more information and motivation to the original story, which does not include these elements.

Blocking – Positioning of actors within the *mis-en-scène*.

CGI (Computer Generated Imagery) – See *Digital Imaging*.

Chiaroscuro – Distribution of light and shadow in the *mis-en-scène*.

Close-up/close shot – Face or head and shoulders, used to reveal inner or emotional state of character.

Continuity editing – Cutting the film to sustain continuous and clear story action, relying on matching screen direction, position and temporal relations from shot to shot.

Crane/overhead shot – Moving around at a significant height above ground level.

Critical flicker vision – Phenomenon whereby the 24 still frames/second at which films are shot and projected is the speed at which the film appears to produce moving images without 'flicker'.

Cross-cutting – Editing that alternates shots of two or more lines of action occurring in different places, usually simultaneously.

Deep-focus – Use of camera lens and lighting to keep both close and distant planes being shot, in focus.

Depth of field/focus – Distance between planes in front of the camera where everything remains in focus.

Diegesis – The world of the film's story, including events presumed to have occurred and actions and spaces not shown onscreen.

Diegetic sound – Any voice, music or sound presented as part of the screen world we are watching.

Digital imaging/compositing – Techniques of editing or altering images in filmmaking that use computer technology and software.

Dissolve/mix – Gradual merging of the end of one shot into the beginning of the next.

Dolly – Wheeled truck or trolley on which the camera and cameraperson are mounted; used for *Tracking shots*.

Downstage – Front of a theatrical stage, nearest the audience.

Edit – To assemble a complete film from its various component shots and sound tracks.

Establishing shot – Usually long shot involving distant framing to show spatial relations among important characters, objects and setting in a scene, before moving to closer shots.

Exposition – The early scenes in a film laying the foundations of situation and characters in the plot.

Eyeline match – A cut in which the first shot shows a character looking off in one direction, and the next contains what they see.

Film noir – 'Dark film': term usually applied to detective or thriller genres using low-key lighting to create a sombre mood.

Flat – Part of a painted scene mounted on a wooden frame, pushed horizontally or lowered on to a theatrical stage.

Focaliser/focalisation – Character with whom we are made to sympathise/the process of bringing about such sympathy.

Hand-held shot – Moving about bumpily at eye level.

High angle – Shot taken from above; can convey sense of power over objects shown.

Identification – Process whereby we closely align our feelings and thoughts with a character.

Image system – Repeated *Motifs* of shape, colour or sound to sustain a theme, or to link together characters or stages of a narrative.

Internal diegetic sound – Sound represented as coming from the mind of a character, which we and they hear, though we assume other characters cannot.

Leitmotif – Musical sound or phrase recurring as a kind of theme tune, often linked to the appearance of specific characters.

Long-shot – Framing in which scale of object is relatively small; a standing human figure fills the screen.

Low angle – Shot taken from below. Can convey sense of threat or danger.

Match-cut/match on action – Continuity cut placing two different framings of the same action together at the same moment in the gesture.

Matte-shot – Where a painted backdrop is photographically incorporated into a shot to suggest a particular setting.

Medium or mid shot – Scale of object shown of moderate size e.g. a human figure from waist-up filling the screen.

Medium-close shot – Scale of object shown quite large e.g. a human figure from chest-up filling the screen.

Medium-long shot – Making an object about four to five feet high fill the screen e.g. a human figure from shins-up filling the screen.

Metacinematic – Film using visual devices to expose the constructed nature of the visions the film provides.

Metatheatre/metatheatrical – Theatre using devices to expose the constructed nature of the drama shown.

Metonymy – A kind of cinematic shorthand in which details, objects, gestures, colour, etc. visually convey meanings or ideas e.g. at the opening of Olivier's *Richard III*, the crown shown is a shorthand for kingship, the monarchy and its associated powers.

Mise-en-scène – Everything we see in the frame, literally, the visual elements 'put into the scene' and theatrically arranged before shooting starts. Such elements typically include setting, *Props*, positioning, behaviour, facial expressions, body language, costume, hair and make-up of characters and their setting within the frame, as well as lighting and colour.

Montage – A 'dialectical' process in which meanings are built up or information is provided over a succession of shots; often contrasted with the *mise-en-scène* approach of creating meaning and information in a single frame.

Motif – Image, theme or element frequently repeated throughout a film. The use of the colour red to denote blood and bloody violence is a good example in Polanski's *Macbeth*.

Narrative film – A film in which a story is developed from beginning to end, made up of a chain of events in cause–effect relationship occurring in time and space.

Non-diegetic sound – Any sound not coming from a source within the screen world, such as voice-over, background music or any sound effects added in post-production.

Open wide/narrow – Film shown at large/small number of theatrical outlets on its first opening.

Pan/panning shot – Moves from side to side from a fixed axis, producing a mobile framing on the screen scanning the space horizontally; an aerial pan makes the same movement high up in the air.

POV – Point of view.

Props – Short for 'properties': any moveable object in a scene (term used in stage, film or TV drama).

Proscenium arch – 'Picture frame' opening separating the stage and acting space from the auditorium in many theatres.

Reaction shot – Showing the reaction of a character to something said or done.

Shot – In shooting, one continuous run of the camera exposing a series of frames (also called a *Take*) in the completed film, one continuous image with a single static or mobile framing.

Shot/reverse shot – Two or more shots edited together which alternate characters, usually in a conversation situation.

Slam-zoom – Extremely rapid enlargement of the image using a zoom lens.

Sound bridge – At the end of a scene, the sound from the next is heard briefly before the new scene begins; at the beginning of a scene, the sound from the previous scene is heard briefly before the sound from the new scene begins.

Steadicam – Gimbal-balanced camera mount enabling camera operator to produce mobile shots of great smoothness while tracking uneven movements of actors.

Stop-motion shooting – Crude trick photographic technique often used in silent films, splicing together separate shots to make them appear continuous.

Subjective camera/ shot – Showing exactly what the character sees from their point of view. Rarely used without an *establishing shot* to orientate the viewer.

Take – During filmmaking, shot produced by one continuous run of the camera; a shot in the completed movie may be chosen from among several takes of the same action.

Thrust stage – Open stage projecting into theatre auditorium permitting audience to watch the performance on three sides.

Time-lapse cinematography – Accelerated motion cinematography that secures a moving picture of a slow process (such as the passage from night into dawn at the opening of Polanski's *Macbeth*) by exposing the film frame by frame over a considerable time interval.

Tracking shot – A mobile framing that travels through space forward, backward or laterally, the camera often being mounted on a *Dolly* moving along specially laid tracks.

Two-shot – Close shot of two persons with the camera as near as possible while keeping them both in shot.

Upstage – Rear of a theatrical stage, furthest away from the audience.

Voice-over – When a screen character's voice or the voice of an unseen narrator is heard over the image on screen.

Whip (or zip) pan – Extremely fast movement of the camera blurring the image between two points in a *Pan*.

Wide shot – Distant shot containing multiple elements in frame (as in landscape-like *establishing shot*), or emphasising a horizontal composition, e.g. in Branagh's *Hamlet*, Hamlet's soliloquy beginning 'How all occasions do inform against me' begins with medium-close shot on him, the camera moving back (going 'wide') until the wide shot shows him as a tiny figure in the snowy landscape.

Wipe – Form of transition from one shot to another in which a margin moves across the screen to eliminate the first shot and reveal the second.

Zoom shot – Act of rapidly enlarging or reducing the image in the frame using zoom lens.

Index

Page numbers in **bold** denote a glossary entry